THE MONGOLS

From Genghis Khan To Tamerlane

W. B. Bartlett is a writer and historian. His other books include *Assassins: The Story of Medieval Islam's Secret Sect*, *The Road to Armageddon: The Last Years of the Crusader Kingdom of Jerusalem*, *An Ungodly War: The Sack of Constantinople & the Fourth Crusade*, *The Last Crusade: The Seventh Crusade & the Final Battle for the Holy Land*, *God Wills It! An Illustrated History of the Crusades*, *Legends of Blood: The Vampire in History & Myth* and *Islam's War Against the Crusaders*.

He lives in Bournemouth.

THE MONGOLS

From Genghis Khan To Tamerlane

W.B. BARTLETT

AMBERLEY

To all those I met in Mongolia, with thanks for the memories

This edition first published 2010

Amberley Publishing Plc
Cirencester Road, Chalford,
Stroud, Gloucestershire, GL6 8PE

www.amberley-books.com

British Library Cataloguing in Publication Data.
A catalogue record for this book is available from the British Library.

ISBN 978 1 84868 191 0

Typesetting and Origination by Amberley Publishing.
Printed in Great Britain.

Contents

Prologue

> The greatest event of the past millennium beyond comparison was the one nation domination that once took place and brought together Europe and Asia tied by one administration, trade and civilisation.

Such was the opinion of the widely respected *Washington Post* on 31 December 1995 in a statement that summed up the impact of the Mongol conquests. It is quite a claim, but one that bears closer examination, for the story of the Mongols is indeed an amazing tale. They were a phenomenon that came from nowhere and went back there again in the space of just three centuries. From being a small tribal clan, not even particularly significant in their own immediate environment, they ruled over the greatest empire that the world had ever seen.

Their empire spread from the shores of the Pacific to those of the Mediterranean, from the frigid tundra of Northern Russia to the edges of the Arabian Desert, from the marshes of Poland to the mountains and forests of China, making it the largest contiguous empire ever known. Its extent could have been even greater if two *khans* had not died at propitious moments, one when the Mongol hordes were ravaging Central Europe, the other when they were on the edge of destroying the largest remaining Muslim power in the Middle East.

But for these events, and the frequent succession disputes that inevitably bedevilled such a gigantic and diverse imperial polity in the latter years of its existence, they might have gone further. They might even have been able to govern the entire known world, an achievement that no other empire has ever been able to match, though, as we shall see, in practice there were always limits to what these incredible imperialists were likely to achieve.

Theirs was not the first great empire to be forged in the steppes. For centuries warriors had emerged from nowhere to unleash terror on unsuspecting enemies, right across to the shores of the Atlantic even. The most famous of these nomadic raiders had been Attila, who had brought his own brand of terror to Europe nearly a millennium before. But there had been others, especially the Turks who emerged from Central Asia and sent shockwaves reverberating out in all directions.

But none of their empires matched that of the Mongols. As one writer remarked, the Mongols represented 'the last and most dreadful of all the nomadic assaults on civilisation'[1]

One stupendous man, Temüjin, later known as Genghis Khan, laid the foundations of this stupendous achievement. Without a doubt he is one of the greatest conquerors in history. Few could claim to match his achievements, Alexander perhaps being the closest. Even at the time, men were aware of his greatness, and comparisons were made between the two mighty warriors. The near-contemporary Persian writer Juvaini remarked that had Alexander lived in the time of Genghis, he 'would have been his pupil in craft and cunning, and of all the talismans for the taking of strongholds he would have found none better than blindly to follow in his footsteps.'[2]

Amazingly, after his death his empire continued to grow, in marked contrast to that of the ancient Macedonian. This was because he left behind him a military arm that no other world power of the day could match. The political inheritance he left was less secure, but it would not be until many years after his demise that his empire would begin to disintegrate. He left behind him a dynasty that carried his achievements forward. This means that the story of the Mongols is far more than just the story of Genghis Khan, incredible though that tale is.

Despite its vast extent, it may seem that the Mongol empire made far less impression on the modern world than that of, say, Rome or even the British Empire. However, that view would be an error, for the Mongols helped to shape much of the world we know. Perhaps there is an image problem. The conquests of the Mongols are accompanied by mental images of the acts of incredible ferocity that accompanied them. Genghis and his successors were certainly capable of acts of stark ruthlessness and savagery. Conquest was often followed by wholesale slaughter. Acts of unbelievable cruelty, almost beyond the imagination, followed in so many cases where a particular city had had the temerity to resist the Mongols, rather than meekly surrender when called upon to do so. This has understandably coloured perceptions of the Mongols. The positive impacts of their conquests are much harder to find.

In addition, the Mongols made little permanent cultural impact on those they came into contact with, unless the obliteration of so many cultural icons in the form of cities and magnificent architecture, in regions such as Persia and China, as a negative result of their conquests. Rather, the Mongols tended to be overwhelmed by the cultures that they theoretically vanquished, particularly for example the Chinese or the Persians. They left little in the way of a permanent cultural footprint, in marked contrast to the long-term results of empires such as that of Rome. They were always hugely outnumbered by their conquered subjects who in the end vanquished them by assimilation more than by the force of arms.

In some ways the origins of the Mongols are what make their story even more remarkable. Mongolia, the modern Mongol homeland, is a vast and ruggedly beautiful country, but even now it is remote and one of the most sparsely populated countries in the world. Before the emergence of the Mongols, Mongolia was virtually unknown outside of its immediate environs. Trapped unfortunately between Russia and China, two great superpowers who have certainly got their own back on the Mongols for the damage done to them in the past, the Mongolians of today are jealously proud of their past conquests. In particular, Genghis, who is regarded as a national hero, is revered in a way that few other countries would understand. Devotion to him was subdued in the days of Communist domination, but now that he may be freely worshipped once more he has been well and truly rehabilitated. Chingis beer is the most popular brew around, (Chingis being one variant of his name) though he is better known as Genghis in the West, and that is therefore what I will call him in this book. The marketing departments responsible for selling vodka, now the most popular alcoholic drink in Mongolia, have inevitably claimed him too. Hotels and restaurants are named after him, as are streets. On the 800th anniversary of his founding of the Mongol state in 1206, the centre of Ulan Bataar (modern capital of the country) came to a standstill, as a massive statue of him was erected outside of the parliament building. It seemed to take forever to complete it, but few seemed to mind. It symptomized the restoration of Genghis to his rightful position and cemented the personality cult that has grown up around him.

So Genghis' legacy lives on, in Mongolia at least. Visiting the country now though serves to emphasise the true extent of his, and his successors', achievements. Mongolia's sheer scale is incredible, but its size contrasts with the sparsity of its population, for although it has a landmass approximating to that of Western Europe, it has less than three million inhabitants. Once one leaves the capital, even today, one can travel for hours without meeting anybody. One of the great sources of wonder is how a country with so few people to claim as its own could have exercised such widespread domination.

The true Mongolia (though the impact of urbanisation is making it less so) is a country of wide open spaces, of self-sufficient herders living in *gers*, felt tents that can be easily collapsed, moved and re-erected elsewhere when the land around them has been grazed to the limit by their flocks. (The term *yurt*, which is often used instead of *ger*, applies more accurately to the landholdings around the tent–*ger* is the term used universally in Mongolia in my experience). The portable homesteads of the Mongols, married to their advanced horsemanship skills, made them incredibly mobile. Indeed, this combination explains much about their past victories. Although the car has impacted on Mongolia as it has everywhere else, a Mongolian's proudest boast is still the number of horses that he owns.

Mongolia is a land of extremes and hardships. It is widely claimed that it has the greatest range between maximum and minimum temperatures of any country in the world, a situation that owes much to its landlocked situation and its high altitude. Certainly, on one May day in 2006 I witnessed this firsthand. One sunny Sunday afternoon I went for a walk in the hills. It was a frazzling day, probably in the region of thirty degrees centigrade, and as a result of my lack of preparation I was badly sunburnt. The next morning I woke up and saw snow covering the car park outside of my apartment. The temperature had dropped to minus ten. For an unprepared foreigner, a temperature swing of forty degrees in the space of just over twelve hours was mildly interesting. For many of the nomadic people of the country, though, the full impact of these variations is much more profound. In recent times, the country has been frequently hit by *zuds,* cold winter spells when the ground is frozen so hard that the grazing animals cannot feed. It is effectively a drought, though one attended by intense cold rather than heat, and its effects can be devastating. It is by no means unusual for 10% of the livestock population to die in such periods. This has the natural effect of producing a very hardy and durable people.

The landscape too is extreme. The towering Altai Mountains in the west of the country reach up to the sky itself, well over 4,000 metres high (an affinity with the sky, seemingly at times so close that it can be touched, is a feature of the Mongolian psyche and perhaps helps to explain the Mongols' past ties with Shamanism), but these rocky battlements provide a significant contrast to the wild wastelands of the Gobi Desert towards the Chinese border. In between are rolling steppes, wide forests of pine and silver birch and long, slowly rolling rivers. All these extremes have helped to forge a hardy, resilient people, and these qualities were at the heart of their achievements.

At the outset, I should make a brief reference to spelling. There is randomness about the anglicised spelling of Mongolian names which makes any attempt at consistency a virtual impossibility. Traditional

Mongolian characters were pictograms, similar to Chinese. With the onset of Russian control in the twentieth century – the country was dominated by the Communist Soviet Union, even though it stayed nominally independent – a Cyrillic alphabet was used which is very similar to Russian, with the addition of two extra characters.

This makes any consistency in spelling virtually impossible – the root language simply does not lend itself to anglicised translation. Some authors who have written several works on the Mongols have even used different interpretations of the same Mongol names in different books that they have written. I have chosen to use in the main the most familiar versions of Mongolian names, hence the use of 'Genghis' rather than 'Chingis'. The only exception is when using quotes from elsewhere, in which cases I have used the original spelling. Otherwise I have tried to be at least consistent throughout this book.

Just over 800 years after Genghis (or Chinggis, Chingis or Genghiz) had founded the first Mongol state, it appears a good time to re-examine the history of the nation that he founded when it was in it's prime. There has been something of a recent resurgence in interest about the Mongols. A number of documentaries have appeared on various satellite and terrestrial television channels, where modern-day adventurers journey to fascinating, little-known lands, therefore allowing us to vicariously participate in the wild wonders they uncover, from the comfort of an armchair. Several biographies have appeared about Genghis, that most famous of Mongols, but also Kublai Khan and Tamerlane, the latter part-Turk, part-Mongol, but closely connected to Genghis and his family and aspiring to emulate their achievements.

But such books tend to concentrate on one particular aspect of the Mongol story rather than the whole sweep of it. Perhaps the vastness of the subject is an inhibitor, since the literally universal scope of the storyline means that a huge amount must be covered. It means that any general history of the Mongols must necessarily try to cover a large volume of material at a fairly frantic pace. This makes it difficult to do the story justice, but it does not mean that such an attempt should not be made, for the story is one of the most amazing in all of human history.

I would also like to explore the reasons for the Mongols' success. Some of this was down to things that they did well, but part of it was also down to the weaknesses inherent in other cultures at the time – a consistent feature of all great empires. Given the sweep of the story, this book becomes almost like a miniature history of the world at that particular moment in time. There were few cultures in Asia or Europe that were unaffected in one way or another by their activities. They shaped the world that they lived in, in a way that had not been seen since the heyday of Rome. Sometimes that impact was direct and blunt, but at other moments they acted as a catalyst for a chain reaction. So when, for example, the Mongols conquered the Khwarismians, a powerful state in parts of Central Asia and Persia, the end result was that thousands of the subjugated state's warriors became mercenaries and ended up depriving the Crusader states in Palestine of Jerusalem several decades later.

It must also be remembered that the sequence of events we are about to follow is not only one of history on a grand scale but also a story of a dynasty. Genghis Khan was the founder of this great empire, but his sons and grandsons took it on to even higher heights. The high-water mark of the Mongol empire came half a century after his death. Without him it would not have been possible, but others of his family, such as Ögedei, Hülegü, Batu, and Kublai, played a massive part in the evolution of this incredible tale. Therefore, another aim of this book is to give them due credit for their part.

Despite the scale of their achievements, the Mongols inspire paradoxical emotions. The stunning extent of their conquests, their rags-to-riches tale (and then back to rags again), perhaps fosters a sense of amazement. Yet at the same time their savagery and their destructive impact encourages a plethora of far more negative feelings. All of this makes it high time that the place of the Mongols in world history is re-assessed. They were men (and women, whose role is largely unwritten but nevertheless highly significant) capable of extremes of emotion, just as many modern 'civilisations' are; at the same time brutal, nihilistic yet also brave, and capable of acts of generosity towards a gallant enemy.

Their story is much more complex than first meets the eye. They left few histories of their own, and most of the surviving accounts of their activities were written by their enemies – not likely to be the most balanced of observers. The very universality of the accounts of them is also a problem. For, as well as Latin – the everyday language of Europe at the time – sources exist in Persian (these are crucial), Chinese, Japanese, Russian, Turkish, Arabic, Mongolian and others. This makes the full range of sources hard to access to all but the most accomplished of linguists, a problem that is exacerbated, as a number of sources are not widely available in English translation.

The histories, then, are generally from outsiders and not from Mongols, who in any event, did not have a written language when their expansion began. There is one notable exception. *The Secret History of the Mongols* tells things from the Mongol point of view and is an invaluable source of information. However, as it is in some ways hagiographic, caution needs to be used in interpreting it. The version that currently exists is a Chinese transcription from the original Mongolian, many centuries old, so this too may be subject to some error. That said, the book is in my view invaluable, and in the main reliable as a source of firsthand evidence.

On a recent visit to Mongolia, a Mongolian colleague who had been of the greatest help to me during my work there presented me with a copy of this book, encased in a beautiful leather box. It will remain one of my most treasured possessions to my dying day. As a result of writing this book, *The Secret History* – previously a highly valued memento of a happy time – has now been opened, and as a result it has found its rightful place in my life.

The Secret History tells an amazing story of an incredible leader, and a relentless people who emerged from the dark frontiers of the world: a twilight zone that none in the West were aware of. The West, however, appeared for a time to tottter on the brink of oblivion. World conquest was an impossible dream and it would be sheer stupidity to think that it would ever come true, but that did not stop such an eventuality from seeming at one stage to be distinctly possible. What follows is an attempt to put that story in context, for it touched virtually every corner of the known world. Even today, the Mongol legacy lives on, in the shape of countries across much of the globe. From China to Europe, theirs is a long-forgotten presence that has done much to shape the world in which we live.

CHAPTER 1

The Coming of Genghis: The Birth & Rise of the World Conqueror 1167-1208

In the early decades of the thirteenth century, a Persian man of letters, Ata-Malik Juvaini, was born. He would later be an able administrator who worked with the Mongols that conquered his country, and he would do their bidding, because he had to do so if he wished to live. He would walk and talk with men who had lived with giants, and from them he would glean tales of one of the most incredible men who ever walked on the face of the earth.

Their stories began, as many great stories do, in the land of myth: a netherworld of gods and mystic spirits who governed the fate of men. It was said, so Juvaini tells us, that there was once a shaman who wandered the wastes of Mongolia naked in the depths of the coldest of winters, alone as he wandered across the desert and through the mountains. Like a Far-Eastern John the Baptist, he one day came in from the wilderness with a message. He told those men he met that 'God has spoken with me and has said: "I have given all of the earth to Temüjin and his children and named him Chingiz-Khan … " '.[1]

Mongolia was a land of myths. It was also a land of shamans, interlocutors with the spirit world, and men of extensive unworldly power in the region of the steppes. The Mongols traced the genealogy of Genghis back to Boerte Chino, 'greyish white wolf', who had mated with Qu`ai-maral, the 'beautiful doe'. The Mongols were always close to nature (though the closeness was, and is, ambivalent – the Mongols are great hunters) and it is entirely understandable, in the light of our knowledge of other native cultures, that they believed they were directly descended from animals.

And so, in a time far removed from our own, in a land that few outside of the Far East had any inkling of, a man came out of the clouds of myth and brewed a storm unlike any other tempest that anyone in history had yet raised. But, on his arrival in this world, few knew of his birth outside of his own immediate family. The year 1167 was an unremarkable one as far as the West was concerned. England and France as ever were on tenterhooks. In the former country Henry II ruled, that mercurial character with the difficult family, whilst in Italy the armies of the German emperor Frederick Barbarossa fought for supremacy against those of the Pope. The rest of the world was oblivious to the birth of a man who would one day threaten to destroy what appeared to most men to be the natural order.

Far away in Mongolia, an event that was to change world history went largely un-remarked. No one even knows for sure in which year the man who would become Genghis Khan was born, though a clue that he was born in the 'year of the pig' suggests that it was 1167.[2] The name 'Genghis' would come later in life; he was given the name 'Temüjin' at birth. It was not the name especially of a warrior for it literally means 'blacksmith'. It was said that he was born clutching a mass of blood in his hand, a clot so large that it was the size of a knucklebone, an augury of what was to come. This might well be an example of hindsight: it is by no means unusual to find that such references are planted to create a suitable picture retrospectively. Nevertheless, if it were true, it would certainly be appropriate.

The achievements of Genghis would re-echo down the ages. Juvaini, who lived in a time and a place where Genghis' personality still towered over the contemporary world, said, 'God almighty in his wisdom and intelligence distinguished Chingiz-Khan from all his coevals and in alertness of mind and absoluteness of power exalted him above all the kings of the world … .'

In contrast to his future greatness, at the time of his birth the Mongols were a large tribe, but one whose significance was in the main localised. Within the tribe were a number of clans, of which one was the Kiyat to which Temüjin belonged. His father was at least the chief of this grouping, so if he was not a dominant figure he was at least important. The Mongols were positioned on the borders of China, within which were found the undoubted regional superpowers of the time (simplistically, China was then divided into three main groupings, a theme to which we will return). From time to time, tribes like the Mongols would play a part in Chinese politics. This would normally be in the form of raids, which were undertaken by the Mongols and by other tribes that lived in the area, as well as perhaps paying the occasional tribute to the Chinese. In return for their good behaviour, the Chinese regimes often employed these unruly tribes as mercenaries.

In the wider scheme of things, Temüjin's birth was a relatively minor event. He can have inherited no great expectations of becoming even a chief of the Mongols, let alone anything else. But from this humble acorn, a monumental oak would grow. Before he came to greatness, however, Temüjin's position would deteriorate significantly, at least if *The Secret History* is to be believed. Not everyone is convinced that this intriguing mix of folklore and history is reliable. However, there is enough mentioned that can be verified from other sources to suggest that it should not be dismissed out of hand.

Temüjin's father, Yesugei, had abducted and forcibly married his mother, Ho'elun. There was nothing unusual in this: such things happened on the steppes all the time. Women were chattels, to be filched and traded like other precious goods. As a result of this act, there was an ongoing feud between Yesugei and the Merkits, the tribe from which Ho'elun's original husband had come (she had been kidnapped whilst travelling to her marital home for the first time). Such feuds lived long in the memory, and opportunities for revenge were patiently awaited. At the outset, Ho'elun's fate was a bitter one. As she saw Yesugei and his brothers riding down from the hills to capture her, she instructed her husband to flee for his life. She took off her blouse and gave it to him as a parting present, so that he might remember her by her scent (scent was an important connector of persons on the steppe, in a way that western cultures would find hard to understand). She would never see him again. Ho'elun had been snatched from the life of a hopeful young bride, with the promise of future happiness, and was now destined to make her way in a camp full of strangers. To compound her misery she was not even Yesugei's first wife, and the clan into which she had been forcibly conscripted lived on the margins of steppe society, eking out a life in conditions far harsher than those enjoyed by most of the tribes in the region. As a lesser wife of a poor tribe, her situation in the world had gone down significantly.

Not long after, her eldest son was born. Nine years passed, and Temüjin grew into a promising youth. His father decided that a suitable bride should be found for him, and he set out for the main camp of his wife's former clan, the Onggirat. Whilst on his way, he came across a subsidiary Onggirat encampment where Temüjin made a great impression on the chief, so much so that a marriage between himself and the chief's daughter, Boerte, was arranged there and then. It was to be an event, in retrospect, of the profoundest importance, far beyond the borders of the small Mongol territories. For Boerte, a year his senior, would become Temüjin's greatest confidante and closest intimate adviser, an unrecognised but very real power behind the man (as indeed was his mother).

As was the custom, Yesugei left Temüjin in the hands of his future father-in-law, where he would grow up for the next few years. He would have to prove his right to be a son-in-law. Once time had passed and they were considered mature enough, Temüjin and Boerte would marry. Well satisfied with the marriage arrangements, Yesugei rode homewards. As he went on his way, he stopped overnight in the camp of some Tartar tribesmen. Yesugei did not recognise them, but it seems that someone there knew and resented him, for his food was laced with poison.

Yesugei set out on his way again, but he had not travelled far when he felt ill. He quickly realised what had happened. Knowing of no antidote, he hurriedly sent for his son, but by the time that Temüjin had arrived he was dead. In one fell swoop, Temüjin's position had plummeted. His status at his young age was dependent on his father. Temüjin was now in great peril. He along with his family became outcasts in his tribe, shunned by them now that Yesugei had gone. They had no wealth, no status, and no rights – a stark contrast to what they had known before. The resentment that Temüjin felt as a result must have been great – as was his thirst for vengeance. The parlous position into which Temüjin, his siblings and mother had now been thrown soon became clear. Every so often the tribes would hold a great feast. Meat would be distributed amongst the people, not just as a way of enjoying a good meal but also as a way of reinforcing mutual bonds of kinship. At such a feast held soon after Yesugei's death, Temüjin and his family were not invited. The symbolism could not be misconstrued: Ho'elun and her brood were beyond the pale.

Not long after this rebuff the tribe rode off without Ho'elun and her family, leaving them deserted, with what might have been a bitter fate. She however, was a fighter. As they rode off, she ran after them carrying the horsehair standard that had once belonged to Yesugei. This trophy was more than just an item of decoration: it contained the very soul of Yesugei. Ho'elun was trying to shame the tribe into remembering their obligations, and for a short time at least she succeeded. Not for long, however. That same night the tribesmen and their families left the camp under the cover of darkness. The next morning Ho'elun woke to find herself and her family alone. It could have been a death sentence, but luckily it was not. The still–young woman eked out food wherever she could find it, from plants, from small animals, from anything that could be eaten. She and her brood lived as scavengers, on the very bottom rung of society's ladder.

There are various stories in *The Secret History of Mongolia* which tell of Temüjin's subsequent upbringing, and to our eyes some are far from complimentary. He had three brothers and a sister. He fell out with one of his brothers, Bekhter, who was in fact a half-brother. Mongols had many wives, a convention that Temüjin would enthusiastically embrace. The only limit on how many wives a man could have was his wealth and his position. The two youths became rivals. Eventually, Temüjin and another sibling, Kasar, decided that matters must be resolved once and for all, and they shot Bekhter dead with their arrows. It is an example of the ruthlessness that later typified the grown man's tactics. It is also perhaps significant that Bekhter was an elder brother: he could therefore claim to be superior to Temüjin, and was a potential barrier to his progress. His mother was enraged at this rash and un-brotherly behaviour. Given the parlous position of the family, the only way to survive at all was to stick together. She admonished Temüjin, reminding him that a family in such a vulnerable position could not afford such infighting.

However, this elimination of a potential rival did not improve Temüjin's lot: his position was about to get worse still. The Kiyats had been allied with a clan called the Tayichi'ut during his father's life, but they the latter had repudiated the alliance and been less than kind to Ho'elun and her brood. They now decided that the young Temüjin was a threat and must be dealt with. Accordingly they launched a surprise raid on the family's little camp one night. Realising that Temüjin was the target, his mother hurried him from the tents to some nearby forests, but after hiding there for days he was caught when trying to break out. He was taken into the camp of the Tayichi'ut and treated as a common criminal, with a huge wooden yoke around his neck. Here he was taunted constantly and in all probability death was not far away. Now, at the lowest point in his life, the gods smiled on Temüjin. He managed to make his escape by knocking a sentry unconscious with the yoke, and then when he hid nearby in the reeds, he was found, not by an enemy guard, but by a youth who, for whatever reason, had no wish to betray him. This boy, Sorkan, managed to send his pursuers the wrong way and then took Temüjin back to his camp, where the yoke was removed and he was given a horse to speed him on his way. It was a kindness that would later be returned by a grateful Temüjin. If he could be a harsh punisher of treachery, so too could he be a generous rewarder of loyalty. Many had subsequent cause to regret Sorkan's kindness. Temüjin returned to his family, but the life he came back to was as harsh as ever. *The Secret History*, which might exaggerate the hardships that Genghis faced to make his later achievements even more impressive, paints a gloomy picture of a difficult existence, living on mere provisions in an unforgiving environment. On one occasion, all but one of the family's remaining horses were stolen and only recovered when Temüjin and his brother stole them back again.

They were helped in this act of recovery by a young friend, Bo'orchu, who would later become a close associate of Temüjin. It was soon after this that Temüjin decided to make good on his betrothal to Boerte, which he had entered into some years before. On his return to her father's camp, he was made welcome, which, considering the decline in his fortunes since the match was made, must have come as something of a pleasant relief. The wedding went ahead and, as a dowry, the bride came with a stunning black sable coat, which was to play a largely unsung part in the history of the Mongol empire. Temüjin needed allies, and the coat, which was highly valued and valuable in the steppes, gave him a bargaining chip, which he used astutely. The Kerait tribe were much more powerful that Temüjin's people and the ambitious young man made his way to the camp of their chief, Toghril, seeking his help to advance his position. Temüjin reminded Toghril that Yesugei, his father, had been a loyal ally, and he asked if that relationship could be reinstated with his son. As a token of his loyalty to the man who would become akin to an adoptive father, he presented the coat to Toghril, which was accepted with grace. This was a crucial event in the rise of Genghis Khan: it brought the vulnerable Temüjin under the wing of a more powerful ally who would give him a degree of protection that had previously not existed. It also shows, incidentally, that there is more to the life of the great conqueror than mere military genius: the need for diplomacy and alliances was also a vital part of his, and other Mongol commanders', armoury.

This was a personal turning point. Temüjin was now a married man with a powerful ally. The youth had metamorphosed into a man. However, he was still more vulnerable than he would have liked, as was about to be proved in cruel fashion. News of his marriage had reached the Merkits, and they remembered keenly the insult that had been delivered to their tribe when Ho'elun had been abducted many years before by Temüjin's father. Grudges were carried for a long time on the steppes, and they now decided to exact their revenge. A party of some 300 Merkits descended on Temüjin's camp, and could be heard from a distance. *The Secret History* says that an old woman, a servant, woke the sleeping party by saying that 'the earth is shaking! I can hear the sound of swift horses' hooves.'[4] But even though the camp was roused, there were not enough horses for everyone in the camp to escape. Temüjin and his brothers made off, as did Ho'elun, but there was no horse for Boerte. As a result, she and the faithful old servant were left behind, being regarded as the most likely to survive in captivity and the most expendable respectively. The old woman put Boerte in a cart harnessed to an ox and attempted to hide her, but her plan failed, and Boerte was soon found by the Merkit soldiers who searched the cart. She was taken off to their camp, where she was forced to become the concubine of the younger brother of the prince from whom Ho'elun had been taken. Such was the way of revenge on the steppes.

Temüjin turned for help to his new mentor, Toghril. The chief of the Keraits was pleased to assist: it seems as if Temüjin had become a favourite. Besides, alliances of this nature were treated seriously: a man who had offered his allegiance as Temüjin had had a right to expect help when needed in return. Toghril assembled an army of 20,000 and summoned help from an old friend of Temüjin, Jamuka. The story of Temüjin and Jamuka was far from over, as it transpired. A night attack was launched on the camp of the Merkits and met with overwhelming success. Temüjin was reunited with Boerte and they returned to their home together. Soon after, she gave birth to a child who was named Jochi. It was almost nine months to the day since her abduction, so there was, to say the least, some doubt about the paternity of Jochi. *The Secret History*[5] has Temüjin boldly saying as soon as Boerte was taken, that he had lost not only a wife but also an unborn son, but the statement smacks of a slightly desperate retrospective attempt to establish Jochi's legitimacy. Even the name is suggestive: Jochi means 'visitor' or 'guest'. If Temüjin wished to dispel doubts about his paternity, it was perhaps not the wisest choice of name he could have made.

The story of the Mongol empire is a story of mighty events, massive battles, and great campaigns across half the known world. It is therefore very easy to overlook the fact that it is also a very personal story, for it is the tale of a dynasty every bit as much as the story of Egypt and its Pharaohs. Temüjin's family were known as the Altin Uruk or the Golden Kin. Temüjin would always give the appearance that he had no doubts at all about being the natural father of Jochi, but uncertainties would raise their heads in other quarters at a later stage. Family disputes were to play a key part in the history of the Mongol empire. However, Temüjin's star was at last in the ascendancy, even if his was not to be a meteoric rise. It was more a patient, step-by-step climb up the rungs of a long ladder – Temüjin would be forty years old before he had even started to become a prominent Mongol chieftain. As his reputation grew, so too did the number of warriors who were prepared to offer him their allegiance. He was generous in his gifts to those who followed him, and this undoubtedly helped to gain their loyalty. A generous lord was highly regarded by his followers. He also had the help of the shamans, the holy men of the steppes, who promulgated the tale that he had been born to rule the world. As the effective link between the earth and Tengri, the mighty god of the sky, their status and influence were immense. The myth they promulgated about Tengri's bequest to Temüjin to rule the world would become widely believed by the Mongols and evolve into a policy rather than a legendary bequest. The end result of this attitude was that the Mongols regarded unconquered nations who refused to accept Mongol supremacy as states in rebellion against the natural order of things.

Jamuka remained by Temüjin's side for a number of years. But appearances of friendship were deceptive, for the men were rivals seeking the overall leadership of the Mongols, and not just of respective clans within the tribe. Temüjin and Jamuka were sworn brothers, that is, they had made a solemn pact to act as allies. There was a name for this brotherly process amongst the Mongols - *anda*. It was a common practice on the steppes for men who were not relatives to adopt, in a formalistic way, a relationship that bound them to act as if they were. Such arrangements went far beyond simple alliances: adherence to such arrangements once made was almost a sacred duty on the steppes. The reality, however, was that the men were opponents. Jamuka could claim a more illustrious ancestry than Temüjin. Socially, the latter was an inferior. Matters came to a head in an almost biblical manner when Jamuka took the best land for himself when their tribes went on their nomad wanderings, and took the horse herd with him: he suggested that Temüjin take more inferior land to go and look after the goats. To modern eyes this does not seem to mean much, but on the steppes it was a statement about status as much as anything else. Horses were a Mongols' pride, animals of status and power; goats were the domain of the shepherd.

Faced with what amounted to an insult, Temüjin did not know what to do. It was allegedly Boerte who made up his mind for him. Realising that it was time for Temüjin to stick up for his rights, she told him that they should make their way away from Jamuka's camp in secret, so that he could start to find his own way in the world. So, under cover of darkness they did so. Temüjin and his family crept away and a new life had begun. As well as a supportive and strong wife, Temüjin was blessed in one respect above all others: his band of generals. Even at this stage, he had a band of loyal devotees who would accompany him throughout his life. Ever since the start of his career, Temüjin had been accompanied by a loyal servant, Jelme. Later Jelme's brother also came to serve him. His name was Subotai and he would become perhaps the greatest Mongol military strategist of all – which makes him, by definition, one of the greatest strategists in history.

Subotai was born in around 1176 (years did not have a lot of meaning for the Mongols, hence any birth-year quoted must of necessity be a best guess) and was therefore about ten years younger than Temüjin. He commanded his first army before he was twenty-five years old, which means that he must have been a man of outstanding talent, for Temüjin made sure that he appointed his generals on merit rather than societal rank. Even at the time, men recognised Subotai's brilliance – a western visitor to the Mongols in the thirteenth century noted that the Mongols regarded him as their greatest soldier.[6] It may be a coincidence that Temüjin's rise to power neatly matches the emergence of Subotai, but then again it might not. As well as being tactically and strategically unrivalled (some modern military commentators believe him to be one of the most outstanding strategists of all time), Subotai had great personal bravery and cunning. On one occasion, it was said that he made his way into the camp of an enemy and gave them false information so that they would unwittingly make their way into a trap. He would undoubtedly be Temüjin's most formidable military lieutenant, a role that he would carry on during the reign of Temüjin's son when he succeeded him many years in the future as *khan*. But this is to get ahead of ourselves. Before Temüjin could rule the Mongols he must become chief of his own clan. When he was about eighteen, the people of his own small nation elected him chief. As soon as the election was over, Temüjin instituted a number of changes in the way affairs were run. The camp was organised and men were required to undertake military training.

Two groups of warriors were developed: one was lightly armed and relied on archery, the other more heavily armed and armoured – the heavy cavalry. This made his clan much more organised and efficient as warriors; however, it is unlikely that everyone took kindly to this unprecedented interference with their personal freedoms. The greybeards amongst the tribe, in particular, cannot all have been over-impressed at this intrusion into their way of life. Toghril welcomed the accession of his protégé, but Jamuka, who was also intensely ambitious, knew that it was time to make his move if he were to stop the now significant rise of Temüjin. His youthful friend was getting ahead of him and threatening to outshine him. He sent messages to other chiefs to join him in putting down this arrogant upstart. They were quick to join him, and soon Jamuka was at the head of an army perhaps 30,000 strong. Perhaps they sensed in Genghis a threat, which must be put down before he became too powerful.

Battle between the two opposing blocs was joined soon after. Temüjin had almost as many men as Jamuka. In light of this, and of Temüjin's later reputation, it might be thought that the result would be a stunning triumph for him. It was not. Jamuka emerged victorious. But Temüjin inspired something that Jamuka did not – loyalty. Although defeated, many of Temüjin's men stayed with him. Jamuka in contrast acted cruelly in victory. Some of the clans who had not turned out for him were attacked, and seventy prominent prisoners were killed by being boiled alive in huge cauldrons. This infuriated and alienated a number of his supporters: although the steppes bred hard men and punishment for offenders could be swift and brutal, gratuitous cruelty was not popular. Before long, thousands of warriors had deserted Jamuka and joined up with Temüjin. A seminal turning point had been reached, a fork in the road brought about by Jamuka's inadequacies. Following these events, something strange happens: Temüjin disappears from view for about nine years. We can only speculate what happened in this time. They must have been years of learning for the still inexperienced clan chieftain, a time when he became familiar with the tools of his chosen trade. When we next catch sight of him, he has taken his men to fight on behalf of the Chin in China against the Tartars, who had for a time been the most formidable force on the steppes, in-itself a useful educational experience for a young warrior with much to learn. In a fierce battle against the Tartars in 1196, Temüjin and his soldiers broke through the spiked barricades that their enemy had erected, and committed considerable slaughter amongst them. Soon after, there was something of a role reversal when Toghril, Temüjin's sponsor, came to seek his help. A tribe from the West known as the Naimans had deposed him, and he asked Temüjin to assist him in recovering his throne. This was the way of the steppes. Personal fortune ebbed and flowed and a man might meet someone on the way down the ladder that he had once helped to climb the rungs in the opposite direction. Temüjin won this particular battle without a fight. The reputation of his soldiers was perhaps now growing, which would explain why the Naimans took flight rather than face him.

Temüjin's time with the Chin had won him much kudos with them. His warriors had proved excellent mercenaries. In recognition of his service, it was Toghril who vicariously received a benefit when he was given the honorary title of Wang Khan by the Chin. The Mongols could not pronounce the name so he became known as 'Ong Khan'. It is ironic that skills learned fighting for the Chin would later be used against them, and that the Mongols would one day bite the hand that had fed them. In 1199, Toghril and Temüjin rode out once more against the Naimans. They pushed one army into the towering crags of the Altai Mountains only to find that another then materialised and threatened them as they made their way back. As darkness fell, Toghril slipped away and left Temüjin's men to fight alone: little good it did him. Temüjin cautiously extricated his men and took them home via a circuitous route. However, Toghril was ambushed and was soon sending frantic messages to Temüjin to come to his aid once more.

A familiar figure was about to rear his head again. Jamuka was still on the scene and as much a rival as ever. He managed to persuade most of the unaligned tribes in the region to accept him as their overall leader, and sought out a decisive battle with Temüjin. The former friends led their respective hosts towards a climactic confrontation. The stage was set for a dramatic conflict as the two armies faced up to each other. Nature, however, intervened, and a huge snowstorm blew up, making battle an impossibility. Jamuka's army drifted away, but now, during the retreat, Jamuka again showed his unsuitability to lead. The missed opportunity had soured Jamuka and he was a disappointed man. Cursing his luck at nature's unhelpful intervention, he raided the camp of one of his allies. Seeing him for what he was, a grasping opportunist, most of those who had been on his side now deserted him. Jamuka, it seems had learned nothing from his past mistakes. The alliance fell apart and the threat from Jamuka subsided, for the time being at least.

To the east, the Tartars still posed a great threat to the rise of Tem jin, and in 1202 a decisive confrontation was fought out. In a battle on the River Kalka, the numerically superior Tartar army was destroyed. A bloodbath followed. Women and children were taken into slavery; However, any male higher than the axle of a wagon was killed. The Tartars had been bitter rivals of the Mongols in the past, and the depth of the hostility between the two tribes meant that the losers of this particular fight could expect nothing but death if they were defeated. Jamuka still sought to oust Temüjin, and he resorted to treachery to achieve his aims. Toghril had a natural son, Senggum, and he resented Temüjin's influence with his father. Just at that moment, Temüjin sent messengers to Toghril, suggesting that his son Jochi should marry Senggum's daughter. Senggum replied with outrage: no daughter of his would marry a Mongol ruffian. But then he had a change of heart. He sent messengers back to Temüjin, accepting the proposal and inviting him to participate in a celebratory banquet. Surprisingly, Temüjin failed to smell a trap. He set out for the banquet, but was intercepted en route by an ally warning him that it was a ruse that would lead to his assassination.

Temüjin turned around, and Senggum, realising that his plot had been uncovered, set out with Jamuka and an army to catch him. They had numerical superiority over Temüjin's men, and the battle that followed was hard fought. For a while it seemed as if Temüjin might be bested. The course of the battle ebbed and flowed throughout the day. But then Senggum was wounded by an arrow in the neck. It did not give Temüjin the chance for victory, but he was offered the opportunity to escape to fight another day as a result, and he took it gratefully. The setback (for such it was, as a decisive victory was beyond his powers) showed that Temüjin was still relatively weak. His was not an overnight success story. Senggum's army perhaps outnumbered him ten to one, showing that Temüjin was still a relatively minor chieftain. But he was in possession of two great assets: those who followed him were devotedly loyal to his cause and they included in their number some outstanding strategists and tacticians. He retreated to the swamps, something of a last resort location if there ever was one, a Mongol Alfred in a Mongolian Athelney. Amazingly, men started to join him, sensing something of his latent greatness. Temüjin realised that these men were making a great sacrifice on his behalf and swore in return that any plunder they took in the future would be divided evenly amongst them all – a successful recruiting tactic, much appreciated by the horsemen of the steppes. He drank to their success by dipping his cup in the brackish waters of the swamp and drinking from it. They followed suit. In years to come, it would be a point of pride for warriors to say that they had drank from the waters of the swamp with their great leader in his darkest hour.

In 1203, Temüjin and his men came out of the swamps and advanced on the Kerait camp. They completed their approach at night and caught their enemy by surprise. The camp was in a narrow gorge, an appalling defensive position reflecting complacency on the part of the Kerait leaders. Temüjin posted men either end of it to ensure that no one could escape. Then he unleashed his mounted archers, who swarmed around the camp from all sides. So heavy was their fire that death was virtually guaranteed for any who dared to move out of the camp. A breakout was launched on the first night of the attack, during which Senggum and Toghril managed to escape. The rest, after three days of fighting, exhausted and desperate, surrendered.

On this occasion, there would be no wholesale slaughter. The Keraits were not Temüjin's natural enemy, in fact in the past they had been allies. Now, Temüjin was formally adopted as their leader. He then took measures which he would repeat many times in the future. He integrated the captured Keraits in his army by splitting them up so that in future their loyalty would be to their comrades and not to their tribe. As a result, a kind of regimental pride was formed. This was a policy that would enable the Mongol army to grow exponentially as foes were bested, and formed the basis for later building a vast empire. Temüjin secured his position by arranging a number of marriages between his family and leading members of the Kerait hierarchy. His youngest son, Tolui, married a niece of Toghril, Sorkaktani. Ironically, it was this, perhaps one of the less noteworthy of the matches, which would have the greatest impact. She would bear three sons, Hülegü, Möngke and Kublai, who would all rise to positions of greatness in the future, two becoming great *khans* and the third the ruler of Persia. For Senggum and Toghril, the end was nigh. Senggum would be killed in the Gobi Desert, dying the death of a common bandit. Toghril's demise was tragedy personified, almost Shakespearian in its pathos. He made his way, an old, wrecked man, into the territory of the Naimans. Here he was taken, and no one would believe that he was a great chief, so he was killed. When the chief of the Naimans discovered his true identity, he had his skull made into a drinking cup.

In 1204, Temüjin moved against the Naimans, who were now allied with Jamuka. As the latter saw the Mongol forces draw into battle formation, even Jamuka knew that all was lost. There was something different about the army facing him. Every man knew his place, every one of them looked determined. They moved in perfect order, with no obvious shouting of commands. It was as if the army was one discrete entity with a common mind and purpose. They were drawn up in ranks, neat and tidy. At their midst, atop a white horse (a colour that was reserved for the highest ranks in the Mongol army) sat Temüjin. Despatch riders moved up and down the lines carrying messages. Banners were spread throughout the army, in readiness to be used for communication once the battle was underway. They the men were calm, disciplined, determined. Every move had a purpose. Everything was slick as if the army were a well-oiled machine of war. Jamuka had seen enough. Before the fight had even begun, he and his men were off. The Naimans who remained fought bravely but were annihilated. Even Temüjin recognised their gallantry, though at the same time perhaps deprecating their lack of organisation. Jamuka's men sensed that his time was past. They deserted him in their droves, until in the end he was betrayed by two of his own men and taken into Temüjin's camp.

It was a poignant moment. The two men were blood brothers, but even the endless steppes were not big enough to hold both of them. Jamuka had to die. Before he did so, he witnessed the death of his two betrayers. They were beheaded in front of him. Temüjin could never stomach betrayal: if a man could betray one lord, he could do the same to another. Almost invariably, men who betrayed their lords to Temüjin would die. *The Secret History* gives Jamuka a glamorous end. It says that Temüjin wanted to let him live and he offered him his life. However, according to this account, Jamuka proudly disdained the offer. The steppes were, after all, not big enough for the two of them. He asked only that he should be given an honourable death, and that his blood should not be spilt. Temüjin agreed, and so Jamuka's back was broken. It was a bitter end to what had once been the closest of friendships. If this painful end were an act of kindness, then it was one that few would surely appreciate.

The year 1206 arrived. It would be a momentous one, for the Mongol tribes now recognised that there was in their midst a man of greatness. One by one they paid Temüjin homage at a great *kuriltai* by a river on the steppes. Here Mongol mythology steps in once more. At the beginning of time it was said that the world was an ocean, and that at the appointed time one man would come to rule over all of it. That moment had come, so they gave Temüjin the title of 'Genghis Khan' or in English, the 'oceanic king'.

800 years later, the Mongol people celebrated the anniversary of this day as the moment that the country of Mongolia was formed. In the modern, and rather polluted, city of Ulaan Baatar, proud Mongolians walked around with an extra spring in their step. The stern face of the greatest man in Mongol history looked down rather disdainfully on his modern-day descendants. Mongolia paid its homage to their foremost hero. No such country existed back in 1206, but it was in truth an epoch-shaping event. The world would never be the same place again. Already some of the traits that would lead to Genghis and his successors conquering half the world were apparent. There were a number of features that over time would make the Mongols the irresistible force that they would become, and it would be an opportune moment to consider what these attributes were. Before doing so, due recognition needs to be given to the fact that Genghis first moulded the Mongols, but others were adept in picking up the mantle and perfecting the good habits that Genghis started. It would be a mistake to assume that Mongol greatness was down to him alone – but his role was seminal.

Genghis inherited some great raw material in the shape of his warriors. The Mongol way of life undoubtedly helped to make each warrior a durable, tough soldier, wedded to his horse and capable of astonishing individual feats of endurance. The harshness of the steppes, where each human being had to cope with incredible extremes of climate and some of the toughest terrain in the world, gave each horseman an innate ability to ride for hundreds of miles and then fight a battle. The terrain shaped the nature of the Mongols and the other warrior tribes of the steppes. Superficially, one gets an impression of vastness when thinking of the steppes, but the grasslands on which the nomadic people of the time relied were not in fact endless. Mongolia itself, and the lands that immediately surrounded it (for the Mongols did not conveniently fit into the boundaries of the modern country) was not an uninterrupted expanse of plains, fertile and endless; it was also characterised by mountain and desert. The land was suitable in the main only for supporting the vast herds of sheep, goats and horses that the Mongols pastured. Little of it was suitable for cultivation. As one early European visitor commented in the thirteenth century, 'the land is only in the hundredth part fruitful and cannot support crops unless irrigated.'[7]

The region was in fact a patchwork quilt of terrain, and finding decent grazing ground for all the tribes that lived thereabouts was far from easy. There was often not enough to go round, and tribes were constantly on the lookout for new pastures. The vast herds denuded stocks rapidly. This inevitably led to conflict and meant that the nomadic tribes were, taken as a generalised whole, a combative lot. This was a harsh world, characterised traditionally by infighting and the need to make the most of every scarce source available in their native environment, as the Persian writer Juvaini noted when remarking how Genghis changed everything:

> Before the appearance of Chingiz-Khan they had no chief or ruler. Each tribe or two tribes lived separately; they were not united with one another, and there was constant fighting and hostility between them. Some of them regarded robbery and violence, immorality and debauchery as deeds of manliness and excellence. The Khan of Khitai used to demand and seize goods from them. Their clothing was of the skins of dogs and mice, and their food was the flesh of those animals and other dead things; their wine was mares' milk and their dessert the fruit of a tree shaped like the pine, which they call qusuq and besides which no other fruit-bearing true will grow in that region.[8]

Some of those comments still hold true, though perhaps when he talks of making clothes from mice, what Juvaini is really saying is that anything that is capable of having clothing made from it was exploited. A nobleman would most certainly have his robes made from fine furs of deer or bear: he would wear two, one with the fur next to his skin, the other facing outwards against the cold. On the other hand, an observer from Western Europe, Friar Giovanni Carpini, who visited

Mongolia in 1246, verified the comment about the Mongols, eating habits. He said that, 'they eat dogs, wolves, foxes and horses, and when in difficulty they eat human flesh'. He went on to mention that when they were fighting in China and were short of food, they took one in every ten men to eat. He even said that he saw them eat lice.[9]

From his comments we can detect the truth of Mongolian life, then as well as now. Above nearly all others, this is a country animals are crucial to the existence of life, for there is virtually no arable farming practised. Animal life was needed for meat, for clothing, for milk, for the sinews which provided the bowstrings for the archer, for the felt with which their round tents were made, for transport. Even their dung was crucial as the principal, and, in many cases, the sole, source of heating fuel. On campaign, extra horses were taken, partly because they were needed to ensure the efficiency of the warrior, sometimes so that they could be used for their meat. Occasionally, the weakest horses would even have their veins nicked so that their blood could provide a source of nutritious liquid. This way of life was one where the land shaped the people far more than the people shaped the land. There was little available other than meat that the people could eat, even if they wanted to. The pine Juvaini refers to is now believed to be the Siberian cedar, only available anyway during the autumn months of the year.[10] It was a predictable diet, though the Mongols loved their feasts, when huge chunks of meat would be boiled up in vast cauldrons the size of several people. Vegetables were virtually unheard of: even now the rather mediocre specimens that can be found in Mongolia are expensive and are shipped in from China. In days long before refrigeration, no such luxury was available. The climate too was extreme. One writer noted that:

> The weather there is extremely variable. In fact, in the middle of summer, when other areas usually have the greatest heat, there is a good deal of thunder and lightning which kills many people, and a great deal of snow actually falls there then. There are great cold windstorms too, so that often men can ride horses only with difficulty.[11]

These attributes helped to shape the Mongols' fighting skills. First and foremost in the Mongols' armoury was their amazing manoeuvrability. As people of the steppes, they had been wedded to their horses literally since they had learned to walk. In a nomad society such as that of the Mongols, the ability to move around freely and quickly was a vital attribute, which could be a matter of life or death in times of peace or war. It was a rule in Genghis' empire too that every male of adult age was liable for military service whenever the Khan decreed that it was due, so every man was effectively a warrior. As one renowned historian commented 'they were a suitable instrument for an expansionist leader'.[12]

Almost all the Mongol warriors were cavalry, though some were heavy, and others were light horsemen. Typically, in battle they would be lined up in five lines, the first two of heavy cavalry in their great carapaces of lamellate armour, the last three light. The first move would be for the light cavalry to make their way through the gaps in the front two lines and charge forward towards the enemy. The Mongols, greatest weapon was the composite bow, the pulling power of which comfortably exceeded that of the English longbow. But not only was the weapon itself awesome, so too was the archer that unleashed it. He was taught how to shoot when just a tiny boy, scarcely capable of walking. His most crucial skill was the ability to unleash his arrow, with accuracy and strength, whilst riding at a gallop, going forward or retreating. He ensured his accuracy by releasing his arrow when the horse was off the ground in between steps. These skills married a fearsome weapon to the asset of manoeuvrability – a lethal combination.

At the outset of the battle, it would be the light horsemen who would unleash their arrows against the enemy. The effect of this might be to create alarm amongst their foe, who might as a result begin to disintegrate. If this were the case, then all was well and good. The heavy cavalry, armed with lances (some with hooks on the end to pull enemy horsemen off their mounts), swords, maces or axes, could then smash into their demoralised foes and crush them. If, however, the enemy were made of sterner stuff, then another tactic could be used. It was employed successfully on many occasions, which is surprising as it might be thought that opponents of the Mongols might have learned from the mistakes of others. The tactic was for the light cavalry to retreat if repulsed, as if they were disheartened. This was meant to encourage the enemy to break formation and chase after the apparently fleeing Mongols. Once the enemy formation had broken up then the fleeing Mongols would suddenly wheel around and turn on the pursuers, now no longer in a compact mass. Arrows would rain down on the enemy, picking them off, and then the heavy cavalry would come crashing in, usually overwhelming their opponents. Although mention of the Mongols might summon up visions of lightly armed warriors, the heavy cavalry in fact wore solid lamellar armour (made of overlapping metal scales) and many of their horses were protected in a similar fashion. They were not too different from Western knights.

These tactics were delivered with perfect discipline and cohesion. The Mongols used carefully coordinated battle-plans. They would be

directed in the fray by the use of flags telling different units what their
next move should be. However, their discipline was honed on the steppes
of Mongolia. It was in the hunt that coordination was perfected. And,
to ensure that the skills of the Mongols did not turn rusty, every year
a great hunt was acted out over a huge area. Juvaini said that Genghis
saw great potential for instilling discipline in his men through the hunt.
He writes:

> He paid great attention to the chase and used to say that the hunting of
> wild beasts was a proper occupation for the commanders of armies; and
> that instruction and training therein was incumbent on warriors and men-
> at-arms, who should learn how the huntsmen come up with the quarry,
> how they hunt it, in what manner they array themselves and after what
> fashion they surround it.[13]

The hunt would cover an area of scores of miles, and would take place
at the beginning of winter. The thousands of horsemen taking part in it
would sweep out in a huge arc, the shape of a semi-circle. They would
then advance together in perfect synchronisation with the widest wings
of the semi-circle, moving in almost imperceptibly towards each other in
a vast pincer movement. It all sounds very simple, but in fact the great
hunt could last for up to three months. The circle would eventually close
and a huge amount of game would be encircled in the middle. The noise
of the trapped and terrified beasts, seeing a wall of humanity enclosing
them, must have been deafening. The outer rims of the circle would then
move in on each other, and the hunt would begin. At the end of it all, the
old men of the tribe would ritualistically approach Genghis and ask for
the life of the few animals that were left. Juvaini chillingly compared the
scene to the aftermath of a Mongol battle, when just a few broken-down
wretches would be left alive amidst the carnage. He even compared the
Mongol army to 'trained wild beasts out after game'.[14]

Of course, the spoils would be massive, and the feasts afterwards would
be long, as would the headaches from excessive consumption of *airag*
'fermented mare's milk'. But all of this had another point to it, for the
coordination that was so evident in the great hunt could be transferred
to the battlefield. The whole event, both organisation and execution,
was meticulously planned, with each small part of each *tumen* deputed
to undertake certain parts of it. Each unit took great pride in performing
its role meticulously, and there were even fines for any of them who were
inefficient in closing the ring on any trapped animals and let any of them
escape. The beauty of this system was that it allowed individual men

to know their place and to develop a working relationship with their colleagues. The Mongol regiment, the *tumen,* consisted of 10,000 men. In times of war, each would have its own commander, who would operate for some of the time at least autonomously, though working within the framework of a wider pre-determined strategy. However, beneath this level the army was sub-divided into smaller units based on a decimal system that a Roman legionary would not have felt uncomfortable with. The smallest of these was a company of ten men. Each man felt pride in belonging to his unit and there were severe laws governing its integrity. A man must at all costs stay with his unit and not seek refuge elsewhere. If this law were broken then the miscreant would be executed in front of the others to prove a very harsh point. If three or more men fled in battle, then the remainder of the troop could be summarily executed. This fostered a sense of collective discipline which, as well as being very effective, was also unusual for the period.

Genghis gathered around him his elite, his own personal guard. Like Xerxes' famous 'Immortals' or Napoleon's Imperial Guard, they were the crack troops of his army. But like Roman Praetorians, they were also his own picked men, and in their ranks his great generals honed their skills alongside their remarkable leader. The secret of Genghis' success lay not just in his own brilliance, undoubted though that was, but in the men around him. Greatest of all his abilities perhaps was his ability to spot talent in others. The *esprit* that this close-knit system produced was fostered in the great hunt. These exercises, a surreal variant of the war games that modern armies might use, were very effective in forging cohesion between the different units of the army. The coordination of the Mongols was so well developed, and their ability to move around the battlefield quickly was so devastating, that their enemy often believed that they were heavily outnumbered. In fact, however, the reverse was often the case, and the Mongols routinely fought at a numerical disadvantage. Genghis reflected on his situation and developed in his mind the tactics and the strategies by which his empire would grow. He built on the skills of his men, shaped by the harshness of the steppes, honed by the lifestyle of warrior hunters. These evolved in the light of experience throughout the rest of his reign, and indeed beyond it, but certain key features would emerge.

The Mongols were at their most deadly when in pursuit of a broken enemy. They would rarely complete an envelopment in battle so thoroughly that there was not a gap through which some of the foe could escape. This was quite deliberate, as an ensnared army has nothing to lose in fighting to the death. However, given the chance to escape, the men would be sorely tempted to take the opportunity of life proffered and make a break for freedom. In the retreat they could then be picked off. The cohesion of the enemy would disintegrate during the retreat. The agile Mongol horsemen would chase after their broken foe in a horrific re-enactment of the great hunt, this time with human prey. They would be ruthless too, rarely showing mercy (though sometimes this general rule would be broken in honour of a brave enemy). One of the most controversial of Mongol attributes was the use of terror as an instrument of subjugation. Even given the fact that the history of the Mongols which remains to us is almost exclusively written by its enemies, it is obvious that the Mongols, from the days of Genghis onwards, deliberately employed terror tactics. Cities that surrendered to them without a fight stood a fair chance of survival (albeit at the price of an exorbitant tribute as a ransom), but those that resisted and were taken after a siege were often brutally decimated as a result. The roll call of victims is long: we will come across names such as Nishapur, Merv, Baghdad, and Kiev, which represent just a sample of the horrific punishments that the Mongols meted out to any who dared resist.

All of this appears to be part of a deliberate policy to 'encourage the others' to seek submission rather than death. Mongol excesses were particularly marked when a kinsman of one of the ruling dynasty was killed in a siege, though it seems unlikely that mere vengeance was the motivator for reprisals, but rather a desire to be seen to be publicly punishing malefactors for their disobedience, so as to ensure that others did not follow their lead. Exemplary justice was the *Leit/Motif* of the Mongols. At the outset, they did not take easily to siege warfare. Their preferred form of combat was naturally a mobile one, based on their skills of horsemanship. They had no history of undertaking long sieges, and at the outset of their attempts at world conquest this gave them a problem. They overcame this issue by assimilating forces and skills from the peoples that they conquered. Thus, they developed a capability for siege warfare by learning it from the Chinese. They also gained skills in basic artillery from them too, so we find references to the use of 'fire-bombs' in battle. From others they gleaned the ability to undertake naval warfare, which they had no natural ability for, coming from a completely landlocked country. The latter was an area that they never really mastered convincingly.

To conquer the vast regions that they did, the Mongols had to employ a number of weapons, and many of these extended far beyond the immediate environs on the battlefield. Before any campaign began ,for example, they would put their well-developed spying network into action. They would find out as much about the country they planned to subdue as they possibly could: who the key players in the ruling administration were, which of them were dissatisfied, what the strengths and weaknesses of their armies were. Only when they were satisfied that they had this sound basis of knowledge would they then launch their attack. The grand strategies to be employed would be debated by the ruling Mongol council in a great *kuriltai* or 'council of war'. The Great Khan, who had been appointed to rule the world, was of course all-powerful, but it would be wrong to assume that he always took decisions without advice. In so vast an empire he could not be in every place at once, therefore he would have to rely on generals to win his battles, and governors to control his conquered territories. The Mongols developed a very centralised system, but even then there was a need to rely on the initiative of subordinates on the ground. The *kuriltai* was a way of making sure that every general knew his part in the war that was to come, and the peace that was to follow. The Great Khan had to trust to his followers, ensure that the plan was properly followed through, given the vast area that the empire would eventually cover and the unsophisticated communications of the epoch. Such trust was, however, not always merited, and over time became increasingly fragile. The Mongol communications system which developed was better than most others at the time. Known as the *yam*, it was based, naturally, on the efficient use of quality horses to speed messengers along as quickly as possible, though a series of runners might also be used in some areas where the terrain mitigated against the employment of horses. There would be a series of staging posts where such envoys could pick up a fresh mount, which always stood ready to speed the next despatch rider on his way. It is believed that the Mongols built on Chinese models of the postal system and rolled them out over their empire.[15]

In times of emergency, a rider was even empowered to requisition the horse of any traveller on the road that he came across. In return, he would hand over a token to the traveller to say that he had done so. This could later be redeemed either for the same horse when it was left at the next staging post or a horse of a similar quality could be taken in its stead. By such means messages could be sped across the Mongol lands at a relatively rapid rate of knots. When the Mongol attack came, it would often arrive from a number of different points of the compass. The Mongols routinely undertook their campaigns by arriving from a variety of directions and then reuniting at the optimum moment. The strategy, in other words, was to divide forces in the build-up to a battle, but to re-concentrate them when battle was about to be joined. This was for several reasons. In the first place it meant that the enemy would be overwhelmed, unaware of where the major strike would take place. It also meant that he would dilute his forces in preparing to repel the invaders. The Hungarian campaign of 1241 was a supreme example of such an approach. The key to this tactic of course was coordination, and ensuring that the separate forces reunited prior to the main attack. It did not always work that way. In the attack on Poland and Hungary in 1241 two parts of what should have been the same army ended up fighting major engagements on the same day hundreds of miles apart. Although on that occasion both emerged victorious, it went against one of the basic tenets of warfare, to ensure that you had your maximum force available when a decisive battle was fought.

There were other practical reasons for splitting their forces. The Mongols relied completely on their horses and these needed to feed. They were used to living off the grasslands that they passed through. As a Mongol army numbered in the tens of thousands and was accompanied by large numbers of camp followers, there was not sufficient capacity to carry the huge volumes of fodder that would be needed to feed the horses if grasslands were not available. Given the fact that each Mongol warrior took a number of horses with him on campaign, an army would quickly denude a location of all the supplies of grass that were available. This was indeed a problem on several later Mongol campaigns, possibly in Hungary and certainly in Syria, where the aridity of the terrain, especially in the south and the eastern approaches to the country, posed a major problem for the Mongol armies. This made it sensible for the Mongols to split their forces when advancing on an enemy's country so that the stocks of grass in any given area would last for longer.

However, it would be wrong to assume that the Mongols resorted to war as their only means of conquest. Invasions would almost invariably be preceded by a delegation of ambassadors warning the target nation to surrender or suffer the consequences. A number of rulers became client kings rather than take on the Mongols in battle. It was said that countries could buy off the Mongols by giving a tenth of all property (including people) to them. Not that the Mongols were vainglorious though: if the odds against them seemed too great, they would simply make sure that they avoided battle. Conquest was always a priority, but not at all costs. The Mongols were patient and could always return when they were stronger. Subterfuge too was an oft-used Mongol trick. By using this, countries could be picked off one at a time. Today's ally would become tomorrow's target. None of this gave the Mongols a problem of conscience: Heaven had decreed that the world should belong to the Great Khan and the means by which this end was achieved was to all intents and purposes an irrelevance.

All of these strategies developed over a period of a century or so. Others would take up the mantle of Genghis and drive his people on inexorably towards greater things. The target was always conquest and no Great Khan would be happy until the whole of the known world owned his sway. In fact, his reputation and position relied on carrying on with the quest. But it was Genghis who was the genius behind it all, the Great Khan whom all his successors would seek to emulate. It was he who formed the Mongol state and who shaped the army on which it was founded. It was he who perfected their battle tactics and it was he who formed their strategies. Long after his death, his successors would refer back to his ambitions and his rulings and he would remain a shadowy, penumbral figure who dictated affairs for decades after his demise.

It is important to ask just why Genghis wished to conquer the world. Naked ambition was part of it of course, as with all would-be conquerors. It is quite likely that he also believed that he had been given a divine mandate. Given the frequent repetition of the claim in various chronicles, it is probably an accurate supposition. But it has been suggested that there were more practical reasons too. One scientific analysis of the climate at the time has suggested that changes in the weather had led to a reduction in the yields of the grasslands in Mongolia, and that this had led to the impulses which led the Mongols to move further afield.[16] Another possibility is that the Mongols had been finding it difficult to trade with the various Chinese dynasties that lay to the east, which would have been a very serious development for them. Given the volatility of the Mongolian climate in all periods, the Mongols had to frequently rely on trade in grain to stock up their supplies of food. Closing off the possibilities of trading would have had serious repercussions for all of Mongol society.

Whatever the motivations, now all of Mongolia accepted Genghis' rule. It was a state of affairs that would have caused barely a ripple beyond neighbouring states, and would have been completely unknown in the Middle East and the West. So, across the world, men and women went about their daily lives, oblivious to the storm that was brewing in the East, and would not in their darkest nightmares have dreamed of the tempest that would soon threaten to overwhelm them all.

CHAPTER 2
The Mongols Head East: Genghis Invades China 1209-1218

For a young chieftain who had seemingly been on the edge of oblivion on more than one occasion, it was no mean feat to become the undisputed head of the Mongols. For most men, perhaps it would all have stopped there with ambition satiated. But for Genghis Khan, unlike most other men, this was simply not enough. Ambition burned fiercely inside him and his vision extended far beyond the steppes and hills of his homeland. He had already seen the makings of something great in his army, which had been turned from a collection of brave but individual warriors into a well trained, superbly disciplined fighting machine. For many years Genghis had been the underdog, and his record in battle was not unblemished. In defeat, however, he learned lessons that he would apply thoroughly: the raw (and probably headstrong) young man had developed with experience. The presence of some outstanding leaders at his side also helped. It was a combination of the lessons bitterly learned and the superb skills of his generals, plus the evolution of a longer-term strategic vision, that made him into what he became. Over time, he sought to integrate, rather than obliterate, defeated opponents, a policy that would enable his often-outnumbered Mongols to fight way above their weight. The steppes, though, lacked sufficient plunder to keep his burgeoning army happy, and, for any self-respecting Mongol leader, there was only one way to satisfy the latent need for booty to keep his men on board. This was crucial: loyalty was a tenuous commodity (as Genghis himself had found out when his father died) and to a certain extent had to be to be bought. Away to the east was a country where large numbers of sedentary city-dwellers lived, surrounded by luxury and highly desirable portable goods. For centuries, its people had been subject to raids from the unruly tribes that settled the steppes. Sometimes these raiders had been bought off. At others, they had been successful in their raiding and had caused a great deal of suffering.

Most of this suffering, though, had been short-term. The raiders had struck, done their harm and gone away again, much richer for their depredations and a major irritant no doubt, but in essence a temporary though deadly problem. Great walls had been erected in an attempt to keep these terrifying hordes away – a policy that had developed over hundreds of years in an always volatile area, where civilisation met the wilderness. At other times, the barbarians had been integrated into the ruling administration's army as mercenaries. As such their loyalty had often been suspect, but it was a way of keeping them in check to an extent. It is important to note that the walls that then inefficiently protected China were not part of the Great Wall, as we now know it (a much later sixteenth–century creation). However, walls had been built to keep out raiders from the steppes for years. These now proved completely porous when faced by such a manoeuvrable enemy. The static defences were incapable of fighting a foe that simply went around them. A twentieth–century US President, Richard Nixon, when looking at that later wall remarked of the Chinese that, 'a people that can build a wall like this, certainly have a great past to be proud of'. A Mongolian historian, B. Batbayar (better known as Baabar) riposted with the comment that, 'the people that forced the building of a wall like this certainly have at least as great a past to be proud of'.[1]

China, as we now know it, did not exist as a coherent entity as Genghis was coming to power. The modern state was roughly divided into three power blocs. These divisions would help the Mongols no end, as the three great powers in China were often at odds with each other, easing the Mongols' path into China. On the borders with Mongolia was a state known as Hsi-Hsia, which was always likely to be the first to feel the weight of the Mongol army's blows, given its geographical location. Elsewhere were the Chin dynasty (the name means 'golden'), broadly in the north of modern China, and the Song, in the south. Genghis, however, was in no hurry. He was a meticulous planner and he realised that the conquest of a region as large as China was a long-term enterprise. In this case, patience truly was a virtue. He therefore ensured that the time was right before marching his armies east. He needed even now to consolidate his position in Mongolia itself, before embarking on foreign adventures, and so some time was spent in mopping up any residual opposition there. However, he was not slow to lay a marker in the sand. In 1208, a new emperor came to the throne of the Chin dynasty who ruled much of northern China. The Chin had been the prominent power there for about a century before the birth of Genghis. The regime had stayed in power partly because, rather than subduing the perceived barbarians surrounding them, they had played one off against the other. The policy that they used was termed in Chinese *i chi i,* which means 'use barbarians to control barbarians'.[2]

The Mongols were nominally vassals of the Chin, having acted as their mercenaries for a time, and an embassy was despatched to Genghis to claim his loyalty to the new ruler. When they demanded that he offer his fealty, he spat in the direction of the south where the emperor sat on the imperial throne. It was a statement, not eloquent perhaps, but more telling than any words could be. It was also a brave one, for the resources available to either side were totally unbalanced. The Chin had fifty million people; the Mongols three million.[3] The relative size of the armies that each side could put in the field was similarly out of proportion. But numbers alone could not disguise the fact that in terms of tactics and discipline, the Mongols had advantages that outweighed the huge odds against them, for whilst most of the Chin warriors were poorly trained levies or mercenaries, all the Mongols had been taught the arts of war almost from the point when they began to walk. The style of war that either side fought was different too. Whereas the Mongols were exclusively cavalry forces, the Chin had large infantry battalions, in addition to having mounted units of their own. Their preferred infantry tactic was to fight in large, massed phalanxes. The problem that this gave them was that it was a very immobile form of warfare, and it was virtually useless when faced by the large hordes of mounted archers that could buzz around their flanks like a swarm of angry bees, loosing their missiles and then sped away again, with little possibility of being caught. However, the Chin did possess a major advantage over the Mongols. If they were vulnerable in an open battle, they still had massive fortifications to hide behind. The first line of defence was the line of vast walls that marked their borders, but this was backed up by several other walls, which acted as further layers of defence behind. In addition, the cities who were also exposed to raids from raiders like the Mongols, and in response to this threat many of them had erected massive fortifications around them. These would prove a hard nut to crack, and explain why the war that was now imminent would last for a quarter of a century until the Mongols finally triumphed.

The Chin and the Mongols had, to say the least, a chequered history as regards their relationship. Genghis had at one stage voluntarily allied himself to them, though this was in the early years of his rise to fame, when his position was uncertain, he had many enemies, and he needed their support. The Chin, along with the Song (the dominant force in the region for the past century) had often forged such alliances with steppe tribesmen, in order to protect their position. In return for Genghis' help against the Tartars, mutual enemies of both, in 1196 the Chin had given him the honorific name of 'Keeper of the Frontier'. It was a nice title, which the Chin hoped to give to the savage Mongols as a reward for their assistance, and also to protect them in the future. Despite such outward expressions of amity, it was a false friendship. There was, to use a colloquialism, 'form' between Mongols and the Chin that went back many years. Over half a century earlier in 1140, Genghis' great-grandfather Kabul had been invited to Zhongdu, the Chin capital. Whilst he was there he playfully tweaked the beard of the emperor. To the Mongols this would have been a piece of horseplay, but to their hosts, obsessed with convention, it was a shocking breach of etiquette, and in the ritualistic Chin court such affronts did not go unnoticed. The insult was on the surface ignored at the time but out of sight revenge was plotted. Kabul was later ambushed, though he managed to escape from the trap that had been set. His nephew Ambakai was not so fortunate. He was captured by the Tartars, a tribe whose territories bordered those of the Mongols, as a result of which a long history of mistrust existed between both parties. Seeking to obtain the good graces of the Chin, they handed their valuable prisoner over. Ambakai was subsequently executed in the most brutal manner by being crucified on a device known as a 'wooden donkey'. It gave Genghis ample reason to hate both the Chin and the Tartars. But the time was not yet quite ripe for vengeance.

In 1209 an event of great significance occurred. A delegation from the Uighurs in the west of Genghis' lands came to offer him allegiance and tribute. This was a crucial development, because, instead of being for any particular military reason (though it did strengthen the western borders of the Mongols), it was an indication that the Uighur's had something that the Mongols lacked: literacy. Their scribes would, as it happened, be even more useful than their warriors, for if the latter were needed to conquer a country, the former were required to administer it, and Genghis had none of his own to fill the gap. He accepted the offer of tribute with good grace, showing that he was as happy to accept supremacy through diplomacy as he was through force – a trait of Mongol leaders that is easy to overlook if one focuses purely on their martial prowess. His relationship with the Uighur ruling family was secured by marriage. It was an important development and a timely one too, for Genghis still had internal division to subdue before he could feel confident of his rule. Some of the trouble came from an unexpected source. Genghis and his successors generally encouraged religious toleration, but he himself was a shamanist. His chief shaman was Kokochu, son of one of Yesugei's old servants and he was something of a liability. Outspoken and arrogant, he attracted dissension almost without trying. And there was much of it about too, especially from freedom-loving steppe dwellers who did not wish to be forced to provide military service when they did not want to. Not everyone welcomed discipline.

Convinced of the power of his own medicine, Kokochu started to tell Genghis that his own brother, Kasar, was a rival for the role of world leader. Genghis at first believed that the threat was genuine, and Kasar was subsequently deprived of his command with absolutely no evidence that he was indeed plotting to depose his brother (and was possibly lucky to escape worse). Genghis trusted holy men perhaps a little more than he should have done, as it gave the opportunity for charlatans to take advantage of him. Inevitably, it was not long before Kokochu went too far. He had his own camp, even his own soldiers, and his mix of encouragement (he offered men who supported him prospects of great rewards in return) and fear (as a shaman, a quality he was well placed to generate) was very successful in increasing his powerbase. As his power grew, so did his confidence, until it translated into arrogance of the most dangerous kind.

One of those to suffer was Temuge, Genghis' younger brother. He lost many of his soldiers to Kokochu, and sent a messenger to his camp to demand that they be returned. The envoy returned with a whipping for his pains, so Temuge went in person to face down Kokochu. However, when he arrived he was seized, threatened and forced to bow in obeisance before the shaman. It was a huge miscalculation on Kokochu's part. When this happened, Temuge was incandescent. It was an enormous insult to his own, and his family's, honour. He rode post haste to Genghis and strode into his *ger* without being announced (which as a member of the ruling caste he was allowed to do). He knelt beside his brother and told him what had happened. It was a terrible insult to the ruling dynasty and it might well have led to instant retribution anyway, but it was the intervention of Boerte that was to prove decisive. Calmly she told her husband that her sons could never be sure of their inheritance whilst Kokochu was alive. We do not hear much about Boerte, other than that she was famed for her great beauty, but Genghis seems to have been genuinely fond of her, despite the great number of other wives and concubines that he was involved with over the course of his life. Genghis saw that his reliance on the shaman was misplaced and must be ended. He told Temuge that Kokochu would soon be at his camp, and that he could do what he wished with him. Vengeance was sweet. Soon after, Kokochu arrived at the camp. There was a delegation waiting for him and Temuge challenged him to a wrestling match, a sport much loved by the Mongols. However, when the proud shaman accepted, he walked straight into a trap. There were three experienced wrestlers waiting for him, who quickly broke his back and left him to die in the dust. This domestic issue being settled, it was time to move on China. Before attacking the Chin – his major enemy in the region, given its power in the lands bordering Mongolia – Genghis had to neutralise Hsi-Hsia. The region was the domain of a tribe called the Tanguts, and they had already been subjected to several Mongol raids. In 1209, the Mongols returned for real. They were not yet skilled in siege warfare though. It was an alien environment for them, and although several towns fell, they did not yet have the skills to subdue larger cities.

Their first serious experience of siege warfare ended in an incident that was so strange that it is hard to think of it as being other than legend. This took place at a fortified town called Volohai. The siege went on for weeks and there was still no sign of a breakthrough, so Genghis made an extraordinary offer to the townsfolk. He would raise the siege, he said, if the town would provide him with a tribute of 1,000 cats and 10,000 swallows. Those inside were delighted at what seemed to be an amazingly generous offer, so they promptly collected the animals and handed them over. They rejoiced at their good fortune but celebration was premature. Genghis ordered that the swallows be released and they naturally flew back to their nests inside the city. The cats were then released and chased them back. However, Genghis had ordered that firebrands should be tied to their tails so that when they rushed back into the town, a huge conflagration quickly erupted. Soon the town was a flaming ruin and was taken. It is a nice story, though probably not true: apart from its inherent unlikeliness it does not appear in print before the seventeenth century.[4]

During the campaign, the Mongols were also faced by another challenge that they were unused to. Most of their enemies in the past had been, like them, cavalry forces. Now they came up against infantry for the first time, forces that relied in the main on pikes for their defence in the same way that Chin armies functioned. It was not, at first, an easy experience for Genghis' men, and on one occasion infantry forces were able to successfully resist Mongol horsemen until their own cavalry came up. Nevertheless, by August the Mongols were laying siege to the capital of Hsi-Hsia, Ning Hsia. This was situated on the mighty Yellow River and its walls proved stubbornly resilient against the as yet poorly developed siege skills of the Mongols. By October, with the city still holding out, Genghis lost patience. If the

Mongols could be resisted, the mighty Yellow River could not be. Genghis ordered that it be dammed and diverted into the city. Even this, however, did not prove decisive. By January 1210, the dam had broken and flooded the Mongols out rather than the city, but both sides were feeling exhausted by what was turning into a stalemate. The ruler of the Tanguts offered to pay tribute to Genghis and gave the hand of his daughter in marriage as a way of emphasising the point. However, he refused absolutely to give any of his soldiers to Genghis, claiming that if the *khan* were as strong as he claimed to be he did not need them. For the moment Genghis, with bigger fish to fry, accepted the rebuff, but it was one that he never forgot or forgave.

This was just the warm-up for the main event, though it had given the Mongols valuable experience, which they would put to good use in the future. Before marching on the Chin, Genghis did what some other great men have done over the ages, and took himself off to the wildernesses of the sacred mountains of his homeland to meditate, and ensure that he was spiritually prepared for the challenge that was to come. Like an athlete on the verge of his greatest trial, he ensured that he was mentally, as well as physically, prepared. There was much to ponder on for, to the untrained eye, that challenge looked an impossible one. The Chin had over half-a-million men to protect their administration. Against them, Genghis could deploy perhaps 65,000, although those numbers would rise as more tribes were recruited to the Mongol army.[5] The odds were fearful, but they were also deceptive. Absolute numbers did not adequately demonstrate the qualitative differences between the troops. The Chin were poorly led, poorly trained and poorly armed. Their morale was low and they had little confidence in their commanders. In contrast, the Mongols were rapidly becoming battle-hardened veterans with absolute faith in their general.

Genghis, as was his wont, prepared meticulously for the invasion of Chin China. After returning from the campaign in His-Hsia he had ordered that all his commanders should assemble for a great *kuriltai,* the council of war where every man could be briefed on his role in the days and months ahead. In case anyone thought about missing this, he warned that if they did so they would be treated like a stone dropped into water – that is, they would disappear from sight. He reflected on what he had learned from the previous campaign, and in particular the need to prepare for siege warfare. He assembled camel trains that could carry large stores of wood and other supplies that would be needed in the months ahead. He deputed his son Ögedei to take charge of siege operations and instruct the senior commanders in the techniques required to conquer a city.

All of this was commendable, but it was still in essence a futile gesture, for the Mongols still lacked the experience required to take a major city. They knew next to nothing about how to assemble powerful siege engines, and they did not have the engineering corps available to instruct them how to do so. It was hard for Ögedei to train anybody in siege warfare when there were so many fundamental failings to deal with. The moment to depart had at last arrived. The Mongol army, which by their standards was huge with over 100,000 men[6], set out across the arid wastelands of the Gobi, which was a fearsome undertaking in its own right. Adopting a tactic that would be used many times in the future, the army was divided into several columns, partly to help provisioning and partly to confuse the enemy. They then set off into the barren wastelands of the Gobi, where the sun scorched by day and the wind froze by night, an arid, desolate region with little to sustain an army.

Great secrecy was observed, as the element of surprise was crucial. Anyone unfortunate enough to get in the way of the army was taken captive or killed on the spot. Three *tumens* went ahead, one led by Subotai, the second by Mukali, and the third by Jebei. The rest of this vast force was under the direct control of Genghis in person. They came out across the desert and were then faced with a part of the Great Wall that offered a false sense of security to the Chin. This Great Wall was not quite the awesome fortification that is so well known to the modern world; it was not as long and it was crumbling. Further, it was manned by nomad mercenaries, who had little interest in putting up much of a fight. However, this did not excuse their next move. Instead of fighting against Genghis, they joined forces with him. Without an arrow being fired in anger, a further 10,000 men had been added to the Mongol army. The Chin were faced with a fatal weakness which this early defection epitomised all too well. They were an occupying force, and as such there was little love for them amongst many of their subjects. The peasantry were happy to exchange one conqueror for another, perhaps hopeful that this was just another raid, though they might not have been so philosophical about the regime change if they knew of the tribulations that lay before them. Crucially, large elements of the army were composed of mercenaries, and even some of the foremost generals of the Chin forces were from nomad tribes.

The war that followed would be a long one. The conquest of China took the best part of a century to complete. However, the campaign started well for the invaders, helped no end by the lack of fighting spirit demonstrated by some of the Chin commanders. During these early years, with siege warfare still a strange black art, the Mongol approach was a simple one. Cities that surrendered of their own volition or were not capable of offering resistance were hungrily gobbled up. But if a city promised to be a tougher nut to crack, it was for the time being left alone. Genghis divided his army into three different units. One under Kasar, Genghis' brother, made its way to Manchuria. The second under Jochi went south, whilst the third under Genghis moved southeast across the vast plains of China. They left a trail of death and destruction in their wake, and possibly hoped that the use of terror tactics would lead to a collapse of morale. Life was cheap to the Mongols, especially when they did not understand or value the way of life that the peasant population lived, alien as it was to their nomadic ways. To their surprise, despite the advent of this reign of terror, morale did not collapse, and the Chin, refusing to accept that they were beaten, fought on.

The Mongols, though, quickly became famed for a quality that would forever be associated with them: the ability to appear as if from nowhere, and the art of moving at lightning speed in order to catch their enemy unawares. Siege skills proved harder to develop, and, as a result, another stalemate developed. The Chin tried on two occasions to fight the Mongols in open battle, and both times they came off much the worse for it. So, instead, they retreated behind their mighty walls, and waited patiently for the Mongols to get fed up and go away.

By the summer of 1211, the Mongols had gained their first sight of the Chin capital, Zhongdu, close to the site of modern Beijing. It was a city unlike any other that the Mongols had yet seen; protected by an 18-mile long wall, rising 50 feet high and surrounded by 900 towers. There were four mighty forts protecting the approaches to the city, each connected to Zhongdu by an underground tunnel. Three deep moats offered further protection. Even a cursory glance demonstrated that there was no chance at this stage of taking the city by assault.

It was not long, perhaps a month, before the Mongols experienced a problem that was to beset them again in the future. As they relied on their horses for practically every facet of warfare, they were also forced to rely on good quality grazing to sustain them, and within just a few weeks the grass around Zhongdu was much depleted. As their horses weakened, so did the fighting capabilities of the Mongol army. Genghis was therefore forced to consider retiring, before fate intervened. The Chin emperor sent a Khitan official to negotiate with Genghis. At least that was the formal line. In reality, given the large numerical advantage that the Chin enjoyed, it was more likely an attempt to ascertain just how weak the Mongols really were. However, the emperor had made a grave error of judgment. The Khitans populated much of north-west China, though they too were originally nomads rather than city-dwellers. They were kindred spirits to the Mongols, being steppe-dwellers by nature too. They felt no real empathy towards the Chin, and the general was soon telling Genghis that within the city dissension was rife. The emperor could trust virtually nobody, and was constantly under threat from the Song dynasty to the south. In addition, the many Khitans who lived within the borders defined by the walls that the Chinese had erected were restless and ripe for rebellion. This did not mean that Genghis was yet strong enough to take Zhongdu, but it encouraged him to stay in the region and not return to Mongolia for the time being. Instead, he wintered in Manchuria, where there was an abundance of good grazing land for his horses. Indeed, he even added to his stock by taking over the vast stud farms that the emperor had maintained there. Before long, the Chin were suing for peace.

Next spring, the Mongols returned under the command of Jebei, one of Genghis' most trusted commanders. He encouraged the Khitans in the region of Manchuria to rise up against their Chin masters. They attacked the ancient capital of Liaoyang. At first, they were resisted. However, Jebei then resorted to a tactic that would become a favourite of the Mongols: subterfuge. Jebei tried a trick that uncannily resonates of the more famous one played at Troy. He led the Khitans and his men away for two days and left the camp for the defenders of Liaoyang to loot. This quickly threw them off their guard, and when the Mongols and their allies came storming back they caught their enemy completely by surprise, with the gates of the city wide open. A rout followed. The garrison of the citadel were soon overpowered and were slaughtered to a man.

There was a legend concerning the recruitment of Jebei to Genghis' cause many years before, which demonstrates the resourcefulness and courage that he displayed on this particular occasion. During Genghis' early years, when he was not yet all-powerful, Jebei was at one time on the other side, fighting against the young Temüjin, and he was captured whilst trying to run away on foot. Genghis' cavalrymen ran him down, and would probably have killed him when he proudly declared that he would match any of them if he too were on a horse. Spurred on by this defiance, a horse was duly provided, whereupon Jebei had slashed his way out through the surrounding horsemen and rode off to freedom. However, he had clearly seen enough to know which way the wind was blowing, and a few days later had ridden into the camp of Genghis, and offered to serve him or die. Genghis wisely chose the former option, a decision he never regretted.

Whilst Jebei (whose full name – Jebei Noyon – means 'the arrow') was winning great victories, Genghis was leading another Mongol army in battle within the Chin lands. He was wounded by an arrow and forced to delegate command to his son Tolui as a result. But in 1213 he was restored to full health and leading his army once more. Zhongdu was again the target and was soon under siege. On this occasion, a state of panic gripped the city. The Mongols were proving a worryingly determined enemy. Inside the walls, those responsible for the defence started to lose their grip. Several leading generals defected to the Mongols, who this time did not kill those who were betraying the city, but instead encouraged others to follow suit. Above all else Mongol policy was pragmatic.

As the noose around Zhongdu tightened, there were those who smelt the opportunity for personal gain, though such profit that transpired would be transient if the city were to fall to the Mongols. One of them was a eunuch named Hushasu. He plotted against the emperor, killing him and the governor of the city and installing a child emperor, a prince of the royal blood, as a puppet. But this did nothing to improve the situation of the populace, and it was not long before Hushasu too fell victim to a plot when he was murdered and his head delivered as an unusual present to the new emperor. Despite all this intrigue, the Mongols were still not adept enough in siege warfare to take the city, and retreated once more to the fecund lands of Manchuria. Although still not possessed of sound siege skills, the Mongols were getting better at this aspect of warfare. As they captured engineers who knew about such things, they were forced to join the ranks of the Mongol army and each Mongol regiment, the *tumen* of 10,000 men, would have a siege train attached to it. Although Zhongdu had not yet fallen, the Mongols had managed to capture dozens of towns and cities.

In 1214, the Mongols returned to Zhongdu once more – they were nothing if not persistent. This time they were better prepared for the siege than they ever had been. Their ranks were swollen by ever more skilled engineers, and they themselves knew through experience what to expect. They had also taken the four forts that represented the outer defensive ring of the city, which was now naked before the terrifying Mongol horde. The Mongols were short of supplies, so in an attempt to force the issue Genghis sent in messengers calling the emperor's bluff. Surprisingly, he bought it, unaware of the true position of his enemy. He recognised Genghis as his lord, married one of his sisters off to him and presented 3,000 horses and 500 child slaves to him, a sizeable tribute.

Genghis marched off, well satisfied. He had taken a number of prisoners in the recent campaign. Those who were of use, engineers, scientists and artisans were spared to live a life of miserable servitude in the service of their Mongol masters. The rest, useless mouths to be fed, were slaughtered. It was not abject cruelty, though it might seem to be such. It was another example, a brutal one to be sure, of Mongol pragmatism. The spirit of the Chin was broken by the surrender, and the emperor, terrified within the increasingly unsecure-looking walls of Zhongdu, deserted his capital and ran off to the city of Kaifeng (modern Nanking). Genghis was on his way back to Mongolia when he got the news. He was convinced that it was an attempt by the emperor to raise an army and fight back against the Mongols. It was a fatal mistake for anyone to make an enemy of the Great Khan, and Genghis rapidly turned his men about and made once more for China. This sealed the fate of Zhongdu. Genghis led his army towards it whilst Subotai moved men into Manchuria. From all sides the Mongols descended on the city, paralysed with fear by the looming storm clouds that swept down on it from all directions. Another Mongol commander, Mukali, ravaged the south of Manchuria, drowning all who dared stand in his way in a sea of blood.

By September, Mukali stood on the threshold of Zhongdu. He encircled it, cutting it off from the outside world, and slowly suffocating it like a python smothering its prey. The Chin emperor sent reinforcements up to relieve it but they were unable to get through. The situation of those inside the city assumed nightmarish proportions. They were soon so short of food that they resorted to eating each other. In May 1215, the commander of the garrison exhorted his men to follow him in a sortie against the enemy. It was effectively an invitation to participate in a suicide mission. His men declined the offer, so instead the commander signed off with a final dramatic gesture of his own when he killed himself. Such abject acceptance of defeat was an appropriate symbol for the state of the city, which by now was on its knees. One cannot begin to imagine the feelings of those inside the city. They were exhausted and hungry, out of food and out of hope. Outside it stood an enemy that was pitiless, and on the verge of achieving what he had struggled to attain for years. Many of their comrades would have perished in the attacks on Zhongdu, and now retribution was at hand. Those frightened citizens must have known that there was no escape from their fate, and that that fate would be an awful one.

In the end, their morale was so shattered that an assault by just 5,000 Mongol soldiers succeeded in forcing entry to the city. The rape and pillage that followed lasted for a month. If a Mongol saw a citizen that he did not like the look of, he killed him on the spot. It was said that when foreign ambassadors visited the city a few years later, the streets were still slippery with human fat from those who had died in the apocalypse. It was not the last time that such analogies would be used of a city that had fallen to the Mongols.

The Chin dynasty had not reached its end, at least not just yet. It would take another twenty years for the Mongols to complete their conquests of this land. It perhaps was a small consolation that by the time this happened, the author of the tragedy that overwhelmed Zhongdu, the Great Khan, Genghis, was dead. Nevertheless, there was no doubting the size of the Mongol victory, even though it was not yet a final one. The walls protecting the boundaries of the Chin kingdom had proved useless. As others have done over the ages, men had outwitted those who built them to keep them out by the simple expedient of going round them. A contemporary song bewailed the fact that 'the Wall was built, with cries of pain and sadness; the moon and the Milky Way seem low in comparison with it. But if all the white bones of the dead had been left piled up there, they would reach the same height as the Wall.'[7]

Mukali was made viceroy of the newly conquered territories in recognition of his leading role in the victory. Genghis returned back to the steppes well satisfied. The land that had been won was rich and full of material resources. Gold and other precious metals were there in abundance, silks, spices and prodigious amounts of other wealth. For a man used only to the scarcity of the steppes, it was a treasure trove of unimaginable riches. But that was not all, welcome though plunder was. Contrary to what some might think, the Mongols were not mindless nihilists. Death was reserved for those with no use. Men who could help to build an empire were kept alive for their skills. The Chin emperor's chancellor was renowned for his abilities, so he now became Genghis' chancellor. Physicians were retained so their medical skills might help Mongol warriors wounded in battle. Yet more engineers were added to the siege trains. The process of empire building was beginning for real.

Subotai was still on the loose in Manchuria. In the winter of 1216 he took the Mongol forces into uncharted territory, crossing the Yalu River and entering Korea. Although the country was relatively small, it was an area that the Mongols would find very hard to subdue, and they never really absorbed it into their empire on a firm basis. However, they would have several attempts at doing so.

Korea was ruled by the Kyoro dynasty. Subotai's excuse for crossing the Yalu was that he wished to get rid of the Khitans who he had chased into the country when he invaded Manchuria. They came across resistance at the town of Kangdong. The Korean winter can be very harsh, and this year was no exception. Snow cut off the Mongol lines of supply. Faced with some very difficult decisions, Subotai decided to ask the Korean government for help. Subotai did not have a massive force with him – perhaps 30,000 men – and the countryside before him was liberally dotted with castles. The Korean army was strong and fairly large but it chose not to fight him. Instead, the Koreans agreed to Subotai's request. Nevertheless, they were nervous. They had no love for the Khitans who had forced their way into their country, but they did not trust the Mongols either.

The reason that the Koreans chose not to fight was because they were used to recognising that whoever was the dominant power in Manchuria was strong enough to dominate them. As the Mongols now clearly controlled Manchuria, the Koreans recognised their supremacy. However, Mongol control over Manchuria proved to be fragile, and when they subsequently recognised this, the Koreans quickly turned on the Mongols. For now though, they helped the Mongols without committing themselves irrevocably to their cause. Supplies were given to the Mongols and cursory assistance given in some of the actions against the Khitans. They took great pains to ensure that they gave the minimum of support to the Mongols. However, they were on their guard all the time, and their commanders were as much spying on the Mongols as they were helping them.

But this action in Korea was not the major concern of Genghis now. Events were about to take place much further west which would divert the attention of the Mongols from China and the region, although desultory action would carry on for some years yet. The Mongol army was about to be put to another great test. The engineers, scientists, administrators, and soldiers who had been recruited, were all to be faced with a period of great challenge, characterised by conquest, great victories and cataclysmic destruction. The Mongol empire was on the move and the world, if it had known what was coming, would have trembled before it.

CHAPTER 3
The Scourge of God:
The Mongols Devastate Central Asia
1218-1222

The shock waves of the Mongol invasions into China reverberated across the Far East. There was a regularly travelled trade route between China and the West, the fabled Silk Road, along which precious fabrics and spices travelled. Western merchants did not make the trip to the Far East in person as intermediaries transported goods to and from East and West along several major arteries of trade. News travelled along these also, and stories of the decline of the Chin dynasty would have reached Central Asia, Persia and beyond fairly quickly.

Ambassadors from these other territories were deputed to make their way to Zhongdu and establish diplomatic relations with the new order. There was no room for sympathy with the deposed rulers. It was imperative that normal trading relations be established as soon as possible. One party of envoys came from the Khwarismian Empire, which occupied large chunks of what is now Persia, Afghanistan and other parts of Central Asia. It was the greatest power in the region, and would no doubt have received reports of the Mongol successes with more than a modicum of interest. This other empire was expanding too, and implicated in this growth was one of Genghis' old adversaries. This was Kuchlug, who was a Naiman, and who had fled west when his people had been severely beaten by Genghis a few years before. He had found sanctuary amongst the Kara-Khitai, who lived on the far side of Mongolia (the name means 'Black Cathay', referring to the fact that at one time these nomadic tribes had populated parts of China). Some Khitans had already been absorbed into the Mongol empire when Manchuria had been added to Genghis' territories.

For some time the kingdom governed by Sultan Mohammed, the ruler of Khwarezm, had been paying tribute to Kara-Khitai, but having come recently to the post, the sultan felt that this was an affront to his honour and must be stopped. Unfortunately for the Khitans, when they accepted Kuchlug into their midst they were inviting a viper into the nest. Kuchlug repaid their kindness with betrayal, and plotted with Mohammed against the ruling regime. As a result, Mohammed invaded Kara-Khitai, overwhelmed the army sent against him and Kuchlug picked up the scraps becoming new lord of the region. This news was not well received by Genghis for two reasons. Firstly, the Naimans had been longstanding enemies of the Mongols, and any growth in their influence through the rise of Kuchlug was not to be welcomed. Secondly, he was required to interfere by the law of the steppe. A steppe lord, Arslan, had a few years previously paid homage to Genghis and in return had married one of his granddaughters. Kuchlug had slain Arslan and, as his lord, Genghis was obliged to seek retribution. There was another reason for the Mongols interest too, based on international *real/politik*. With two empires both on the increase and edging closer to each other's territory, it was probably only a matter of time before a confrontation occurred. Kara-Khitai provided a buffer of sorts but given Kuchlug's debt to Sultan Mohammed and his previous antipathy to Genghis, it was a far from neutral one. It posed a threat to Genghis and therefore he would have welcomed its elimination.

However, Genghis liked to have the appearance of legitimacy on his side when he launched his armies against a foe. Kuchlug's actions against Arslan had given a convenient excuse for him to dispose of an old enemy. In 1218, Jebei was sent into Kara-Khitai at the head of two *tumens*. These were now seasoned troops, hardened by the difficulties of war against the Chin. Kuchlug the interloper on the other hand was despised by many of his subjects, to whom of course he was a foreigner. He had proved a high-handed, cruel and ineffective leader, who was hated by most of those he claimed to rule. In particular, he was a ruthless persecutor of those who adopted different religious beliefs from his own. He was a Buddhist, but most of his people were Muslims. When a prominent Imam had refused to convert to Islam after he came to power, he was promptly crucified on the gates of his college as a result. Such actions were guaranteed to turn an already un-enamoured people violently against him.

The Mongols espoused religious toleration, and the pragmatism of this policy was now demonstrated with telling effect. They had a well-developed spy network, and scouts would have been sent into the country ahead of them. These scouts would have been lightly armed and equipped for speed. They would play a crucial part in the campaign, and would have reported back to their commanders religiously. They would therefore have known all about the grievances of the populace against Kuchlug. Jebei therefore let it be known that all Muslims would be free to worship as they wished if the Mongols were to take over. It was an easy decision for the inhabitants of the capital, Kashgar, to make. As one, the people abandoned Kuchlug and, when he tried to escape, they caught him and killed him, saving Jebei the trouble. And so Kara-Khitai was added to the ever-larger Mongol empire, bringing the Mongol territories flush up against the lands ruled by Sultan Mohammed.

Sultan Mohammed was a lord in control of fabulous wealth. All the great trade routes from the East crossed his lands, adding to the riches of the mythical cities of Bokhara and Samarkand. But his grip on power was illusory, as he was very reliant on mercenaries to keep his lands, and they were never a trustworthy source of warriors. What is more, it would soon transpire that he was a very poor judge of character. Further, he had not been long since he had usurped power in Khwarezm. Most of his people were Persians but he and his men were Turks and this was an uneasy mix. The Persians regarded the Turks as barbarians, and were exploited for their wealth by their new, unloved ruler. Such exploitation was an unwise move on his part: he should have gone out of his way to ingratiate himself to his subjects. Instead, he did nothing save alienate them, a mistake that would come back to haunt him. This attitude was fostered by Mohammed's excessive opinion of himself. The sycophantic courtiers that surrounded him, who uttered words of ridiculous exaggeration in an attempt to promote their own interests, in turn encouraged this. They told him that his conquests were so momentous that he was 'the second Alexander'. In the process, all they did was to kindle idle dreams of glory in the sultan's mind. It is hard to gauge too accurately the psychology of individuals who lived so many centuries ago, but such hyperbole might well be responsible for the rashness of Mohammed's actions, when he came into contact with a man who had a much greater claim to be the reincarnation of the ancient Macedonian conqueror.

Genghis' first instinct was to develop trading relations with Mohammed. Although it was always fairly likely that the two empires would come to blows, the reality was that Genghis still had much unfinished business in China to attend to. In other words, the timing was all wrong. Therefore he would not have, by choice, sought out a confrontation with Khwarezm, at least at this stage. He sent three ambassadors to the Sultan, men of Khwarismian origin from Kara-Khitai who carried with them impressive presents and the following pleasantly worded missive:

> I send you these gifts. I know your power and the vast extent of your empire and I regard you as my most cherished son. For your part you must know that I have conquered China and all the Turkish nations north of it; my country is an anthill of soldiers and a mine of silver, and I have no need of

other lands. Therefore I believe that we have an equal interest in encouraging trade between our subjects.[1]

It was a politely phrased message, though such soothing words did in fact carry something of a coded threat. The use of the word 'son' for example, carries some significance in Mongol political terminology. Such phraseology symbolises that the *khan* is Mohammed's father, and, therefore by definition of the language of the time, also his superior. In case anyone was in any doubt about this, the use of a seal carrying the phrase, 'the Emperor of Mankind' left little room for error. Nevertheless, it was some way short of a declaration of war, and it was an approach that a sagacious man would have treated with prudence, but such a measured response was not to be forthcoming. The same year that Kara-Khitai fell, 1218, the first Mongol-trading-caravan made its way to Khwarezm accompanied by an ambassador. They arrived at the frontier city of Otrar, situated on the mighty Jaxartes River. The great wealth of the caravan, however, soon attracted the unwelcome attention of the governor of the city, a man named Inalchuk Khwadir Khan. He reported to Mohammed that he suspected that the merchants were spies. Mohammed's instinct should have been decisively in the direction of a cautious response to such news, but instead he went the other way. He told the governor that if it could be proved that the men were indeed spies then they should be put to death. Regardless of the proof of the allegations, such an act would be tantamount to a declaration of war on an enemy that Mohammed had not yet faced, and of whose strength he could be in no real doubt.

In fairness to Mohammed, perhaps he was already reckoning that he needed to be on his guard. He had recently tried to depose the Caliph in Baghdad, an event that would have outraged many Muslims. However, his army had suffered appallingly in some awfully inclement weather that assailed them as they moved on the city. Nevertheless, the Caliph was understandably terrified, having no real military power of his own to protect himself. The Caliph's power was exclusively as a symbol rather than a military leader, so he needed the support of a military power to protect his position: a situation which incidentally was surprisingly similar to that of the Catholic Pope in Europe at the same moment. He turned in desperation (or at least so it was rumoured) to Genghis, the rising power in the east, who he believed might be interested in the political capital he might gain from supporting him. But it was said that the *khan* was not interested in such a move and did not take the proposal forward.

Consequently, Mohammed might already have felt extremely threatened by the approaches of Genghis. In the event, the governor of Otrar did not even go through the pretence of establishing the guilt or otherwise of the merchants. Instead, he had all of them summarily killed and their valuable supplies seized. When Genghis got wind of this act, he sent an ambassador accompanied by two envoys to demand retribution. Such missions proved extremely dangerous for those involved in those days, and the envoys were soon back at the court of Genghis with their beards and their hair singed, carrying the head of the ambassador which had been summarily hacked off his shoulders. No man could overlook such an open gesture of antagonism, least of all Genghis Khan. The Mongols did not normally like to go to war without some justification for it, however contrived. It is unlikely that, at this moment, Genghis truly wanted a war with Khwarezm, given his ongoing commitments elsewhere, but the treatment of his ambassadors was in effect an open declaration of war on Mohammed's part. It was unthinkable that Genghis would not respond.

Mohammed at least knew what to expect next, and he was confident of the result of the battle that he realised must follow. He had an enormous numerical superiority, and this made him feel that he would have little trouble in repelling the Mongols. Rule number one of warfare is never to underestimate your enemy, and Mohammed had just broken it. It was a fatal and irrecoverable mistake.

Mohammed did, however, have one asset. His son, Jalal al-Din, was a man of much greater merit than his father and he urged that the Sultan's armies should advance against the Mongols before they could concentrate. This was in all probability a false hope of obtaining victory, and could have led to a disaster equally as great as the one that was now imminent, but it at least showed a fighting spirit. However, it is a strategy that was very unlikely to have worked. The Khwarismian forces were hopelessly out of their depth, and in an offensive battle would probably have suffered as badly, if not worse, as if they had stayed on the defensive. The mistake was in starting the war at all.

Jalal al-Din's words fell on deaf ears anyhow. Mohammed decided that his troops would stay exactly where they were and wait for the Mongols to come to them. Although the Mongol army would be the largest ever raised, perhaps some 200,000 strong[2], they would be outnumbered five to two. Given this superiority and his defensive position, the odds appeared to be heavily in Mohammed's favour – but only if the individual soldiers of the two forces were equally matched, which they quite clearly were not. For the Khwarismians did have a few well-armed soldiers, particularly in the form of their cavalry. However, most of their men were raw levies, untrained in the arts of war. Mohammed had been triumphant in his campaign to subdue Khwarezm, but there the opposition had not been of a very high standard. Most of his men were hopelessly inadequate when matched against the Mongol armies that were heading their way.

In a typical Mongol fashion, the force was split up into four groups. Genghis led the first of these, along with Subotai who was the master strategist behind the invasion. Two of Genghis' sons, Ögedei and Chagatai, led the second group, which swept up to the north. Jebei and Jochi led the other two groups, which came up from the south. The idea was to overwhelm the defences of Khwarezm, and throw the defenders completely off balance. Before they arrived, a vanguard rode through the mountains into the Fergana valley, near to the city of Khojend. When they arrived, they appeared ragged, hungry, tired. Jalal al-Din rode towards them at the head of 50,000 men, giving him a substantial numerical advantage. A fierce battle ensued. The forces clashed violently, sabres and lances clashed on the armour of Mongol and Khwarismian knight, arrows flew, thick clouds of death falling on the massed ranks of opponents.

Jalal al-Din was an inspirational commander, and he rode at the head of the cream of Khwarismian forces. The Mongols were tired and were eventually rolled back. The retreat was slow at first, but then became general. With difficulty they extricated themselves, and rode as fast as they could away from the carnage. The casualties on both sides were great, but the Khwarismians in the end had been victorious. Great rejoicing ensued, but all was not as it seemed, for the Mongols were sophisticated strategists as well as outstanding warriors, and although this might have appeared to be a tactical defeat, it was in fact a strategic victory. The purpose of the vanguard had been to distract the Khwarismians from the main invasion force, and even as the battle was being fought a much greater army was preparing to advance.

It was as if a game of chess was being played out on a giant board. The four main groups now moved forward. The first two of these reached Otrar together but the group under Genghis then disappeared to the north. One of the most terrifying aspects of the Mongols on the march was the amazing propensity of tens of thousands of men to vanish without trace, and then appear, as if out of a cloudless sky, as a terrifying deluge that swamped anyone foolish enough to get in their way. Otrar held out for five months, but as this was the place where the war had started, those within its walls – especially its errant governor – could expect little mercy, and were therefore inspired to be stubborn in their resistance. Eventually, the breach was made and the Mongols poured in, sewing death in their wake. The garrison held out for another two months in the citadel, but then that too fell.

One of the last men to be captured was the governor, who must by now have been regretting his greed. He fled with his wife to the roof of a house and when he had run out of other ammunition he threw tiles down on to the Mongols below. It is in some ways one of the more terrifying images of the Mongol era: a man who had betrayed a trust, faced by an implacable enemy hell-bent on revenge, within minutes of a certain and painful death. One can only begin to imagine the levels of desperation that this greedy and foolish man had now sunk to. The Mongols surrounding him had been given strict orders that he must be captured alive: a special fate had been reserved for him. So rather than kill him, miners dug away at the foundations, and the building collapsed. He was pulled out of the ruins alive and taken away to receive his punishment.

The Mongols did not usually indulge themselves in gratuitous cruelty, but that is not to underestimate their violence. The best adjective to describe them would be ruthless: they killed as a rule with chilling efficiency, but their cruelty did come out when someone had been guilty of a particular heinous act of treachery. This manifested itself now, as the avaricious governor's ears and eyes were filled with molten silver, until he died an agonising death.

The fall of Otrar was just the beginning. Further south, Jebei and Jochi were making their move too. The first attacks were successful, and Jochi decided to divide his force further, leaving part of it to besiege the city of Khojend whilst the rest moved north to create yet more chaos. Khojend fell soon after, but inside the city was a man who at least had a bit of fight about him, and who was to cause the Mongols a headache or two. This was the governor, Timür Malik. He retreated with 1,000 others to an island in the middle of the river. If siege warfare was the first Achilles' heel of the Mongol army, amphibious enterprises were the second. Time and again when faced with even a small crossing to attack an enemy the Mongols would struggle. The most famous example of this would be the attack on Japan half-a-century later, but there were many other smaller-scale engagements when the problem would expose itself. It was not that they were unprepared: Mongol warriors carried a leather sack which was waterproof and could be inflated and when occasion demanded, used as a makeshift raft.

These problems with amphibious warfare were understandable. The Mongols were cavalry soldiers, and of course the particular qualities associated with that arm of warfare were useless when they moved off land. They also came from a landlocked territory, with no naval heritage to call upon. Despite employing experienced sailors from other nations to help them overcome this deficiency, unlike siege warfare – where they quickly adapted and became quite successful – amphibious operations was an area that they never mastered. On this occasion, the short crossing over to the island might as well have been the width of the widest ocean. The Mongol soldiers packed themselves into barges and launched their attack on the small garrison of defenders, but they were repulsed. Next, the Mongols adopted another tactic that the great Alexander had used nearly two thousand years ago at Tyre. When faced with an island, he had attempted to turn it into a peninsula by building a causeway, and now the Mongols did the same. However, this merely encouraged the defenders to launch their own counter-attacks, using barges that they had with them, which served to slow the attack down but failed to stop it altogether. It became clear that the Mongols would succeed with their plan and the end would be a foregone conclusion. So instead, Timür Malik packed the defenders into barges and made their escape.

The Mongols had placed a chain across the river in anticipation of such a move, but it was attacked with such force that the escapees broke it and started to go north with the river current. Jochi, in the meantime, was heading south towards Khojend, when he heard what was happening. He threw a barricade of boats across the river, and packed them with archers to stop the fugitives from going any further. Construction of this had only just finished when in the distance, the barges with the escapees, hove into view. Timür Malik was not ready to give up just yet. Perhaps realising that he might have to take to the land at some stage, he had had the foresight to put horses on board his barges. Seeing the barricades in good time, and realising that he could not force the barrier, he moved his barges to the bank and started to ride off. His pursuers had been riding for days and were tired, meaning he was able to outrun them. Three horsemen chased after him. In traditional heroic fashion he only had three arrows in his quiver to deal with them. With the first of these he shot one of his pursuers dead, and then shouted insults at the other two before outrunning them. He at last made good his escape. Even the Mongols, it seems, were not too unhappy with the flight to freedom of a brave and resourceful adversary. Timür Malik had earned his life.

Sultan Mohammed received the ill tidings of the widespread defeats inflicted on his forces with increasing desperation. He fled to Samarkand

and despatched his last 50,000 reserves to fight against the army of Jebei. What followed was predictable: another rout, with this force also smashed. Mohammed was now naked before a deadly threat. Just as it seemed that things could not get worse, they did. Genghis and Subotai appeared out of nowhere 400 miles behind Mohammed's lines at Bokhara. The city was defended by the most powerful of weapons, a vast desert that was believed to be un-crossable, and acted as a shield against the most potent of enemies. The desert presented a powerful defensive barrier, except for one thing – it was not un-crossable, as Genghis and his men now proved when they appeared out of the desert before the city.

There were 20,000 men defending the city, but most of them were mercenaries. Genghis deliberately left one exit from the city unguarded, hoping to tempt them out. The plan worked a treat, and they came out as hoped. Rather than fight the Mongols, though, they then ran away. This in fact played right into the hands of their foe, who let them run so far, hunted them down, trapped them, and then wiped them out. Few men could outride a Mongol army, even when spurred on by a state of blind panic.

The governor and his guard retreated into the citadel, leaving the city to defend itself. Bokhara was now defenceless and, fortunately for its people, they knew it. They therefore surrendered the city without further ado, and in so doing saved themselves the terrible fate that awaited others who resisted the Mongols. The city was pillaged and everything of value in it was taken, but its citizens were allowed to leave before this happened, at least saving their lives. Many commentators remark positively on the fact that Genghis and his Mongol successors preached religious toleration, but it would appear that this was in part a tactic to divide opposition in the countries that they invaded. For many of the more humble members of society, often oppressed by their overlords, sometimes persecuted on religious grounds, such toleration might appear as a welcome relief from what they were used to. However, based on what happened in Bokhara it would seem that this tactic was little more than a ruse, or at least a matter of expedience rather than an example of a deeply held belief in toleration.

There were a number of *imams* (Muslim holy men) in the city. They were some of the many educated men in the city, which itself took its name from the ancient Persian *bukbar*, meaning the centre of learning. As they walked through the conquered streets of Bokhara to the Mosque, they saw that the horses of Mongol cavalrymen were eating grain out of the boxes in which the Muslim holy books had been stored. Everywhere pages from the books lay scattered in the wind, a sacred detritus trampled underfoot without a second thought by all and sundry. Inside the building, dancing girls had been bullied into performing their worldly gyrations, an insult that struck to the core of the Muslim faith and of its followers' respect for their holy places. It was hardly a demonstration of tolerance in action. Rather than seeing the Mongols as being tolerant to religious belief they were in the main it seems, indifferent to it.

Unfortunately, the city itself did not survive its capture. It was an accident that sealed its fate. The wooden houses of the city were packed close together, a fire hazard and a disaster waiting to happen. The defenders of the citadel still held out, and continued to fire their ballistae at the Mongols in Bokhara. Many of the missiles were firebombs of *naphtha*, which soared over the battered walls of the citadel into the city. This caused a fire to take hold which had soon spread uncontrollably. The conflagration took a vice-like grip over Bokhara, and soon clouds of acrid, choking smoke hung like a pall over this city of wonders.

The fate of the garrison was sealed too. Their position was hopeless, and the Mongols planned a final assault. The tactics they employed for this exemplified their ruthlessness. Thousands of the captive citizens of Bokhara were driven in front of their forces, like a flock of frightened sheep, a human shield that protected the Mongols from the missiles thrown at them by the garrison with their own flesh and blood. It was probably during this last assault that the missiles fired from behind the citadel wall ignited the conflagration that now consumed this tragic city.

Before Bokhara was abandoned to its awful fate, Genghis played out a memorable scene. He called the citizens together and addressed them from an open-air pulpit. Ascending the stairs, he took the place of the *imam* and addressed the people. He first asked who the rich people in the city were, and 280 residents were pointed out. They would of course lose all the wealth that they had now to the Mongols. He then turned to the rest of the populace. By their sins, the people of Bokhara had brought this terrible fate upon themselves. The punishment of the city, he told them, had been brought about by the misgovernment of their leaders. The great spirit had decreed that Bokhara must be punished for their sins. He and his Mongols, he said, were the scourge of God. The people of the city were then forced out into the fields. Most of them were spared, but Genghis conscripted some of the young men into his army to add to the force he was taking towards Samarkand. One man escaped, and relayed the message of what had happened at this wonderful city to those he met in Khorasan. When asked about the Mongols, his reply was simplicity personified: 'they came, they sapped, they burnt, they slew, they plundered and they departed'.[3] It was a statement reminiscent of

Shakespeare's famous speech by Julius Caesar: 'veni, vidi, vici' – 'I came, I saw, I conquered'. As the fortunate escapee had intimated, Genghis and his army had now left Bokhara, after destroying the walls that had once protected the city.

Samarkand was now in a hopeless position. From north, south, east and west the Mongols descended on the city. Its capture would be the crowning glory of the campaign. This city of unbelievable wealth and overwhelming architectural magnificence was the jewel in the crown of Sultan Mohammed. Even the most humble of houses within its vast walls would typically have access to a garden. Fountains flowed freely and canals meandered sleepily in and around it. Skilled workers wove their magic on silk, or meticulously worked intricate patterns on copper utensils and ornaments. Those who knew Samarkand waxed lyrical about it. Juvaini, not an eye-witness to these events but someone who would have known many men who were, wrote that 'it was the greatest of the countries of the Sultan's empire in width of territory, the most pleasant of his lands in fertility of soil and, by common consent, the most delectable of the paradises of this world among the four Edens'.[4]

All this wealth was like a magnet. So too was the political significance of what was effectively Mohammed's capital. The city was powerless in the face of the looming onslaught. The roll-call of commanders descending on the city was like a who's who of Mongol greats. From the north came Ögedei and Chagatai. Jochi came from Khojend in the east. Most terrifying of all, from the west, the land of the dead, came Subotai and Genghis himself.

The Mongols again turned to subterfuge to improve their position. Prisoners were forced to carry standards in the Mongol ranks, making the army look larger than it actually was. This was the least of the prisoners' worries, for many of them were again conscripted into becoming the 'forlorn hope', to be driven before the advancing Mongol forces so that the defenders would waste their energy and their arrows on disposing with non-combatants. Genghis surveyed the town carefully, walking around its walls for several days, looking for weak points. His men were given several days' rest, to prepare themselves for the expected long fight ahead. On the third day battle was joined. The defenders employed desperate measures to drive the Mongols back. Elephants were sent out to crush them but the Mongols held firm. Just like Alexander's Macedonians in India, the Mongols had learned that these monsters were just as dangerous to the enemy as to them if they stood firm. Enraged by the arrows that the Mongols poured into them, the ponderous pachyderms turned tail and lumbered backwards, trampling many of the defenders to death in the process in their panicky flight.

Samarkand was so strong that the battle was expected to last for a year, perhaps longer. It survived for ten days, then, singularly failing to learn any lessons from the disaster at Bokhara, a large part of its garrison was tempted out into the open, where it was predictably destroyed. Another 20,000 of the garrison rode out and surrendered to Genghis, offering to join Genghis' army and thereby abandoning the citizens of Samarkand to whatever might befall them. The city then surrendered without further fighting, which again saved its people from a terrible fate. The citizens were warned that their lives would be forfeited if they tried to hide from the Mongols, so terrified masses assembled in the streets and squares as they had been told to do. The Mongols then helped themselves to the copious amounts of plunder contained within the city. The elephants who had survived in the meantime were let loose onto the plains around the city to fend for themselves. They soon starved to death, as they were unable to find enough sustenance in what, to them, was a strange land: their mahouts had previously provided them with fodder to live off.

Some of the citizens were allowed to ransom themselves and buy their lives and their freedom, but not all. Large numbers of them were conscripted as slaves, particularly craftsmen whose skills were held in high esteem by Genghis. It was as if he was thinking of doing something that no other Mongol had previously done: to build a city, a statement of power that all men might see his greatness. Perhaps he no longer wished to be a nomad, but rather to seen as the master of the world. The skills of people such as these would be invaluable in the future, though Genghis would die before any dreams he might have had, in respect of the creation of a Mongolian capital city, could become reality.

The garrison remaining in the citadel continued to hold out, which meant that when it was captured soon after, they were all slaughtered. Now that the city had fallen, the walls were demolished. As for the 20,000 men of the garrison who had abandoned the city before the final battle, Genghis had them all rounded up and slaughtered. Men who could betray one lord were equally as likely to betray another. The walls of Samarkand were then, like those of Bokhara, smashed down so that the city would be incapable of rising against Genghis once he had moved on.

However, Mohammed was still on the loose, and Genghis determined that he must be captured before he could regard the war as over. Others though, like Subotai, had seen that Mohammed's son, Jalal ad-Din was much more of a threat, although he was as yet unable to convince his *khan* to this effect. Genghis would find out soon enough how difficult an opponent he would be. Jebei and Subotai were given two *tumens* to lead the chase after the Sultan, who was now fleeing for his freedom, if not his life. Mohammed knew that they were on the scent like a pair of hounds after a fox, and did everything that he could to shake them off. He fled to the lands around Balkh but he was about to be involved in a terrifying race for his life. The bulk of the Mongol army followed after him.

The campaign that Genghis now embarked on was to leave the blackest stain of all on his reputation. He and his army advanced on Tirmiz. The people of the city, showing a badly misplaced trust in their ability to resist, sallied out to fight the Mongols. The inevitable rout followed. Then the men and women who survived were divided into groups. Each Mongol warrior was given the task of killing a number of them. They were struck down without a sign of pity or compassion, and crushed as if they were worth nothing more than insects. This was the Mongols at their most ruthless. One woman pleaded for her life, saying that she would give her captors a precious pearl if they let her live. When she explained that she had taken the precaution of swallowing it to protect it, she was slit open. Genghis then ordered that the corpses of the slain should be treated in the same way just in case anyone else had adopted similar tactics.

Genghis now moved on Balkh, a city of great wealth. The chief men of the city, inspired by the chilling example of those who had dared to resist Genghis, rode out to present their city to the Mongols to do with as they wished. However, Jalal ad-Din was still on the loose, and was capable of acting as a figurehead around whom dissidents could rally. Genghis therefore took the decision that none could be allowed to live. Juvaini noted that the only beneficiaries of this callous atrocity were the lions and other beasts of carrion in the area, which were provided with enough food to last them for months.[5]

The fate of the people of Balkh was not yet over. Genghis took himself off to Peshawar for a while but then returned to Balkh. Some of the citizens had saved their lives by hiding when the city had been sacked. Now that Genghis was back they too were killed. Even the walls were pulled down, effectively wiping the city from the face of the earth. It took decades for the city to stage any kind of recovery. When Marco Polo passed through about half a century later, he described how:

> Balkh is a splendid city of great size. It used to be much greater and more
> splendid; but the Tartars and other invaders have sacked and ravaged it.
> For I can tell you that there used to be many fine palaces and mansions of
> marble, which are still to be seen, but shattered now and in ruins.[6]

This was Genghis' fearful legacy.

Jalal ad-Din, however, was proving a troublesome foe. News came in that he had won a victory against a badly outnumbered Mongol army. His temerity, and also that of those who had helped him, enraged Genghis. The people of the lands through which he now travelled were now marked for destruction, and he ruthlessly struck them down in their thousands. Aware that the Mongol avalanche was bearing down on them, the people of the countryside into which Genghis now journeyed,sought refuge in the cities. Here they trembled behind the walls, wondering what fate was about to overtake them. At Bamian[7] there was an incident that was to have the direst of consequences. Genghis' favourite grandson, Mutugen, was killed in the attack when the city refused to surrender. The wrath of the *khan* was raised by this act, and the bitter bile of revenge drove his actions in the campaign that followed. Not in their worst nightmares could the populace have envisaged how awful their fate would be. Genghis was merciless, and a bloodbath of horrific proportions ensued. Every living creature in Bamian was put to the sword when the city inevitably fell. Further to the west, Tolui and Genghis' son-in-law Toghutshar, were sent to lead another Mongol force in the region of Merv.

The Mongols moved in on the city of Merv. The people were divided as to what they should do. Some advocated surrender, but others were up for a fight. At this critical stage, a number of Turcomans made their way to the city, encouraging the citizens to resist the Mongol hordes. They were further encouraged when, in an assault on another town, a small Mongol force was overwhelmed in a small-scale battle. This gave them heart.

At this juncture Tolui arrived with an army, including some local conscripts, of 7,000 men. A small group of these, about 400 in all, approached closer to the city, and noticed a large number of Turcoman cavalry, unaware of their presence, being very casual. Observing this complacency they laid a trap, which, on a jet black night soon after, they sprang on the Turcomans who were cut to pieces as a result.

Replenished by the welcome addition of 60,000 cattle that they seized, the Mongols grew in number and in confidence. Tolui spent several days touring around the walls, hunting for weaknesses that he could exploit. It was not in the end the Mongols who attacked Merv; it was rather the other way round. Small forces sallied out of the city in futile and uncoordinated attempts to drive the Mongols back. These were poor tactics, doomed to fail and, at the same time, certain to dissipate the resources of the city.

The Mongols easily repulsed these attacks and tightened their grip on the city. It was not long before its commander, Mujir-al-Mulk, saw that the only chance of survival was submission. He sent one of the *imams* of the city, Jamal-al-Din, to Tolui's camp, accompanied with gifts of handsome horses, camels and mules. Tolui questioned him closely to find out who the wealthy citizens were, obviously hoping to profit from the information in short order. Jamal-al-Din gave him a list with 200 names on it, and these unfortunate citizens, who must suddenly have regretted their wealth, were ordered to come into the Mongol camp at once. Now that the city had chosen to surrender, the Mongols entered through its gates and drove its inhabitants out onto the plains around. So many people were present at Merv that it took four days for all the people to come out.

Once the citizens of Merv were assembled outside, the men were separated from the women, the Mongols helping themselves to the more beautiful ones amongst the latter group. 400 useful artisans were detached from the rest, along with a few boys and girls who made attractive slaves. The order was then given to massacre the rest. It was said that individual soldiers were ordered to execute up to 400 citizens. By the time that the blanket of night cloaked the plains, they were soaked in blood. It was one of the greatest atrocities in history. It was then that the city itself was destroyed. The walls were pulled down, the citadel levelled, the great mosque set ablaze. One of the few survivors from the city was installed as its emir, though quite what he was emir of is a moot point. A few terrified citizens who had managed to hide from the wrath of the Mongols, some 5,000 in all, joined him soon after. The blood lust of the Mongols was not sated. The rearguard of their enemy put them to the sword too. According to some accounts, 700,000 people died at Merv.[8]

The Mongols then set out on the road to Nishapur. Ahead of them, terrified groups of refugees hurried as fast as they could away from the shattered remnants of Merv, messengers of death carrying grievous tidings with them. The Mongols were soon in amongst them, cutting and slashing, striking them down without mercy. What is most striking about this campaign is the savagery of it, pitiless even by Mongol standards. Groups of Mongols kept coming through Merv and killing any survivors of the recent slaughter that they found there. The Afghan levies that accompanied them were particularly enthusiastic in the tortures that they inflicted on the local inhabitants. Sultan Mohammed had fled from Balkh to Nishapur. Here, his sleep was disturbed by terrifying dreams in which he had seen dishevelled people, their hair wild and their faces scratched, dressed in black like mourners. They struck their heads with their hands and lamented piteously. Everywhere the doomed Sultan saw bad omens. He had lost the will to fight and told the people of Nishapur to flee, for a storm was about to descend on them. When they, in the main, stayed where they were, he urged them to fortify the walls to be as strong as they possibly could, even though in his heart of hearts he believed the outcome of the forthcoming fight to be inevitable destruction.

Jalal ad-Din was still with him and was despatched towards Balkh, but when he heard that Jelme and Subotai were close by, he returned. Realising that the Mongols were still stubbornly bearing down on him, Mohammed went out hunting, or so he said, but as soon as he was out of sight of the city, he fled away from it as fast as he could. When they realised that he had gone, some other notables followed his example. Soon after, the Mongols arrived before the gates. They demanded that Nishapur surrender. The governor of the town, Mujir-al-Mulk, prevaricated, but provided the Mongols with food. As other parties arrived, they were similarly treated. There were, however, ongoing signs of resistance elsewhere, and these seem to have encouraged the people of Nishapur to fight.

A Mongol army of 10,000 arrived led by Toghutshar, the son-in-law of Genghis Khan. This was the vanguard of Tolui's army. The people of Nishapur now resisted his attempt to enter through the gates. Arrows showered down from the battlements and one of them struck home on Toghutshar, causing him to fall from his horse, mortally wounded. The death of a near-kinsman of the Great Khan equated to a death warrant for the city. The Mongols, dispirited for the time being, withdrew. Round about Nishapur, smaller towns were taken and massacres inevitably followed. The savagery can only be explained as an attempt to cow the people into submission, but Nishapur itself was running increasingly short of supplies, and as winter came the morale of its people started to plummet.

Tolui returned with an army in the spring of 1221. They wheeled up their great mangonels towards the city, accompanied by vast supplies of heavy rocks, which the machines would hurl towards the city in an attempt to batter it into submission. Although the defenders were well equipped with mangonels and catapults of their own, in addition to having a number of crossbowmen (a weapon widely feared, even by the Mongols), they now saw that the enemy before them was larger and more determined than before, and so they lost heart.

The death of Toghutshar meant that there was no possibility of quarter being given. The attack, which inevitably followed, was launched at dawn of 7 April and went on for several days. The moat surrounding the city was filled in and the walls breached. As the end drew near, the Mongols scaled the walls, in ones and twos first, then tens and twenties. They gained a foothold, and were soon streaming into the city, fighting in the streets amongst the palaces and mansions. As the hours passed that Friday, the Muslim holy day, the Mongols increasingly gained control of Nishapur. Now fired up by the lust for blood and a thirst for vengeance, a holocaust was at hand.

The destruction of Nishapur was absolute. When the city inevitably fell, its defenders either dead or exhausted, Toghutsar's widow presided over the macabre rituals that followed. All living creatures that were found were killed, their bodies piled in huge pyramids of death: one for the men, another for the women, and another for the children. Even domestic animals were butchered without exception. Then the site of the city was ploughed so that none might know it had ever existed. The scale of the slaughter in this and the other cities taken had never been seen before, and perhaps, in its stark totality, has never been seen since.

The Sultan was now a broken man. He continued to fly away from the Mongols as fast as he could, but became increasingly paranoid, perhaps understandably fearing betrayal, and dismissed many of his servants. The Mongols kept up their furious pursuit. Eventually he took to a boat on the shores of the Caspian Sea. The Mongols were so close behind that they shot arrows at the vessel as it sailed out into the waters, but they fell short. Mohammed managed to escape them at last but it was a hollow victory. Shortly afterwards, on an island in the sea, he contracted pleurisy and died. This great man, at one time possessor of ornate palaces and vast cities richer than any others in the world, was buried wrapped in a torn shirt for a shroud.

The population that he had abandoned cowered before the Mongol onslaught, but Jalal al-Din fought on. Genghis was indefatigable in pursuit of his prey. Everywhere that Jalal al-Din went, Genghis was never far behind. Then word reached Genghis that his foe was going to try and find sanctuary in India. Chasing after him at a frantic pace, 'like the wind which drives the clouds',[9] the Mongols redoubled their efforts to catch Jalal al-Din before he got away, eventually catching up with him on the banks of the Indus. Genghis gave strict orders that Jalal ad-Din should be taken alive. His enemy's army was completely surrounded, with the river at their back. Although Jalal al-Din fought like a lion, seemingly everywhere at once, his army was crushed, but rather than surrender, he drove his horse into the water and managed to swim across, carrying his standard with him still. Genghis, admiring his opponent, called off the hunt for the time being, and remarked that any father would be proud to boast of such a son. His gallantry was not unbounded though: Jalal ad-Din's children were captured, and all the males slaughtered at his command, regardless of how young they were. The seed of such a mighty warrior could not be allowed to live, as they might one day return to haunt the Mongols.

Jalal ad-Din and a handful of his followers sought refuge in the thick forests just across the Indus. Genghis had still not given up on Jalal ad-Din though. He instructed one of his generals, Törbei, to cross the great river after him. He moved into the region of Multan and Lahore and laid siege to the former city. His mangonels were soon wreaking destruction but, just when the city appeared to be on the verge of falling, the heat of the plains proved too much and the Mongols were forced to withdraw. Törbei returned to Genghis for what may have been a frosty reception, given his failure to achieve the overwhelming success that the Mongols were becoming used to.

The fighting in Central Asia was ended soon after. The Mongols, tired from their immense exertions, rested. However, many of them were soon struck down with sickness. They, and their *khan*, missed the steppes, and it was time to go home. They had taken a multitude of prisoners, amongst them Indians. They could not be fed on the march so Genghis ordered that they should all be killed. The *khan*, for a while, chewed over the idea of going back through India, via Bengal, Assam and the Himalayas, but he thought better of it. So instead, he made his way back through Peshawar. This was the end of the campaign, though it did not mean that these lands were securely added to the empire yet. Genghis had other conquests on his mind, in particular, China, where much remained to be done, and his resources were being stretched. It was time to go home, recuperate and then move on to pastures new. The massacres stopped: as Genghis' chancellor Yeh-Lu Ch'u-Ts'ai, former adviser to the Chin thousands of miles away, had bravely told him 'It is time to make an end of the killing'.

The terror that these invasions induced (or at least that portion of it directly affected) cannot be overstated. Nothing quite like it had ever happened to the Muslim world before. To devout Muslims, the Mongols were no more than barbarians in contrast even to Christians like the Crusaders who at least were 'peoples of the book', that is, followers of a God who was similar in some aspects to Allah even though the practices that Christians followed were theologically in error as far as Muslims were concerned. One Islamic writer, Ibn al-Athir, wrote despondently that Genghis' campaign was 'a tremendous disaster such as had never happened before ... It may well be that the world from now until its end ... will not experience the like again'.[10] These are understandable sentiments from a devout Muslim, who had seen some of the pearls of Islam plundered by a people he considered to be savages, but out of line with what would subsequently happen, for in just forty years time, events even more devastating to Islam would occur.

Ibn al-Athir goes on to describe at length the impact of these events on the Muslim world and perhaps it is best to give the last word to him, an Islamic chronicler. At the start of his account of these dreadful years he says:

> The events I am about to describe are so horrible that for years I avoided all mention of them. It is not easy to announce that death has fallen upon Islam and the Muslims. Alas! I would have preferred my mother never to have given birth to me, or to have died without witnessing all these evils. If one day you are told that the earth has never known such calamity since God created Adam, do not hesitate to believe it, for such is the strict truth'.[1]

For the region that Genghis had conquered, the future was as bleak as it could be. This fertile land, well irrigated and prosperous not long before, was now a smouldering wreck, a wasteland where the figure of death now stalked the flotsam of humanity that survived, without pity. Where once towns had hummed to the sound of traders selling their wares, from the caravans that criss-crossed the region from east to west and back again, now the few people that remained trembled in fear. The caravanserais had been subsumed by deserts. In city after city, an unearthly silence was the only presence where once there had been bustling markets, packed streets. Khwarezm was destroyed, never to rise from the ashes. The Mongols would for a time lose their grip on parts of the region, and Jalal ad-Din, tired of a safe life under the protection of the King of Delhi, would lead a fight-back that would, in the end, fail. But the old order had gone, never to return. For the people of this part of the world, things would never be the same again.

CHAPTER 4

The End of an Era: The Invasion of Russia & the Death of Genghis 1222-1227

Whilst the campaign in Khwarezm was still in progress, the Mongols were appearing on another stage for the first time. Russia was about to be visited in what was effectively a preliminary survey designed to gain information with which to undertake a future, more substantial campaign. It is hard to underestimate the effectiveness of Mongol reconnaissance, and the thoroughness of their preparation. Campaigns were sometimes launched many years after the initial fact-finding missions had been undertaken. A full-scale invasion of parts of Europe did not begin in earnest until 1240. However, the campaign that was about to be begin would provide a vast amount of information, which later Mongol expeditions would take full advantage of.

The steppes of Russia sounded very promising to the Mongols. They were vast, reaching to the horizon and beyond, and provided large supplies of grass for their horses. It must have seemed very much like Mongolia, and as a result of its attractiveness it was here that the Mongols planned to move next. Unfortunately, in between the Mongol armies in Persia and the Central Asian steppes stood the Christian kingdom of Georgia. Its king, a vainglorious young man who reigned as George IV, prided himself on his martial prowess, and was spurred on by dreams of glory. Even now, he and 30,000 of his well-armed warriors were assembled, impatiently waiting to set out to join the Sixth Crusade. It was an exciting prospect, this mission to the Holy Land, but it would never leave Georgia, for a new enemy was about to appear and destroy all chances of this army ever leaving its homeland.

George knew that a Mongol army was not too far away, as he had heard of the destruction going on to the south of his country. The tales of refugees and displaced soldiers must have made for harrowing listening. However, the prospect of a Mongol attack did not appear to cause him undue alarm. He believed that his country might well be raided, but he did not imagine that he would have too much trouble repulsing the Mongols who dared to set foot on his soil. He looked upon them as nothing more than a rabble of indisciplined barbarians. He could not have been more wrong. Sure enough, news came into his court at Tiflis (the Georgian capital, now Tbilisi) that a force of Mongols, perhaps 30,000 strong, had arrived. They were accompanied by a few thousand Kurdish and Turcoman allies. George set out to meet them, backed up by 70,000 warriors. The two armies met on the plain of Khuman. The Georgians charged enthusiastically against the vastly outnumbered Mongols, who soon began to retreat. Spurred on by this sign of weakness, the Georgians charged even more excitedly. Soon their army was widely spread out across the plain.

Any student of Mongol military tactics (George was clearly not one) would have realised that this was exactly what they wanted. With the Georgians having lost all formation, the Mongols quickly launched their counter. The cavalrymen rapidly remounted on fresh horses, which had been kept waiting in some nearby woods, specifically for that purpose. Under the protection of an arrow-storm, they charged at the Georgians, smashing a huge wedge in their ranks. George and a handful of his courtiers managed to escape the abattoir, but the cream of the Georgian army was left dead or dying on the plain. George prepared himself for the expected attack on his capital of Tiflis, but it did not come. The only interest that the Mongols had in the kingdom at this stage, was as a thoroughfare to Russia, and had therefore withdrawn. They realised that an extended siege of Tiflis would not be consistent with the primary objective of their expedition. They had been given clear targets by Genghis, and taking Tiflis was not one of them, so they resolved not to be distracted again.

The Mongols returned to Georgia again in the winter, a time of year when their foes were not expecting an advance to be made. They sped up the coast as quickly as they could, but George got wind of their presence and once more led his men against them. Despite the fact that the Mongols wished to avoid a battle, the results of the one that now happened were sadly similar to the previous occasion. Subotai managed to lure the Georgians headlong into a trap, in a pass where Jebei was ready and waiting for their arrival.

Although the Georgians were cautious and tried to retain a solid front against Jebei's attack, as they did so they exposed themselves to Subotai, who had been retreating before them but now wheeled about, smashed into their flanks and crushed them. The Georgians were cut to pieces. Although the Mongols did not know it, there were no reserves left to the king to launch another attack on them. Not only would there be no input to the Crusade now, the Georgians did not even have enough men left to defend their kingdom. George, called 'The Brilliant' (a sobriquet which must have been tarnished somewhat by these heavy defeats) died soon after his dreams of honour and glory had been so totally trampled. His sister Rusudan, who succeeded him, wrote soon after to the Pope, explaining why there would be no Georgian input to his Crusade:

> A savage people of Tartars, hellish of aspect, as voracious as wolves in their hunger for spoils, as brave as lions, have invaded my country ... The brave knighthood of Georgia has hunted them down and out of the country killing 25,000 of the invaders. But alas, we are no longer in a position to take up the Cross, as we had promised your Holiness to do.[1]

The bravado of Rusudan might seem admirable but it was well wide of the mark. The Mongols had only left because Georgia was a transit point and was never the main target. And if the Georgians had really killed 25,000 Mongols, then there would be hardly any left to carry on the campaign further north. What happened subsequently showed how wrong Rusudan's assessment was. Unfortunately for the Georgians, their forces had been so decimated by their efforts that for years afterwards the country was virtually defenceless against raids from neighbouring tribes.

The Mongols next rode against the fortress of Derbend where the Shah of Shirvan was resisting them. He, however, had worked out that the Mongols did not regard him as their main prize, but had set their sights on more distant targets. They wanted to get to Russia, and to do so they would need guides to lead them across the Caucasus in the depths of winter, so he struck a deal with them. If he provided them with guides and provisions then he would in return be left alone. It was a deal that proved acceptable to the Mongols, and it was therefore agreed that the Shah would hand over the guides. However, he was no fool. He picked guides who were known to be loyal to him, and gave them orders that they were to make sure that the route taken was as circuitous as possible. Whilst they were delayed, he would send messengers to the tribes beyond the mountains and tell them that the Mongols were on their way with hell in their wake.

Subotai was too experienced to easily fall for the trick, and the journey started with him picking a guide at random and beheading him to encourage the others to do their part efficiently, but these unsubtle measures did not work. The journey through the mountains was a nightmare in bitterly cold weather, and the artillery was almost all lost.

Hundreds of Mongol soldiers perished in the bitter cold of the harsh mountain winter, which chilled the life out of even the toughest of men. To make matters worse, when they eventually reached the other side of the passes and began to drop down to the plains below, they saw that there was an army of 50,000 soldiers waiting to greet them. This army was composed of various tribes from the steppes. It had been assembled at the instigation of Kotian, king of the Cumans. The Cumans were Turko-Mongol warriors, who in many ways were kindred spirits of the tribes from Mongolia. They made their living by taking booty from others – particularly sedentary states, who grew rich, fat and comfortable, and were ill-equipped to fight off pagan pillagers. Also known as Polovtsians, they are believed to originate with the Kimaks[2], a Central Asian tribe. They were nomads who depended for existence on two apparently paradoxical qualities: the skills to raid their neighbours and the ability to ally with them. The relationship changed from one of conflict to one of amity with bewildering frequency, but such fluctuations were predicated most of all on *realpolitik* and changing circumstances. It is also worth noting that the Cumans had, put simplistically, split into two groups over time, one on the western steppes of Russia, the other much further east.

Kotian had received word from over the mountains that the Mongols were on their way, but he knew enough to suspect that an attack was imminent even before the Shah's messengers arrived. There had been some Cuman tribesmen (those from the eastern tribes) who were already fighting alongside the Khwarismians, when the Mongols had invaded Khwarezm (these were known as the Kanglis). The mother of the late Shah Mohammed came from this latter tribal grouping. Others had been in the Georgian royal guard, and they had spread the word to their cousins in the west, meaning that he already had good intelligence concerning the Mongol threat.

Threatening to cut off the supply of booty that enabled the Cumans to flourish, the Mongols provided a similar challenge to others, such as the Alans, the Khazars, the Bulgars, and other tribes that roamed the steppes. United by this common threat, Kotian formed an alliance with these others, and formed a motley army, a human wall, built of flesh, bone and blood, which blocked the onward progress of the Mongols as they came down from the mountains.

Kotian had put the army under the command of his brother Yuri and his son Daniel, and they waited patiently for the Mongols as the latter fought their way across the mountain passes. The army posed a grave threat, as their position prevented the Mongols from deploying, and removed any chance that they might drive a wedge in the ranks of this blocking force, and push their way through. The Mongols realised that they had been led into a trap (the guides had by this time prudently disappeared so no instant retribution against them was possible). Seeing that their exit was blocked, and that they were effectively like a cork in the narrow neck of a bottle, Subotai and Jebei returned a short way up the pass through which they had come, and took up a defensive position behind some rocks. Here they waited for the armies of the tribal alliance to attack them. However, their wait was in vain as, Yuri and Daniel had no intention of throwing away the advantage that they held by indulging in such a rash action. Their refusal to respond to the challenge meant that the Mongols could either launch a desperately risky attack, retreat to the place from whence they had come, or stand still and starve. None of the options was attractive. After considering the limited options open to them, the Mongols came up with a plan to extricate themselves from this tricky position. They were not inclined to go on with the attack against impossible odds, and were quite prepared to use other means to gain their ends, should the occasion demand it. Now was one such occasion.

The Mongols and the tribes whose armies stood in their way shared a common language: booty, which the Mongols had picked up plenty of on their travels thus far. So, the next morning, as the Cumans slept off the hangovers induced by the celebration of their 'victory' during the previous evening, a Mongol ambassador rode into camp. He came with an offer. He explained that the Mongols and the Cumans had no reason to be fighting. The Mongols desired to be friendly towards the steppe tribes, and as a token of their goodwill, they were very happy to hand over half of the loot that they had garnered. The ambassador suggested that the Mongols and the Cumans should fight together against their common enemies: the Christian and Muslim principalities that surrounded them. It was an obvious bribe, but it achieved its purpose spectacularly. Yuri and Daniel agreed and accepted the booty with alacrity. They would fight together, they told the ambassador, in return for this most generous gift. Only the Cumans were involved in this pact, which meant that the other tribes were, as a result, exposed to the full wrath of the Mongols. The Cumans for their part happily took the booty and then quickly disappeared as soon as the Mongols' backs were turned; thus in one day they had betrayed both their allies and the Mongols. The latter would be fastidious in exacting their revenge for this duplicity in the near future.

The allied army that remained was swept aside with all the ease of the wind blowing a pile of leaves out of its path. Mongol scouts were soon hot on the heels of the treacherous Cumans. Like a hunter stalking its prey, they soon tracked the Cumans down, and messages were despatched to the Mongol commanders with the main army not far behind, reporting the enemy position. With a speed that no other soldiers of the time could match, the Mongol army quickly caught up with the Cumans, and the inevitable battle followed. Once more, Jebei and Subotai were triumphant, Yuri and Daniel were both killed and the booty was returned to its original owners. The rest of the Cumans scattered before this terrifying force, which then descended on Astrakhan. The steppes that they had come to reconnoitre now lay naked before them. For a short time the Mongols relaxed. Horses ate and grew fat; warriors rested and replenished their own depleted reserves of energy. Now that the Cumans no longer stood in their way, Jebei and Subotai decided that it was time to split their forces in two.

Subotai rode off to the southwest, to the vicinity of the Sea of Azov. En route he left the traditional trail of destruction in his wake, setting ablaze all the towns that had given refuge Cumans sanctuary. It was now that he met for the first time men from a strange, and as yet unknown, land, far to the west. He understood that these men were merchants, coming from a far-off place called Venice. Both sides quickly saw that there was mutual benefit in staying on good terms with each other. The Venetians were not part of an army, they were traders, and clearly had no real interest in the people of the region other than as a source of trade. On the other hand, to Subotai they offered a glimpse into a world of which he knew nothing. He offered the Venetians generous hospitality, which they happily accepted.

At the end of this extraordinary meeting, a secret treaty was signed between the Mongols and Venice. The Venetians would provide economic reports of all the countries that they visited on their travels in the region, and in return the Mongols would destroy any trading stations that they found, leaving the Venetians with a monopoly. When all is said and done, the Mongols and the Venetians shared one striking attribute – they were marvellous opportunists.

Jebei meanwhile had been active along the River Don. Subotai now believed that the time was ripe for a push towards the borders of Hungary. Before he did so, he was determined to show the Venetians that he would be a useful ally to have. The Genovese, fierce rivals of Venice, had a trading outpost on the Crimean Peninsula. It was called Sudak and it stood on the fringes of the Black Sea, over which the Genovese trading galleys rode to and fro, plying their trade. The port was burned with typical ruthless Mongol efficiency. Just a few terrified survivors managed to escape by sea, returning to the west with the first eyewitness accounts of the horrors of being attacked by the Mongols. Now reunited, Jebei and Subotai set out in the direction of Hungary, in the company of 5,000 Brodniki tribesmen, to whom they were allied. During the latter months of 1222, the Mongols marched up and down the banks of the Dniester River. The Cumans had wisely retreated before them. From the Mongol base, scouts were despatched to spy on the land further afield, whilst conscripted cartographers pieced together maps of Russia.

Chinese associates of the Mongols now provided a sophisticated administrative support function for the warriors, and they drew up censuses, and detailed information on Russia and the surrounding lands, including Hungary, Poland, Silesia and Bohemia. It was not used for two decades, but it epitomises the attention to detail which the Mongols employed in support of their campaigns. In this case, the title of 'Doomsday Book' for this evidence would have been particularly apt.

Kotian, King of the Cumans, however, had not been idle. He foresaw that the Mongols might be here to stay or, if they were not, then they might well be coming back again in the future on yet more devastating raids. It was important that they were discouraged from doing so. However, his forces had been badly depleted by successive reverses. He could not face up to the Mongols alone and so he hunted around for allies. He approached the rulers in the south of Russia (approximating to the modern Ukraine) for help. It was, on the face of it, a strange move. The people there had suffered greatly at the hands of Cuman raids in the past, and must have been absolutely thrilled that these troublesome tribes had now been firmly put in their place. But Kotian was not apparently quite the unsophisticated savage that a caricatured and superficial assessment of him might suggest. He won the support of the Russian princes of these lands, with the simple summary that 'they have taken our lands today; tomorrow it will be yours'.

His persuasive oratory did the trick, though the generous gifts that he doled out undoubtedly helped too. Kotian had won some allies, although, ironically enough, he would not see the benefit of this personally, being ousted soon after by an internal coup. This incident in fact reflects the ever-precarious position of a Cuman prince. As it turned out, in the long run, this was far from a personal tragedy. Without him at its head, his army was soon slaughtered, and by escaping this bitter fate, Kotian could go on to live and fight another day. He would subsequently return to lead the Cumans once more. His dealings with the Mongols were far from over.

The internal divisions within Russia at the time – a not unimportant consideration in the light of later Mongol conquests – were reflected in the cosmopolitan leadership of the army that came to the rather unexpected support of their traditional Cuman enemy. There was the Prince of Galicia, Mstislav the Daring, who had married a Cuman woman (they were renowned for their satisfying skills in the intimacy of the bed-chamber). He was a prince who had led something of a chequered existence so far, taking control of various cities and then losing them with rather worrying frequency. He was brave but reckless. The princes of Kursk and Chernigov were also included in this alliance. So too was the Grand Prince Mstislav Romanovich of Kiev, who had also watched his family fortunes rise and fall, at one stage even losing Kiev altogether. But his reputation was now at a high point – just two years previously in 1221 he had won a major victory over the Hungarians. The Grand Duke of Suzdal, Yuri, did not come in person but sent a contingent to swell the ranks of the allies. All told, there were perhaps 80,000 men or more in this hotchpotch army, although only about 20,000 could be regarded as well equipped.[3]

The Mongols, however, had no wish for a fight. They had come to the region with a clear strategic purpose, namely to provide themselves with as much information about Russia and the neighbouring steppes as they could possibly gather. Of course, they would collect a rather handsome haul of plunder in the process, but that was not the main purpose. Once their main objective had been accomplished, it was time to report back to Genghis thousands of miles away.

Yet, as it turned out, they were not able to extricate themselves so easily. Jebei and Subotai were increasingly perturbed by reports they received about the substantial army that was being gathered against them. From all over the region, small groups of warriors were converging at a rendezvous point, collectively representing a massive threat to the Mongols. By this time, reinforcements were on the way from Jochi, but it was a race against time for them to arrive before the now-imminent battle took place.

Jochi had been campaigning further east against the Bulgars, another warlike tribe who presented the Mongols with a significant threat. He had a great stake in all these events in the steppes, far to the west of his homeland. By Mongol tradition, a father's lands, even if he were an emperor, would be divided amongst his sons. It was also conventional that the eldest – in this case Jochi – would be given the rights to the land (his territory would be known as an *ulus*) furthest away from home. This move was now a reconnaissance – it was likely that at some time in the future, Jochi would be instructed to return and conquer all he could in order to win his *ulus,* and he therefore had a vested interest in the outcome of the campaign. However, he was far away, even allowing for the superb communications system of the Mongols. The Russian and Cuman forces were gathering at Zarub, about forty miles south of Kiev. The cavalry, naturally enough, arrived on horseback, but many of the infantry arrived in riverboats, a conventional form of transport in a region where there were many conveniently navigable rivers: their presence would be life-saving to some of them at a later stage.

Jochi had not yet arrived when the powerful army of Russians and Cumans, which was chasing the Mongols, caught up with them on the Dniester. Jochi had sent word claiming to be ill, an assertion that not everyone believed, and which may have put him on the wrong side of his father. At any event, he would not be coming, and Subotai and Jebei were on their own. The two armies moved closer to each other, and it was clear that the Mongols were now faced with little option but to fight. The Mongols did their best to avoid a battle. They sent envoys to the Russian princes. The message that they carried was that the Mongols did not wish to fight the Russians, and their dispute was with the Cumans. These tidings were not well received: the envoys were promptly executed, which seems to have been the fashionable way of declaring war at the time.

The Mongols accepted this harsh message for what it was, and sent back another ambassador to pass on the news that the Mongols were now at war with the Russians and their allies, tidings that cannot have come as a surprise to anyone. This brave man received the just desserts of his fearlessness, and was allowed to return to the Mongols unharmed. However, those who were responsible for the death of the ambassadors were now marked men. Such an act was considered the gravest of insults, and meant that not only was this a fight to the death, but also that this death would be terrible indeed. The gruesome message of the slaughtered governor of Otrar loomed large, as a warning to all who dared to do such a thing. But there were also wider operational reasons why the Mongols now had to fight. Genghis had only given Jebei and Subotai permission to undertake their reconnaissance so that they could join up with Jochi, who was conducting operations further east against the Bulgars. They were on the way to join him when the Russian threat loomed down on them. It would be suicidal to leave a hostile force at their rear when it was of this magnitude – it would threaten both them and Jochi – and they therefore had no choice but to wipe this army from the face of the earth.

It was imperative that they fought the battle in as advantageous a position as possible, and to facilitate this, a rearguard action needed to be fought. At this point a hero emerged, the Mongol equivalent of Leonidas at Thermopylae or Travis at the Alamo. His name was Hamabek. His role was to lead a force of 1,000 men; their mission was to slow down the Russian army as much as possible. There was next to no chance that any of the men would survive the impossible odds they now faced.

This brave band, vastly outnumbered but still contemptuous of their enemy, mustered on the far banks of the river. Their enemy, though, did everything they could to demonstrate why the Mongols were so successful at this period. In contrast to the tight knit group facing them, the Russians could not agree on who should lead their mishmash of an army. They argued incessantly until Mstislav the Daring took the bull by the horns and led a large contingent over the river against Hamabek.

They outnumbered the Mongols ten to one, but the arrow-storms that rained down on the attacking force thinned their ranks considerably. Despite this, the odds were too long and the Mongols were overwhelmed and killed almost to a man. Hamabek did not act out his valorous part quite perfectly. He was found hiding in a ditch (he had apparently sought refuge in a burial ground) and summarily executed. The Russians on the far bank, witnessing Mstislav's triumph, hurried across to join him in what they now anticipated would be a joyride against the demoralised Mongol army fleeing before them.

The thinking of the Mongol commanders had now gone full circle. From initially seeking to avoid battle, they now actively sought it, but only at a time and place of their choosing when their advantages were maximised. It is notable how great commanders of all eras seem to share characteristics in common. There is a well-attested story that Wellington had identified the ground around Waterloo as a place where he would fight Napoleon well before the battle took place. And so, centuries before, had Jebei and Subotai (probably the latter) marked out a spot for a decisive fight months before they fought it. The Mongols were luring their enemy into territory where they knew that they would feel comfortable and the Russians would not, in order that the odds would be stacked in their favour. The steppes felt like home to the Mongol. Although they did not of course know every nook and cranny as they might have done in Mongolia, they knew better than anyone how to fight on terrain such as this. As they moved slowly eastwards and the Russians and their allies followed on, it was as if the spider was luring the fly into its web.

The terrain was not just important in terms of winning the battle either. The Mongols were ruthless, and a key part of their strategy was to commit as much slaughter on their foe as possible. By trapping their enemy in the open as they fled from the battlefield – the result that the Mongols were hoping for – then they would be best placed to kill huge numbers of them. The Mongols could use their greatest weapon, their mobility, to best advantage on the wide-open spaces of the steppes, and the result for the Russians and their allies if caught in the open would be catastrophic.

The spot chosen was near the western bank of the River Kalka (now the Kalymus). The Mongols were not retreating at all; on the contrary, they were actually slowing down so that the Russians and their allies could catch them up. When the vanguard of this force eventually caught them, they were already positioned ready for battle in a river valley by the Kalka. The allied army was led by a council of princes, which frankly meant that it was not led at all. Military campaigns do not normally work very well if they are run by committee. The Cumans led the way during the nine days it took them to reach the Kalka. This was a sensible decision, as they knew the ground far better than the Russians, who found this all to be unfamiliar territory. However, as the Mongol army hove into view on 31 May 1233, all thought of further rational thinking quickly disappeared, and was overwhelmed by the scent of victory.

Mstislav the Daring was at the head of the vanguard. The sight of this army before him was too much for a glory-seeker like him to resist. Without waiting for the forces at his rear to catch him up, he screamed to his men to follow him, and charged headlong at the enemy. Some of the other forces were close enough to hang on to his coattails and joined in, but it was an uncoordinated attack guaranteed to dissipate any advantages that the Russo-Cuman force might have had. Soon large gaps were appearing in the ranks of the allied army, as the Mongols began to shoot down scores of men. The attacking force was now dangerously split over miles of broken country. The river itself was not much larger than a big stream, but ravines and deep valleys flanked its banks. The Mongols had timed their attacks to perfection, whilst their enemy were literally spread all over the steppe. The Mongols had been expecting just such an attack. They ignited smokescreens in front of their ranks to confuse and blind their enemy. Almost silently, from out of the smoke, like avenging Valkyries emerging from the clouds, Mongol heavy cavalry crashed into the gaps that their archers had made in the enemy lines, and turned them into gaping holes. It was too much for the Cumans, who had seen more than enough of what these fearsome warriors could do. They turned the heads of their horses around, and sped away as fast as they could.

What was already a debacle soon became a disaster. The princes at the rear did not even know a battle had started when a horde of terrified Cumans (who were exclusively mounted archers in this battle) rode frenetically into them. A huge melee ensued, and before there was any chance of order being restored, the Mongols were in the midst of this confused mass. The Grand Prince of Kiev, fortunately for him, was so far behind that he was able to observe this happening from a safe distance to the rear. Seeing that the result of this battle was now a foregone conclusion, he drew his men up in a defensive circle inside their wagons. Mstislav the Daring, who had certainly lived up to his name, though many might doubt his wisdom in doing so, led the survivors away from the battle. In their wake lay 40,000 dead. The roll of honour included no less than six princes. It was a shattering toll, but it was not yet complete. At their most fierce in the chase of a fleeing enemy, the Mongols now moved in for the kill.

A ride of death covering 150 miles now ensued. Large parties of Russians fell by the score as the Mongols homed in on their prey. It was not until the Russians made it back to the River Dneiper, and gratefully embraced the sanctuary of their riverboats, that they were safe. The fleeing army sank those boats that they could not fill, to prevent the Mongols from following them. The shattered residue of the proud force that had set out less than two weeks before now sailed to safety. Amongst their number was Mstislav the Daring, a born survivor if ever there was one. Not all were so lucky. The army from Chernigov made their way overland, riding as hard as they could back towards their homeland. It was a rare horse that could outrun the Mongols and consequently many of the army were killed. Amongst their number was their prince, Mstislav Svyatoslavich, who died along with his son. The roll call of dead princes was growing, and still it was not complete.

In the meantime, the other Mstislav, the Grand Prince of Kiev, fought a heroic action inside the improvised laager that his men had built. This was not a static defence, as the laager crawled slowly rearwards like a giant tortoise. Mstislav and his men fought gallantly, but after three days, water was running desperately short, and there was no hope of fighting their way out. They were then overcome by subterfuge. The Mongols sent envoys to negotiate their surrender, and whilst the garrison was distracted by these discussions, they stormed the camp and slaughtered those inside. This completed the Mongol victory. That night a great banquet was held in celebration. The victors chose the occasion to engage in one of those acts of gratuitous violence that tarnished their reputation. Jebei and Subotai took their meal on a specially manufactured table in the shape of a box. Inside this, three captive princes (including Mstislav of Kiev) were placed. As the box was almost airtight all three of them suffocated. It was cruel no doubt, but also, as has been pointed out, a method of killing a prince without shedding his blood, which was the way that Mongol tradition demanded such executions should be carried out.[4] The details of this macabre execution come with several variations. Some accounts say that the Mongols made a floor from planks and buried the captured princes alive beneath it. They then danced on it, crushing them to death. However they died, it is clear that the end of the princes was brutal and horrific. They had broken a sacred trust when they had slaughtered the ambassadors that the Mongols had sent not so many weeks before, the gravest of insults, which merited, in Mongol eyes, the cruellest of deaths.

These violent events marked the effective end of the formal campaign against Russia for the time being. In terms of military strategy, the Mongol's moves had been outstanding. They had retreated deeper and deeper into inhospitable territory, luring the enemy into a trap, with their forces widely dispersed and uncoordinated. Students of military tactics might recognise this strategy, for it was one adopted with considerable success by the Soviet army against the Germans in the Second World War. The mopping up operations continued thereafter, but they were soon to come to an end. A messenger arrived from Genghis ordering the army to join up with that of Jochi and return to the Great Khan's side.

There were, in fact, dark clouds looming over Jochi. He was headstrong, something of a free spirit, and a number of his senior generals were not happy with his performance. Complaints were being muttered against him which Genghis had clearly got wind of. The suspicions that he had been malingering also counted against him. Jochi was expected to take Genghis' place when he died, but people were increasingly certain that he was not up to the task. The very origins of Jochi, with his dubious paternity, undoubtedly added fuel to the flames ignited by these rumours (as discussed previously, he had been born soon after Boerte was restored to Genghis' bed, before which time she had been held as a captive concubine by the Merkits). Genghis, however, had always been supportive of all of his sons, and wished to preserve unity amongst them, a stance that perhaps was fostered as much as anything by a desire to remove the bitterness of his own earlier family life when he had killed one of his own brothers. He hoped that joining Jebei and Subotai with Jochi might create a united front, which would put a quick stop to all the hostile gossip.

So Subotai and Jebei started to make their way back towards Jochi. The campaign, however, was starting to take its toll. It had, after all, been a large raid that these men had been involved in rather than a major campaign, and the numbers of soldiers with them reflected this. Despite their victories, they had suffered many casualties. Of the men who had survived, it is safe to assume that a number were wounded and most of them were tired. The fighting power of the army had inevitably diminished as a result of their almost superhuman exertions.

Before the retreating Mongols joined up with Jochi, they had to pass through the lands of the Bulgars. They crossed over the River Volga into Bulgar territory. The Bulgars, however, were not going to give them easy passage through their lands, and launched a fierce attack. Depleted by their exertions in Russia, the Mongols were not strong enough to fight them off, and crossed back over to the west bank of the Volga rather than push the point. It was a blow to Mongol morale, and it would not be forgotten. The Bulgars would be a marked tribe from now on. Eventually Jebei and Subotai joined up with Jochi and moved back towards Genghis. En route, there were many opportunities for further pillaging, which they took full advantage of. A large Bulgar force was crushed and then the Mongols moved on into the lands of the eastern Cumans, known as the Kanglis, who had fought in support of Khwarezm. The Mongols bore a grudge for a long time, and were ruthless in avenging those who fuelled their ire for whatever reason. They smashed the Kangli army in battle, killed their *khan* and extracted a massive tribute from his people.

The army continued their journey back to Genghis. Spirits were high and their march had something of the swagger of a Roman triumph about it. But the sweet taste of victory was suddenly soured. Subotai had played a key role in the glorious victories recently won. However, Jebei had certainly played an important part too, and it must have come as a shock when he was struck down by fever and suddenly died. Somewhat sobered by this untimely reminder of man's mortality, the army at last arrived back at the camp of Genghis after an epic journey, which had taken them far into lands previously unknown. The loss of Jebei would have been felt deeply by him, having been by his side ever since those early far-off days on the steppe. However, the results of the campaign had been very useful. The knowledge gained would be locked up in a metaphorical box, to be brought out again when the time was right. Genghis met the returning army seated in a vast tent which could hold 2,000 people. He seemed well suited to playing the part of a world conqueror. He sat on a magnificent throne that had formerly been the property of the now dead

Sultan Mohammed of Khwarezm. He supped freely on the Shiraz wines of the conquered region, which were a personal favourite, a satisfying reward for victory. A robust and determined campaigner, Genghis was also a man who knew how to enjoy the fruits of victory to the full.

The Mongol court had its protocols, like all others, and they were jealously protected. The senior commanders were all granted the privilege of strolling unannounced into the court, and now they all did so. Jochi, the senior son, strode in first. He walked deferentially to the throne and knelt before his father. He placed his father's hand on his forehead, a traditional sign of submission. Realising that he was on shaky ground, he went out of his way to play the part of the Prodigal Son, seeking his father's forgiveness for not acting in strict accordance with his original orders during the recent campaign. Jochi sought to ingratiate himself further by the stupendous present of 100,000 captured horses. Genghis made no further reference to any perceived misbehaviour, and it seemed that no permanent damage had been done to the relationship between father and son.

And so the Mongols disappeared from the fringes of Europe as quickly as they had descended upon them. Inevitably, Christian men in Russia and Europe remarked that they were indeed the scourge of God, come to punish men for their sins, rather like the Vikings half a millennium previously. As a chronicler from Novgorod reflected pensively, 'we do not know where these evil Tartars came from nor where they went'.[5] Collective sighs of relief were breathed, and men hoped to God that this was the last they would see of them.

Unfortunately for them, the Mongols had not yet finished with Europe. However, Genghis had a good deal of unfinished business to attend to first, much further east in China. He had left his trusted lieutenant Mukali to carry on the war there, but he had subsequently died and, following his demise, all momentum had gone out of the prosecution of the conflict. A war of long, hard sieges followed, the kind of campaign that the Mongols were most unsuited to. It was time for some impetus to be instilled into the process. Genghis therefore made his way back from Khwarezm. His men had been recuperating for a while. Chagatai and Ögedei had been indulging in that favourite of Mongol pastimes, hunting, this time with swans as the game. It was said that they sent caravans carrying fifty camel loads of the elegant birds back to Genghis. There were other more bloody diversions as well: a group of Uighur nobles who had been accused of plotting against Genghis were executed for their crimes.

In the Far East, there was also Korea for the Mongols to deal with. The Mongols had left the peninsula in 1219, when the Khitan garrison at Kangdong had surrendered. This was, however, far from the end of Mongol interest in Korea. Some troops were left in the border town of Uiju. They were given the rather unsubtle instruction that they should try and learn the Korean language so that they could use it when the main Mongol army returned. The Mongols were too stretched to deal with the peninsula for now, but they fully intended to return in the future. Korea and the Mongols were at peace until 1225. There was then a very serious incident which did not bode well for relations between the two. Mongol envoys came to the Korean capital at Pyongyang. The envoys had been treated well enough, and returned bearing gifts (not that they had necessarily appreciated them that much: they were pleased to be carrying back the otter pelts they had been given, but they apparently dumped most of the other presents on the way.) Unfortunately, the envoys were attacked and slaughtered. It was probably nothing more than common banditry at work. The Mongols, however, blamed the Korean government for this perceived outrage, something that may have been a convenient excuse for an invasion – the Mongols always liked to have the appearance of a legitimate excuse for their campaigns. The time was not yet right, but the insult, as the Mongols considered it, was marked down for future reference. It was time to return to China for now.

There were two major powers left to subdue here, the Chin in the north and the Song in the south. There were also the Tanguts in the border regions. The Mongol propensity to bear a grudge still fuelled a desire to settle a score as far as Genghis was concerned. Years before, when he had first invaded China, the Tangut king had paid him tribute, but disdainfully refused to provide him with troops. Because he had other wars to fight at the time, he had been forced to let the snub pass, but it rankled deeply within him, burning away like a festering sore. Genghis was a dangerous man to make an enemy of, something that he planned to demonstrate with spectacular effect. The army of retribution readied itself for the task ahead.

There is one enemy that even a world conqueror cannot overcome. The spectre of death had been sensed moving closer to Genghis as the years advanced. He was, by the standards of the day, if not old, close to being so, at about sixty years of age. Those long years of campaigning had taken their toll, along with the damage caused by the wounds, the hardships, and the stresses of command, which had worn him down over the years. Genghis felt a shadow moving over him. He summoned wise old sages, including a Taoist teacher who claimed to have found the secret of eternal life. His name was Changchun and he was popularly supposed to be 300 years old. Genghis had sent one of his confidantes, Liu Zhonglu, to find him and bring him back to his court. When he did, Changchun did not want to come. It was a huge journey to the court of Genghis and he was old. However, the great *khan* could not be denied, and Changchun had set out on a trip that would take him four years to make. His journey is described in a book called *Travels of an Alchemist*. He reached the mountains by Lake Baikal, where an escort provided by Ögedei led him on towards Genghis. By the end of 1221 he had arrived at Samarkand. Here Changchun was treated with great honour, being housed in the former palace of Shah Mohammed. He stayed here for the winter as Genghis was out on campaign trying to chase down Jalal al-Din.

When spring came Changchun had been taken to Genghis, who was camped up near Kabul. The *khan* quickly got to the point: did Changchun have any potions with him that would prolong life indefinitely? No, replied the sage, he had treatments that would protect life but none that would make it everlasting. That was beyond his gift. Despite the disappointment this must have caused, months of leisurely discussion followed. Some of the wise man's advice would not have been welcome: Changchun disapproved of hunting and told the *khan* so. He also advised sexual abstinence as a way of ensuring a longer life. It is difficult to guess which piece of advice would have been the most unwelcome to Genghis given his love of hunting, his many wives and the number of concubines he enjoyed. One modern estimate claimed that some seventeen million people in the twenty-first century world, are descended from Genghis Khan, including the British Royal Family, Iranian royalty and the family of Dracula (one assumes the medieval Romanian prince and not the fictitious vampire count!), which gives us an insight into Genghis' prolific activities in the bedchamber.[6] However unpalatable the advice, though, Changchun was greatly respected by Genghis. His words were meticulously recorded and his followers were exempted from taxation.

This visit from Changchun showed how disturbed Genghis was at the inevitability of death. As Genghis returned east and prepared to move on China, he was acutely aware of strange and troubling omens. His dreams were disturbed; his daytimes haunted, and the pleasure of living became foreign to him. Nevertheless, he pressed on regardless. He sat at the head of his war machine as it rumbled towards China, but not for long. He always loved the thrill of the hunt, and one day, as he was out indulging his passion for such sport, he fell from his horse. There were no bones broken but the Great Khan had done himself terrible internal injury. The days passed; seemingly unable to recover, he became progressively

The Mongols

weaker.[7] Soon after this event, shattering tidings were received from the west. Jochi, that troublesome son of dubious provenance, was dead. Not everyone liked him; a number of senior advisers did not have a good word to say about him. But one man was devastated by the news. Genghis retired to his tent and refused to see anyone for days. This was a man who once admonished one of his own sons for grieving the loss of a child excessively. There seems little doubt that, regardless of any suspicions as to the parentage of Jochi, Genghis loved him dearly.

The business of war still went on. The Tangut king, trapped in a bleak stronghold in the mountains, unhelpfully died – Genghis would have loved to have taken his revenge in person. There was an extraordinary battle on the frozen ice of the Yellow River. The Mongols, in their element, covered the hooves of their horses with cloth so that they might get a better grip. The Tangut cavalry slid all over the place, their horses struggling almost comically to stay upright. The inevitable Mongol victory ensued. Soon after, the son of the dead Tangut king sued for peace. Under terms of truce, he made his way into the camp of Genghis. By now the *khan* was an embittered, dying man, and showing a disdain for convention that did him no honour, Genghis ordered that every one of his party should be slain. It was an act by a great man who knew his last day was imminent. Even a world conqueror must, after all, die. His sons were summoned to his side: Chagatai, in command of the reserve army, stayed where he was, but Ögedei and Tolui hurried to their father.

They made their way into his tent, dimly lit, and, as their eyes adjusted to the near darkness, the figure that appeared before them was unrecognisable. Huddled in his blanket, almost paralysed, this was not the man who had made the world tremble. Towards the end, Genghis descended to the depths of despair and self-pity. It was said that, in a bitter outburst, he had declared that, 'my descendants will wear gold, they will eat the choicest meats, they will ride the finest horses, they will hold in their arms the most beautiful women, and they will forget to whom they owe it all'.[8] He was in part wrong: he would never be forgotten. His shadow would lurk like a wraith over those that came after him. Future *khans* remained in awe of his legacy. Nearly two centuries later, another great conqueror, known as Tamerlane, would reverence Genghis and his descendants as if they were gods. In many ways this was not surprising. Honouring prominent ancestors was a key part of shamanist tradition, and none would be more distinguished than Genghis. The spectre of Genghis still managed to shape Mongol policy decades after he died. Towards the end, it seems that he worried that his sons might fall out, and that a civil war might follow. He had seen such things in his youth, and it seems that he retained an almost paranoid fear that he would be usurped even during his days of greatness. He extolled Tolui and Ögedei to make sure that such division did not mar their relationships, nor should there be any dispute with the absent Chagatai. He was right to fear, though the dissension would in the event skip a generation. But such great events were in the far future. Now, in these last moments, was the time for more intimate concerns. The care of his beloved Boerte was entrusted to a devoted friend, Kilugen, and his favourite poet was summoned to his side to compose some suitably eloquent and moving funeral verses.

The succession had already been decided. In Juvaini's flowery (and highly suspect) words, Genghis had not long before called his sons together and told them that his advice, or to be more precise his command, was that 'Ögedei should ascend the throne of the Khanate in my place, because he stands out among you for the excellency of his firm council and the superiority of his perspicacious understanding'.[9] His end is shrouded in myth. It is meant to be so of course, with supermen who have rewritten the natural order. During his last moments, his prescience was finely tuned. He remarked that he had seen one of his seed who was destined for greatness, not a son but a grandson by the name of Kublai. His breathing slowed and then, at last, it was over. It was August 1227 and the world had lost one of the greatest military commanders in history. Word of his death, which occurred in Gansu Province in northwest China,[10] was kept from his army for several days, almost as if those close to him could not believe it was true. But there was no resurrection, no miracle: Genghis, after all, was born in the same way as every other man, and so he died. So, soon after, the unbearable news was broken to his army. There would need to be a great *kuriltai* to agree on Genghis' nomination of Ögedei as his successor, but that could wait for now. First of all the Great Khan must be laid to rest with all the great pomp and dignity that such a man deserved.

The emotions of Genghis' soldiers at this moment in time are not recorded in detail, but this must surely have come as a hammer-blow. He had taken the Mongols to previously undreamed-of heights. The secret of his success was that he had taken a previously fragmented group of peoples, and united them under a centralising influence – him. There was delegation in this system for sure, but his decision was in the end final. It was not clear whether anyone else would be able to repeat the trick. In the event, no one would to anything like the same extent. Deprived of his over-arching control, the Mongol dream was already doomed to die a death, though that death would be a long time in coming.

For three months his body lay in state. From all over his vast empire men came to bid farewell to their *khan*. Then he was buried, not in a vast mausoleum in an opulent city, but at the place he loved best, a sacred mountain on the steppes of Mongolia. Great secrecy attended his burial place. All those who knew where it was were killed and their secret died with them. For centuries after he was buried there, not only was the site of his grave unknown, but also the region in which it was located was closed off to most of the people. A European friar, who visited the country some twenty years after Genghis' death, later noted the burial rituals of the Mongols. The description he provides in all probability outlines what happened to Genghis' earthly remains:

> When one of them dies, if he is a noble, he is buried secretly in a field that pleases them. What is more, he is buried sitting in the middle of one of his tents, and they place a table before him and put a tray of meat and a bowl of mare's milk in it. Furthermore, there is buried with him a mare with a foal and a horse with a saddle and bridle, and they eat another horse and fill the skin with straw and mount it on two or four poles up high, so that in the next world he may have a tent where he may stay, and a mare from which he may have milk and by which he may increase the number of his horses and the horses he may ride.[11]

With Genghis, even the trees did their part. An old myth says that Genghis was buried under a great tree, higher than all the others, but the rest of them then decided to grow to the same height as this distinctive tree, so that no one could distinguish one from another. So his grave was lost, one of the greatest undiscovered monuments that perhaps some future archaeologist may uncover. Certainly they continue to dream that they might do so, the grave of Genghis still being seen as a Holy Grail for archaeologists.

And so Genghis died, leaving a legacy such as no man has ever done – the world. He bequeathed to his sons the responsibility for conquering that part of humanity that he had not managed to subdue himself. His resting place though, was lost, never again to be found, leaving behind the instruction that 'the Tartars must subject the entire world to themselves and have no peace with them unless they submit to the Tartars no matter how long it would take to kill them'.[12] This was the key to his last will and testament, which would continue to act as a beacon for future Mongol policy. But that was in the future: now the world conqueror was consigned to the sacred soil of his homeland, amongst the hills that had shaped his character, and provided the backdrop for much of his extraordinary life.

Somewhere on the steppes of Mongolia to this very day lie the remains of the greatest conqueror that the world has ever seen. From time to time rumours circulate claiming that his last resting place has been uncovered. A report appeared in 2004 claiming that a joint Japanese-Mongolian expedition has found his mausoleum though not his grave, which archaeologists claim lies within eight miles of the site.[13] Such claims should be examined with a generous dose of scepticism.

Despite these continuing expeditions, as yet he remains undiscovered, buried in a shroud of mystery. However, he lies not alone, but in the company of heroes like Arthur of myth and Attila of history, their resting place known only by the gods. And yet, paradoxically, he lives still, not in this world but in the world of legend.

CHAPTER 5
Ögedei & the Golden Horde: A New *Khan* is Elected & a Russian Empire Established 1228-1240

Genghis had transformed the Mongols from being one of the underdogs, into the greatest rising power in the world. The British Empire must have felt similar emotions of loss and uncertainty when Queen Victoria died, so close was the link between him and his people. The great man had made the impossible seem achievable, and with his demise some must have wondered if all his achievements would die with him. Life, however, had to go on, even if it seemed unthinkable without him: even the great were not immortal.

Although Ögedei had been nominated his heir, it was another two years before the *kuriltai* which agreed to his succession would be held. The succession was also not the straightforward assumption of all powers that a western philosophy might suppose, as the empire was to be divided up between Genghis' sons. Ögedei would be the Great Khan, the lord over all, but he would be, more than anything, a first amongst near equals. His brothers would still be immensely powerful, and have a significant degree of autonomy. In this division lay the first inklings of serious trouble ahead. Genghis had been an outstanding ruler but in one thing he had been deficient: he had not left behind a clear succession policy. This meant that with a great empire now to rule, there was a strong possibility that future successions would be fraught with division. In the absence of any clear hereditary direction, there was the real danger that whoever held the strongest army, whenever the throne became available in the future, would try and seize it for themselves.

What followed with subsequent successions was a downward spiral of increasingly tense and bitter disputes. Genghis had been a supreme autocrat who, even if he would listen to counsel, always took the final decision. His word was the law. In this assumption of political supremacy, he would leave an example that would prove impossible to emulate. Even with decades of conquest still to come, the seeds of the ultimate disintegration of the Mongol empire had already been sown when he died, though they had not yet borne fruit. The empire was accordingly split. The Mongol homeland, (symbolically most sacred place of all the Mongolian territories) would be gifted to Tolui, Genghis' younger son. The lands to the south west of the empire, which included the immense riches of Khwarezm, would go to Chagatai. The borders of this territory were still poorly defined, and much remained to be done to secure them. The western steppes further off in the Russian territories were to be divided between the sons of Jochi, Orda and Batu. The latter in particular would play a critical part in future Mongol politics, in spite of his distance from Mongolia. The elasticity of the frontiers here was more marked than anywhere else.

Tolui acted as regent until the formal election of a successor to Genghis took place. In fairness to him, although he had a reputation for acting on impulse, there is no record that he attempted to take the *khanate* for himself, even though his position as regent gave him a good deal of power, symbolic or otherwise. When the *kuriltai* was held, there were no dissensions to the bequest of the *khanate* to Ögedei. Chagatai was the eldest brother now Jochi had gone, but Genghis, being an astute judge of character as well as a warrior, had recognised that his qualities were unsuited to the imperial throne. Chagatai was hotheaded and impetuous. Juvaini described him as 'a fierce and mighty khan, stern and severe'.[1] He was, though, a man who knew well the protocols and legal customs of the Mongols, and he would be an excellent legal adviser. It was a role that he would play in the future with dedication and a great sense of duty.

Tolui was very popular but he was young and impetuous. Genghis recognised that the empire he had fashioned was still fragile, and needed nurturing. There was a great risk that Tolui's youthful exuberance could translate into excessive impulsiveness, with possibly fatal results for the empire. That is why, despite his popularity, Genghis – who, using Mongol convention, could nominate any of his sons or even his brothers as his successor – did not recommend that Tolui should take his place. It was the personality of Ögedei (the interpersonal qualities as we might now call them) that won him the nomination. He was an easy-going man who had the capacity to keep men loyal by the warmth that he engendered. Genghis, the man of iron, was also someone who had a surprisingly good understanding of what was needed to keep his people united, for he recognised that the greatest threat to the Mongols was no other power that they might face, but their own internal divisions. After all, steppe society had been subject to intrigue, plot and coup for centuries, and it was not realistic to expect all of this to change in a generation.

Ögedei did all the right things at his election. He at first refused to accept the result, not believing, he said, that he was any more worthy than his brothers of the honour. It took forty days for him to be persuaded by the chancellor, the venerable Yeh-Lu Ch'u-Ts'ai, that he should accept the imperial throne. Nevertheless, his apparent reticence, feigned or otherwise, more than anything sent a message to his kin that he did not mean to be an absolute ruler, and that they still had a crucial role to play in the government of the empire. Ögedei possessed the common touch, and this ingratiated him to his people. He travelled with a small escort so that he could be approached by the people to whom he spoke warmly and freely. He gave alms to the poor. Most of all, he earned himself a reputation for mercy and balance in his judgements, a contrast perhaps to his father, though it should be noted that, regardless of what his enemies thought of him, Genghis was considered to be a just and fair ruler by most of his own people. His excesses were generally reserved for other races.

Ögedei decided that an empire needs a capital, not of tents but of stone: a permanent statement of power where an emperor could live, merchants could trade, and ambassadors could pay their respects in appropriate splendour. The place that he chose for the city to be built was on the steppes of Mongolia at Karakorum, a Turkish word meaning 'Black Boulders'. By western standards, it would be small and unprepossessing, but its importance was huge in a symbolic sense, representing a coming of age for a nomadic society. As the city grew, the way of life changed. Every day 500 wagons made their way into the city with food for the populace. Ögedei oversaw the erection of what was, by Mongol standards, a great palace. It was large, and longer than an arrow shot (which is considerable, as a Mongol arrow shot travelled quite a long way). Craftsmen came from all over to build it. One of its outstanding features was a magnificent fountain in the form of animals, elephants, tigers and horses. *Airag* flowed freely from it, an acquired taste for visitors from outside Mongolia no doubt, but a rare treat for a Mongol (though Ögedei's preference was for wine). He ordered that the other royal princes should build palaces here too, an important move that added to the grandeur of the place, and helped to keep the family happy. Karakorum grew, a unique development in Mongolia, unprecedented in this nomadic society. Not everyone, however, was impressed. When envoys from Western Europe arrived a couple of decades later, one compared it not altogether favourably with the suburb of Saint Denis in Paris, and described the great palace as a rather poor second to the monastery back in the same place in France.

It was far from an ideal place to build a capital. Although perhaps it was understandable that the Mongols wished their first town to be in Mongolia, it was hundreds of miles away from their new centres of power. In addition, there were few supplies available locally that would be suitable to construct its buildings, hence the need for wagon-loads of construction materials and other provisions to be ferried in. But the reason for this is clear: there was no obvious reason to build a city in the hub of their newly-won territories for they had already conquered plenty of them, which they could, if they wished, turn into a capital should they so desire. That they chose not to do so is a sign that the Mongols were still in touch with their cultural origins.

There was an increasing power from behind the throne: the chancellor Yeh-Lu Ch'u-Ts'ai. Fortunately it was a role he exercised sagaciously and without excessive thought of self-interest. Chagatai too took a part, and Ögedei was seemingly in awe of him. Ögedei had one major weakness, one unfortunately shared with some Mongols both ancient and modern: an unhealthy liking for alcohol. There was an amusing incident when Chagatai demonstrated how bad alcohol was for Ögedei, by putting some in an iron bottle and showing how it corroded. Ögedei, apparently convinced, agreed that he would cut his consumption in half. He then ordered cups to be made that were twice as large as those previously used, and drank the same volume of alcohol but in half the number of cups.

Genghis had left some very specific orders in his will. Even beyond the grave he was a huge influence. The details of his will also give us of course one of the best insights we have into his mind, and his own personal priorities. In it, he told his sons that they were to finish what he started – they were to complete the conquest of Chin China. It was a divine mandate, treated as if it were from heaven itself. The process of conquest here had been going on for several decades. It was a slow war, partly because of weaknesses in Mongol strategy. When the Mongols first burst into Chin territory, the objective was plunder rather than conquest. This meant that, even if a city were taken, it was looted and then either abandoned or garrisoned by a tiny force, which was too weak to hold it. The Chin were nothing if not resilient. They rebuilt shattered cities and decimated armies from the massive materiel that was available to them. Rather like Soviet Russia in the Second World War, heavy losses to the enemy were replenished from large stocks of manpower, and vast supplies of other equipment.

The opening period of Ögedei's reign was a much less energetic time than the years when Genghis had been *khan*. There seem to have been two camps within Ögedei's court: those who wished for a time of consolidation, and those led by Subotai, who were much more aggressive, and argued that the Mongols could continue with their empire-building. Subotai won the argument, which was a hard one to resist given the specificity of Genghis' will. Ögedei, as was his custom, showed good grace in accepting the decision to return to the quest for expansion, and he gave a royal princess to Subotai as a wife, an honour that signified royal approval. The *khan* was at the head of the army of conquest that subsequently left for China, as was expected of him, but Subotai was the man who designed the overall strategy, and he became the effective leader in the field. Tolui was given a force to lead, but, given his reputation as a somewhat headstrong young man, senior and experienced generals were given the prominent positions in his army.

The capital of the Chin was now at Kaifeng, which they planned to make their Stalingrad. This was the logical target for the Mongols' campaign, but it would be a very difficult proposition. To the north of it lay the Yellow River, and to the south the Yangtze. Forty miles of wall guarded it, and an intricate complex of fortifications protected the approach to the city. But if Kaifeng fell there would be no further places for the Chin to run. This would be a fight to the death, and the Chin determined that they would fight it on the defensive as this gave them the greatest chance of success in the critical campaign that was about to be waged. Subotai realised that, however strong the Mongol army was (and a further extended campaign would play into the hands of the Chin) it was crucial that he could find a way of luring the Chin forces off their guard, and bringing them out into the open, where he felt certain they would be annihilated. To do this, he planned to make the enemy believe that the Mongols would strike from the north, whilst in reality the main strike would be from a different direction.

He accordingly launched a major attack from the north. This was exactly what the Chin expected him to do, being the logical direction for an assault. Subotai duly laid siege to several major river fortresses, and the Chin hurried up reinforcements to beat him back. Whilst all this was going on, a major Mongol force was preparing itself in the west. It was under the command of Tolui. Its plan was a daring one: it would cross the Gobi desert, and sweep down to the south into Song territory. Although there was no state of war between the Song and the Mongols, the Mongol command reasoned that, given the constant antipathy between the Song and the Chin, they would be given free passage through the territory of the former when they entered it. This worked exactly as planned. Tolui and his men crossed the desert and then the mountains of

Western China. As they made their way through the passes in the west, they glimpsed in the distance the most incredible mountain ranges they had ever seen, the vast precipices of the Himalaya in Tibet. When they moved into Song territory, they were allowed to pass unmolested and Tolui and his 30,000 men swept through the region. Perhaps the Song felt powerless to intervene, or maybe they were happy to see the end of their rivals in the north. They would be unwise to celebrate too much, for it would be their turn next.

Tolui's move created a state of panic in Kaifeng. Convinced now that this was the main Mongol army, the Chin rushed reinforcements down from the north to the south. As expected, they were panicking like frightened hens. The impact of this was to leave the northern borders undermanned and, faced by a weakened front line, Subotai and his army came crashing through. In the meantime, Tolui had shown much maturity in continually harassing the Chin forces that were sent to face him. Constantly sending in his light cavalry archers to sting the enemy into a reaction, he soon had the Chin chasing after him. It was winter now; the ground was hard as iron, and the air so icy that it burned the lungs of men when they breathed in. Tolui was luring the Chin away from the main thrust of the attack, leaving their backs unguarded. A bitter campaign followed. Tolui lured the Chin deeper into the mountains. His men were in desperate straits by now, tired, many wounded, a number already dead. Food was so short that men took to eating their horses and then, when this source was exhausted, they ate the bodies of their dead. But, if the situation was bad for the Mongols, it was far worse for the Chin, who were in the main city-dwellers and completely unused to such hardships.

Whilst these battles were being fought in such horrific conditions, the sudden terrifying news was received by the Chin soldiers at the front that Subotai was across the Yellow River, and moving on Kaifeng. Realising that they had been duped in a deadly combination of hide-and-seek and blind man's bluff, the Chin defence began to disintegrate. Units in the south were ordered to extricate themselves from the fighting with Tolui, and rush back to the north. Chaos ensued. Tolui saw that the Chin were moving back, and encouraged his men to undertake one more superhuman effort. The enemy had been caught completely off-guard. Tolui set off hot on the tails of the fleeing Chin forces. Before long, the retrenchment was degenerating into a rout. Although the Chin armies rushed back towards Kaifeng, they were little better than a disorganised mob. Subotai and his army moved like lightning. The speed of his movement gave him exactly what he wanted. The Chin armies were cut off from Kaifeng and trapped in the open. The battle that was subsequently fought was a rout. The Chin were ruthlessly cut down and the army destroyed.

Ögedei now saw that the campaign was virtually over, and returned to Mongolia accompanied by Tolui. The final conquest of Kaifeng was left in the hands of Subotai. He was ruthless in his execution of this. A huge wall was built around the city. He then forced captive Chinese prisoners to pile timber against the walls and set fire to them. The defenders were forced to try and kill their own people to stamp out this threat. The siege (which began in 1232) was fiercely fought. Morale inside Kaifeng was low, but the emperor did what he could to raise it by ensuring that his people saw him prominently, as he walked the walls, exhorting his men to greater efforts.

In the meantime, the Mongols had become much more proficient at building and employing siege engines, and these sent fire-bombs into Kaifeng, which caused great damage. One writer, a Chin official inside the city, said that 'the Mongol army intensified the bombardment of the city and the stone balls flew in like rain showers. The crews of the city's own artillery were put in terrible confusion and were partly crushed, partly pounded'.[2]

The city defended heroically. Although their position was perilous, there was one area where they had an advantage. Their artillery was far more sophisticated than that available to the Mongols, and caused heavy casualties amongst the besiegers. Their fire-bombs in particular, primitive combustible devices launched from trebuchets, exploded on impact and could penetrate armour and burn anyone unfortunate enough to get in their path to death. Every man capable of bearing arms inside the city was forced to fight. For some months the battle went on, a bitter, harsh siege prosecuted without pity or relief. Winter passed to summer and, in stark contrast to the icy cold of the former that had hit the armies so hard, the heat was now suffocating. Inside Kaifeng, the conditions were nightmarish. Food was already desperately short, and the defenders had also turned to eating their dead. Then, terrible news swept the city – plague had broken out. Subotai got word of this and offered to withdraw in return for gifts to him and his commanders. The sole intention of the ploy was to let the Mongols move back from Kaifeng before plague attacked them too. Just one month later, with the virility of the disease now expended, the Mongols were back, and this time they moved in for the kill against a city that was on the verge of collapse. They broke through the walls at last, and swept through the streets. The Chin emperor, believing the position to be hopeless, had fled and left the city to its fate. He later committed suicide at Caizhou.

Subotai wished to hand over Kaifeng to his men, to do with as they pleased. If he had done so, then there was no doubt how things would end. But times were changing: Chinese officials, whom his forces had captured over the past years, advised Ögedei that there was more profit to be had from letting Kaifeng live and produce tax revenues in the future than from pillaging it now. So Ögedei ordered that Kaifeng should be spared. Subotai, being an old-school, harsh, unyielding warrior, was no doubt mortified. He returned to the expanding city at Karakorum. Tolui was now dead; it was said as a result of too much alcohol – an unfortunate family trait that had not yet claimed its last victim. By 1235, Karakorum was completed by the addition of a wall that embraced the entire city in a granite grip. Plans were then made for the campaigns ahead, and Subotai, naturally enough, was at the heart of them.

Further conquest continued throughout the next few years of Ögedei's reign: the empire was still expanding in some areas, even though Genghis was now long gone. Expansion was not the name of the game everywhere, however. Many of the conquests that had been made in Khwarezm were not yet permanent additions to the Mongol empire, and only some of the gains in Central Asia were hung on to. The tidemark of Mongol conquests in Persia had receded. It was further east that expansion continued, again giving an insight into Mongol priorities. In China, the fall of the Chin dynasty allowed the Song in the south to grab two of their former enemy's cities. As the Mongols now considered that these belonged to them, this was considered an act that merited the declaration of war against the Song as well. Such a step, however, had long been a certainty. Another council was held, at which Chagatai reported that his armies had started to resume the advance in Khwarezm. Georgia too was being attacked again. The armies of Jalal ad-din, son of Sultan Mohammed, were still active, and needed to be put down. Ögedei replied that he had also ordered two of his sons, Koten and Kuchu, to move on the Song. It was all action in the Mongol empire, with fighting taking place on a number of fronts simultaneously.

All these victories added to the lands of Ögedei and Chagatai, as well as their power and status. Moves were also made against Korea, in the hope of adding that country to the burgeoning empire. Once that fell and the Song territories were conquered, the Pacific Ocean put a natural stop to further eastward expansion (with the notable exception of Japan of course). Operations in Korea had begun afresh in August 1231. The Mongols were at odds with the Koreans because the latter had refused to help in the campaign against the Chin. The Koreans, as noted previously, were expected to act as allies of the prominent power in the region, which was now the Mongols, and they had failed to act the part expected of them. Uiju, the border town, was first to fall to the Mongol armies. They then moved on to Kuju, which was to provide a well-documented account of the Mongols in action during a siege.

The fight that followed was bitter. The Mongols loaded up carts with grass and wood: they trundled these up against the gates and set fire to them in the hope of setting the place ablaze, but the flames failed to take hold. Siege towers were built and miners started to tunnel away into the foundations of the walls. The Koreans struck back as hard as they could. Burning straw was fired at the siege engines and countermines were dug. This was to be no walkover. The Koreans were maybe overmatched, like a middleweight fighter against a prime heavyweight, but they did not lack either pride or spirit. The defence was led by a heroic figure, Pak So. Despite intense pressure, he refused to surrender. The Mongols tried to scale the walls with ladders, but these were met with large improvised devices like giant metal claws, which were used to smash the ladders to pieces. Against the odds, Kuju continued to hold on.

A relief army was sent by the Koreans to save the city. However, it was itself surprised by the Mongols. In a hard-fought skirmish against it, the leader of the relief force was killed, and his army broke up in chaos. The Mongols redoubled their efforts, but at the same time sent raiding parties further a-field, deeper into Korea. This sent the Korean government into a spin, as the Mongols were now dangerously close to their capital. The government therefore decided that it was high time to negotiate. Without consulting Pak So, they agreed to surrender Kuju as part of the settlement. Pak So was beside himself when he heard the news, and refused to give the city up. Some role reversal then followed: the Korean authorities ordering that Pak So should be executed for his refusal to obey their orders, but the Mongols intervened and saved him in recognition of his heroism.

The tribute that Korea was required to pay for being saved the harsh ravages of the Mongols was huge. Gold, silver, 20,000 horses and clothing for one million soldiers was required. This however, was not the end of the war. The government managed to slip away from the Mongols, and found safety on the fortified island of Kanghwa. It was only half a mile offshore, but this might as well have been the width of the Pacific, for the Mongols were unable to subdue it. Instead they raided elsewhere. A Mongol warrior, Sartaq, led his men way down into Korea, south of where Seoul now stands, and laid siege to a mountain fortress at Ch'oin. The defence was led by a warrior monk, Kim Yunhu. It was possibly he who took an arrow and shot it into the eye of Sartaq, striking him dead. With his demise, the Mongols did not know what to do and the siege was raised. This marked the end of the Mongol invasion, which was far from an unqualified success. It had highlighted two major deficiencies in Mongol tactics: the problems that they still had with siege warfare and difficulties with amphibious operations.

Mongol attention was once again beginning to look west, although a *kuriltai* did also decide that Korea must be invaded once more after the unsatisfactory result in the recent campaign there. Mongol pride had been stung, and must at some time be avenged. However, actions further west were the priority. Family considerations played their part in this decision. Orda, whose men became known as the White Horde, held territories on the Russian steppes, but they were to the north and further expansion was constrained by natural barriers in the form of the icy tundra of the region. Batu had next to nothing, a small following, few cities and none of any wealth. It was not fitting that a prince of the blood should be living in such a fashion. Further, there were strong reasons why attention should be turned to the steppes. Their very vastness made them almost completely porous. They had not been added permanently to the Mongol empire, and, until they were, the hostile and unruly tribes there posed a threat. But on the other hand, if the steppes were permanently subdued then they would form an excellent launch pad for conquest further west. They also provided ample stocks of grass to feed the vast Mongol herds.

Although the benefits of any conquest would accrue to Batu, it was Subotai who took the lead in arguing the case for the move west. The long-term vision of the master strategist was such that he believed it would take eighteen years to complete the conquest. A considerable number of men would be needed and, furthermore, those chosen should be the pick of the Mongol army. This would be no raid: it would be nothing short of conquest. The raids on Russia in 1221 had caused havoc. They had been awful for those unfortunate enough to be in their path, with death and destruction left in their wake. Yet they were, for all their horror, incursions rather than invasions. The Mongols had struck like a bolt of lightning out of a clear blue sky, but then they had disappeared back to where they had come from. At the time, apart from the terror, the Russians had been bewildered. Whence had these demons come and where had they gone? No one knew, but all thanked God that they did not stay.

For some, even the raids had taken a toll that could not be borne. The crushing defeats inflicted by the Mongols on the Georgians had broken their power. When that old adversary of the Mongols, Jalal ad-Din (son of Mohammed, Shah of Khwarezm) returned to Persia a few years after, the Mongols had chased him across the Indus, and he was welcomed as a liberator by many of the population who were unimpressed with the high levels of Mongol taxation. He succeeded in taking back chunks of the country and he even held Baghdad for a while. He then turned on Georgia, which was too weak to resist him. Its power was broken, though the end was close at hand for Jalal ad-Din too. The Mongols did not take kindly to defeat and rebellion, and they advanced on Persia to retake the lands recently lost to them. There was no resistance – people remembered too vividly just what defiance towards the Mongols meant. Defeated without a fight and a fugitive once more, Jalal ad-Din met his end in 1231, a prince no longer, murdered by a Kurdish peasant whose brother he had once killed. It was a fitting analogy for the end of one aspiring empire, which had been overwhelmed by another much greater one. The impressive state that was Khwarezm had gone forever.

Apart from these disturbances around the edges of the steppes, life in Russia had returned much to the normality that it had known before the Mongol assaults of 1221, with raids and counter-raids between the various semi-nomadic tribes in the region, and frequent border disputes between the unruly Russian principalities. It was a life of frequent but small-scale disorder, just as it had been for decades. Despite the warning shots fifteen years ago, the Russian world had not changed at all as a result of the raids. But when the Mongols appeared in Russia again in 1236 they had something quite different from a raid in mind. They had sensed weakness in the people who lived in the vast Russian hinterland – the same kind of vulnerability that no doubt earlier Viking raiders to the West would have noticed when descending upon a potential conquest. And just as those old-time pillagers had decided to colonise parts of England and France, the Mongols now decided to add vast parts of Russia (or at least the steppe areas in the south) to their burgeoning Empire.

The impact of this group, later known as the Golden Horde, was massive. They would outlive the rest of the Mongol empire by over 100 years, though towards the end they would be but a pale shadow of their former selves. They also demonstrated something else: the vulnerability of the Mongol empire. Like all dynasties, personal ambition and rivalry did not take long to take root, and these attributes, which in the end would help to destroy the Mongols, were particularly noticeable in these early years of conquest in Russia. At the time, in fact, there was no such country as Russia, but simply a number of principalities ruled parts of the land we now give the name. This of course helped the

Mongols no end. 'Divide and conquer' was to be of help to them on more than one occasion as their empire grew, but the inherent weakness of smaller, disunited and rival states was illustrated perfectly in the Russian campaign. The Mongols also benefited from their hardiness in their efforts to tame the Russians. In stark contrast to later would-be conquerors like Napoleon Bonaparte and Adolf Hitler, winter was not their natural foe. Rather, it was a friend, for it froze the flowing, wide rivers rock-hard and allowed their horses to cross when it would otherwise have been impossible to do so.

The invasion, for such it was, was no opportunistic-spur-of-the moment decision. At the great council meeting (*kuriltai*) held in 1235 the decision to move on Russia and Korea was made. There was sound reasoning behind these decisions. Russia was chosen because it was vast, and its very size would make it hard to defend. It offered the kind of land that was needed, with large stocks of grasslands with which to feed horses and other livestock. Furthermore, the Mongols knew what to expect, for they had been there before, and on that former occasion been very successful. There was no reason to believe that they would not be so again. The results of the fact-finding reconnaissance to the region a decade and more before, were taken out, dusted off and used to plan the campaign.

The army that set out for the west was large – some 50,000 strong. Along with some of the best troops available to the Mongols, there were engineers from China and Persia. Commanding the troops were some very senior figures, including no less than ten Mongol princes. Batu and his four brothers were present, as was Chagatai's son Baidar and grandson Buri. Two of Ögedei's sons were there too, Kuyuk and Kadan, as well as Möngke and Budjek, sons of Tolui. The main beneficiary of any victories would undoubtedly be Batu, but the man with the real vision of conquest was Subotai. Despite the time that had elapsed since the last major raids on Russia, it would be wrong to think that the Mongols had gone away completely in the interim. The Mongols had, from time to time, raided nomadic tribes which bordered on to Russian lands. This may have been partly because the raiders smelt easy pickings, but it also had a more strategic reason: it prevented the creation of a solid buffer zone, which would hamper any future Mongol advance towards Russian lands.

Every now and then a pitiful trail of humanity would stream into Russian territory, seeking sanctuary from the terrible deprivations that the Mongols had unleashed upon them. Such events must have been a cause of serious concern, as they provided a stark reminder that the

Mongols were still on the scene, but the Russians were unable to prepare themselves properly for the apocalypse that was about to descend upon them, or perhaps they simply refused against their better judgement to accept that they too were a likely future prey for the Mongol predator. A preliminary to the attack on Russia was an offensive against the city of Bulghar, capital to the people of the same name. Mongol memories again went back a long way, and the fact that the Bulgars had attacked the Mongols nearly fifteen years before was still remembered. The Bulgars would have good cause to regret their decision.

The army deputed to strike Bulghar was led by Batu and Subotai. Batu was the senior man, being the grandson of Genghis Khan, but Subotai was the strategist *par excellence*, and some see his hand in most of the major strategic decisions that were made during the invasion of Russia. He in particular would prove his mettle yet again during the campaign. At the same time, another part of the Mongol army headed south. This was a feature of the Mongol war machine: the ability to split itself up like some giant amoeba and spread out in different directions, bringing terror in it's wake. This southern army, led by the two warriors, Möngke and Budjek, attacked Kipchak tribes in the region. The people there broke and fled before them and hid themselves in the great forests that abutted the Volga. This was no defence though, for the Mongols were master huntsmen. They formed themselves up in a huge half-circle, enveloping the edges of the woods in the process. Then they moved inwards in much the same way as they would perform the great hunt back in the steppes of Mongolia. The difference was that this time, the prey were not wolves or deer, they were human beings. However, a number of them had sought safety on an island in the river. The Mongols were never comfortable on the water and the Kipchaks may have thought themselves safe where they were. Unfortunately for them, there was a sandbank near the island, making the crossing shallow. The tribesmen on the island were caught by surprise when the Mongols crossed, and were overwhelmed. Their leader Bachman was a proud and brave warrior. Realising that the game was up, he asked to be put to death by Möngke's hand. The honour was refused, however, and Bachman was sliced in half by the sword of Budjek.

Bulghar had become the capital city of the Bulgars who had stayed behind in Russia, whilst many of their compatriots had headed west to establish the state in Europe that still bears their name. Their lands denuded of much of their population, the Bulgars that were left had imported cheap labour in the form of serfs to do the hard work that lined their pockets. In the process, they became wealthy and comfortable, and this resulted in two things happening. Firstly the Bulgars, once nomadic warriors themselves, became sedentary and weak. Secondly, the serfs who provided all the hard labour that made them rich were not inclined to rush to their aid when they were attacked. On the contrary, many of these serfs welcomed the Mongols enthusiastically.

Given all these deficiencies, it is little wonder that the Bulgars were unable to put up much of a fight, that their city fell and was then obliterated in torrents of blood. It was something of a pushover by the sound of it, and the Mongols quickly pushed on towards Russia, where much harder fighting was expected. The city of Bulghar, once the hub of so much trading activity, was left as a heap of charred, smoking rubble: it would never again rise from the ashes.

Batu and Subotai took stock before the real invasion took place. More troops were needed so they rounded up conscripts from some of the tribes they had subjugated into their ranks. Such men were cheap and expendable (a welcome addition to the Mongol army, that was likely to meet with a stern test when faced with the warlike Russians). In the end 120,000 men set out, but the fight was to be nothing like as bad as feared, largely because the Russians were disunited and too distracted with fighting each other to face up to the Mongol threat.

It was December 1237 when the first hammer-blow struck Russia. The timing was significant: few commanders were likely to launch a strike in winter, and such a fact gave the Russians great comfort. But this was, literally, cold comfort, for the Mongolian commander, Subotai, and his soldiers were used to harsh winters, and would not be put off by such a trifle. They welcomed the winter: it gave them the element of surprise and it assisted their manoeuvrability. It was in many ways an early day *blitzkrieg*. Subotai's plan was simplicity itself, but was none the worse for that. Russia was vast, with strong concentrations of power in the north around Novgorod and Suzdal, and another powerful bloc gathered around Kiev and Chernigov. Subotai would drive a massive wedge through the heart of the country, splitting it into two. The Mongols could then pick off one power bloc at a time.

First in the firing line was the city of Riazan, situated on the Oka River. Two outlying cities were taken quickly and then the Mongols laid a siege to Riazan itself on 16 December. This was a perfect place to make their first strike. They were able to advance through the thick forests that prevailed in the region unobserved, and so catch the city unawares. The city formed the outer guard to Russia proper, but it was unlikely to put up much of a fight. Even for Russia, the city was renowned for its bitter infighting, something that the Mongols, with their excellent spy network, knew very well.

The Mongols, as was often the case, offered the option of a peaceful surrender to start off with. They demanded that the city be given up to them and the traditional tax of a tenth of all Riazan's wealth be given. But this plea for Danegeld failed, and the Mongols sharpened their swords and restrung their bows for the fight ahead. Given the decision to fight, the citizens could expect no mercy should the city fall. The Mongol tactics were thorough. A huge palisade was erected around the parameters of the city walls, to prevent those inside from escaping, and also to hamper any relief effort. It was a classic tactic, which even Julius Caesar had used in his campaigns in Gaul. The garrison was outnumbered, whereas the Mongols were able to keep throwing fresh troops into the fray on a regular basis. On 21 December, the Mongols launched their strongest attack yet. Their men charged at the gates with battering rams, whilst others threw firebrands into Riazan and yet more climbed scaling ladders. The ferocity of the assault was irresistible: it was on such a wide scale that the defenders were simply overwhelmed by the assaults of so many troops from a number of different directions simultaneously. Fired up by their success, the Mongols stormed into the city, which fell in a river of blood.

Utter carnage ensued. Prince Yuri, lord of the city, was slain, as was his wife. Huge numbers of citizens were killed, by sword, by arrow, by being burned alive or disembowelled. Few were spared, regardless of age or sex. The Mongols then set alight whatever was left. The author of *The Tale of the Destruction of Riazan* was particularly overwhelmed by the massacre, describing vividly how, 'churches of God were destroyed, and much blood was spilled on the holy altars. Not one man was left alive in the city. All were dead. All had drunk the same bitter cup to the dregs, and there was not anyone to mourn the dead'.[3] Two relief forces arrived too late to do anything more than witness the devastation that had virtually obliterated Riazan. The rest of the province in which it was situated soon shared its fate. The city of Kolomna was the last part of it to fall. By this time, the Russians were thoroughly alerted to the true extent of the threat posed by the terrifying hordes moving towards them, and their armies had been deployed with a view to stopping them.

The Mongols moved on, burning a small town by the name of Moscow as they did so. Although it was far removed from the powerful metropolis that it would become later in its history, it had a substantial garrison. But it was unable to resist the Mongols any better than Riazan had been. The governor was killed, though this time prisoners were taken for the pragmatic reason that more labourers were needed to assist the Mongol advance.

One of Russia's foremost cities at the time, Vladimir, was now isolated, and the Russian leader, Grand Prince Yuri, descended northwards towards the darkness to re-gather his strength, trusting on the substantial fortifications of the city to keep it safe. It was a brave move, for within its walls were the majority of Yuri's family. Part of the Mongol army followed the Grand Duke as he garnered his army for battle, but others moved on to Suzdal, which they took after another brief fight, and then on to Vladimir for an assault on that crucial city. An attack on Vladimir began on 7 February 1239. The Mongols prefaced their attack with a piece of psychological warfare. They paraded the captured Prince Vladimir, son of Yuri, before the city. It was a move calculated to demoralise the defenders. The Mongols demanded that Vladimir be surrendered, in return for the Prince's life. When this was inevitably refused, his two brothers inside the city had to stand on the walls and watch his slaughter. The Mongols then forced thousands of their Russian captives to build a palisade around the city. This was an old Mongol trick, calculated to terrify the defenders with an insight into the ruthless nature of their enemy, and also to discourage them from firing at the conscripted constructors, as they might well be shooting at their own kith and kin by doing so.

The Mongols soon showed that they had learned all the skills of siege warfare in the past two decades of their military education. Their artillery showered the walls with giant boulders, which crashed into the defences, shooting up clouds of dust and falling debris as they hit home. Throughout the day, the city was softened up in preparation for the denouement that was now imminent. On the next day, 8 February, the crisis point was reached. It was a Sunday, which in some ways must have added to the horror of it all for the Russian Orthodox defenders of the place, for it further gave the impression that outside the gates lay the forces of Satan. The Mongols then launched four synchronised attacks on the different gates of the city. It was a tactic that again overwhelmed the defence, which was simply not organised or substantial enough to react to this attack on many fronts. The citizens panicked, and any hope of survival, which was a realistic one as Vladimir was well garrisoned, soon evaporated.

The defence was brief and hopeless; soon the streets were packed with panic-stricken inhabitants doing their best to flee the terrifying packs of rampaging Mongol soldiers who were pouring in from all directions. By midday the two princes in the city, Vsevolod and Mstislav, were slain. The end was a scene of brutal terror. Some of the great and the good, including the Grand Duchess whom Yuri thought would have been safe behind Vladimir's walls, fled into the cathedral in search of refuge. The doors were barricaded against the overwhelming force hammering at them, but soon the Mongols had poured in. The duchess, with her daughters and grandchildren, had fled to the loft above the great edifice that housed the sacred icon of the Virgin. But the Virgin Mother was blind and deaf to the pleas of the citizens that she had, by tradition, protected. The Mongols shouted to those seeking safety in the rafters to come down. They would have made valuable hostages, and would have fetched a sizable ransom. However, they refused to do so, so the Mongols gathered up straw and wood, packed it around the base and set it alight. The flames took hold, destroying what was left of Grand Prince Yuri's family as the building came crashing to the ground, and was soon nothing more than a heap of smouldering embers. The collapsed cathedral was a fitting metaphor for the state of Russian resistance.

Vladimir now conquered, the Mongol army returned to their relentless advance through Russia. It being again split, Subotai led one part of the army, Batu the other. It was the former who headed towards the Grand Prince and his men. News of the catastrophe at Vladimir filled Yuri with grief. He was with his army on the Sit river awaiting reinforcements from Novgorod, but none came. At the beginning of March, a reconnaissance party he had sent out to establish the full extent of the challenge facing him returned with shattering news: they were now completely surrounded. Aware that there was no way out but to fight, Yuri bravely advanced to face the Mongol hordes. The battle that followed was fierce and hard-fought; it was said that 'blood flowed like water.[4] But there was an inevitability about its outcome, and as Yuri lay dead, so did the flower of his army.

It seemed that nothing could now stop the Mongols from subduing all the lands of Russia, but now, as so often in their history, they were saved by heroic resistance from an unexpected source. The city of Torzhok stood between the Mongols and Novgorod. Batu's men laid siege to city, but it proved an unexpectedly stubborn nut to crack. It took two weeks to take it, and by this time the winter, friend of the Mongols, was starting to take leave of the world for another year.

Once Torzhok fell, the road to Novgorod, then the greatest of Russian cities, now lay wide open, but not for the last time in history the Russian climate saved the day in the face of a ruthless invader. For once, it was not the onset of winter that intervened, but the coming of spring. With the melting of the thick snow blanket that had embraced the land during the previous months, the rivers thawed, and the land began to flood. This effectively stopped the Mongols from going any further. The sacrifice of

Torzhok, which had bought precious time, had saved Novgorod and, just sixty-five miles away from the city, the Mongols wheeled around. Frustrated at this final hurdle, the Mongols moved south. There was further raiding of course, and it has even been suggested that some of the foragers may have got as far as Karelia on the borders of Finland.[5] By now Batu and Subotai had joined forces again. Their great tactical awareness was shown by the fact that they carefully avoided all major fortified cities as they travelled. They wanted no distractions. They had other targets to hunt.

Batu now retook overall command of the Mongol forces: he was destined to be the first *khan* of the Golden Horde, which dominated much of Russia. He took his time over his next move, allowing his men to regain their vitality and be ready for the next big push. For most of 1239, the Mongols engaged in mopping up activities against the Polovtsians, also known as the Cumans, the fierce tribesmen who lived in the western parts of Russia. Those that were not killed or captured fled away to Hungary. They had not yet seen the last of the Mongols.

The Cumans had long been infiltrating Europe. Of nomadic stock themselves, they had been seen by some in the Western Church as ripe for conversion, and several missionary expeditions had tried to bring them into the Christian fold, but with limited success. Nevertheless, the Cumans who hastened to Hungary were cajoled into accepting baptism as the price of their refuge. For some of the people of Europe though, especially in Hungary, it was hard to differentiate them from people such as the Mongols, and this would lead to a good deal of uncertainty and confusion in the not too distant future. But that was still to come: the Mongols had further work to do in Russia yet.

It was the southern part of Russia that this time took the brunt of the attack. The campaign started, atypically, with a Mongol defeat. The garrison of Kozelsk, showing more backbone than many of their brothers in arms, went onto the offensive. They attacked the Mongol vanguard, which was poorly prepared to receive it, and it was consequently overwhelmed. Many Mongols were lost, but it was a Pyrrhic Russian victory. So incensed were the Mongols that, when they took Kozelsk after a long and desperate fight that lasted seven weeks, they destroyed it. They were particularly upset that three sons of generals had been killed in the attack, and sought revenge. The Mongols gave a new name to Kozelsk: from now on they referred to it as 'the City of Sorrow' in commemoration of the devastation that had been visited upon it.

That winter was spent in recharging flagging energies in the vast open spaces of what is now the Ukraine. It was a land that would have reminded the Mongols of home, with the wide, flat, sweeping steppes, stretching on *ad infinitum* towards a horizon that was never reached. Above it all, the sky had a vastness that men from the cramped and claustrophobic territories of the West could never understand, until they had seen it, and then its immensity defied description. Mongol horses fed on the grasses, nutritious and plentiful, and restored their depleted fat reserves. There was more fighting, but the nature of it that winter was more of raiding than of set-piece battles or sieges. There were vast numbers of tribesmen in the region: Cumans, Alans and others who were constantly battered by Mongol raids. They were excellent sources of cheap labour, and so many were taken prisoner that it was said that they outnumbered their captors.

In the idleness of that winter, though, there were signs of tensions within the Mongol ranks. Few enemies could stand up to them but the greatest threat to Mongol domination was the Mongols themselves. Even such a man as Genghis could not always keep the lid on rivalries. The most unstable part of his legacy was the succession. He left a divided empire, and the ploy of having one Great Khan, to whom all others were in theory subservient, did not work as thoroughly as he would have hoped in accreting rival interests together. Such division had, after all, characterised other great empires in the past, when the driving force behind it had gone. Alexander's would be the best example of this, with its division on his death. Rome too had gone down the same track on a number of occasions.

Batu was something of an enigma as far as the Mongols were concerned. His father had been Jochi, eldest son of Genghis Khan and Boerte, though the doubts about his legitimacy spread to his son. When Jochi died young, Batu in theory inherited his rights; but he inherited the doubts too. He did not wear them well, and his greatest failing was his insecurity, which was about to manifest itself with worrying effect. The Mongol people are a proud race. They, like Alexander's Macedonians, like a good party and sometimes excessive indulgence at these affairs led to trouble. There was a serious incident during that winter at one such event. There were strict protocols in place on such occasions, and it seems that Batu, inadvertently or otherwise, may have broken them. Two other senior members of Genghis' family, Kuyuk and Buri, were outraged at Batu's airs and graces, and stormed out of his tent. The most sensible way to deal with this would have been a quiet and private word; a declaration of brotherly affection for public consumption, and that would have been it. Unfortunately, Batu chose to escalate the crisis.

He wrote in bitter terms to Ögedei, the Great Khan, complaining of the actions of Kuyuk and Buri. Ögedei, who was Kuyuk's father, was incensed at his son's actions. He knew that maintenance of unity relied on the careful protection of the status quo. Checks and balances needed to be built in, in order to do so, and Kuyuk had threatened the fragile equilibrium of the political balance of power by his public display of pique. Kuyuk returned to Karakorum, where Ögedei was even talking about placing him in the front ranks of the army during the next campaign – a virtual death sentence. He also spoke of recalling Buri for punishment. When Kuyuk arrived at the Mongol capital, for a time Ögedei refused to see him. He relented but only so that he could castigate him firsthand. Chagatai, keeper of the law for the Mongols, was a stickler for protocol though, and said that any punishment should be decided on by the commander in the field, in this case Batu. So Kuyuk made the long journey back to the front.

In the meantime, Batu had calmed down. Kuyuk and Buri were both returned to their commands and nothing more was said of the matter. But beneath the surface the affair must have left a lasting impression, and it epitomised the eggshell-thin veneer of unity within the Mongol governing hierarchy, which could so easily crack. Such frictions would in the end prove the Mongols' Achilles' Heel. Bad blood between Batu and Kuyuk in particular lingered on. In the south of Russia, campaigning began again in earnest in 1240. First of all, the city of Pereyaslavl fell, then Chernigov. At the latter, the defenders were so desperate in their final defence that they resorted to throwing down stones from their own battlements in a vain attempt to halt the inevitable. All this was the precursor to the main event: the conquest of Kiev. It was a city of great heritage and beauty, and even the Mongols were impressed by it. It was commanded by a brave, if rash, governor, Dimitri. When Mongol envoys entered the city he had them executed. It was a move calculated to ensure that the city fought to the death. A number of Kiev's citizens had reasoned that their only hope was to surrender and pay tribute to the enemy. Dimitri put all end to such plans with his summary execution of the ambassadors. It was a defiant gesture, but it served merely to infuriate the Mongols.

The siege of the city began soon after. The walls of Kiev shook as large boulders slammed into them. The air was filled with the screeches of the dying, the blares of trumpets and the braying of camels. The streets of the city reverberated to the howls of anguished and terrified citizens expecting the worst. The initial attacks were concentrated on the Polish Gate, which was weak, with even the battlements made of wood. The city echoed to the battering of rams on wood, and of catapulted boulders crashing on stone. Although the walls were soon breached, another day and night of fierce fighting followed, with hard-fought street battles amongst the rubble of the shattered city. But the result was once more a massacre of a conquered city that had dared to resist the Mongols. The last defence took place in the Church of the Virgin; again, she seemed unwilling to protect her sponsors from their fate. In fact, so many people crammed into the building that it collapsed under their weight and the defence of Kiev ended in a cloud of dust and broken timbers.

That was the end of Kiev. The brave Dimitri was captured, though severally wounded. Surprisingly, his fierce resolution had impressed the Mongols, and he was allowed to live. His city was not so lucky. Six years later, an envoy from the Pope in Rome, Giovanni di Plano Carpini, travelled past the ruins of this once great city on his way to the Mongol court. His description would not have been out of place if it had been describing the streets of Hiroshima after the dropping of the atomic bomb there in 1945:

> When we were journeying through that land we came across countless skulls and bones of dead men lying about on the ground. Kiev had been a very large and thickly populated town, but now it has been reduced almost to nothing, for there are at the present time scarcely two hundred houses there and the inhabitants are kept in complete slavery.[6]

But six years was a long time in the life of the Mongol empire, and by that time the victors of Kiev had moved on to yet more conquest. Out of nowhere, Russia had been decimated once more, but the triumphs of Vladimir and Kiev were not yet enough to satiate the conquerors. Another region would soon feel the unexpected and most unwelcome edge of the Mongol sword. This time, it was Europe that stood in fear, trembling at the hurricane from the east.

CHAPTER 6

Europe & the Mongol Nightmare: The Mongols Raid Eastern Europe 1241-1246

Europe was not a major field of operations for the Mongols. The raids that they made were in the main opportunistic, and conducted in search of plunder, but they did not lead to permanent settlement in the main land mass of Europe (this applied to large chunks of Russia too, with the forest lands there in the main unpeopled by the Mongols). The primary motivation for them moving into Russia was that, in keeping with Mongol tradition, Genghis had told Jochi, his eldest son, to conquer lands far away from the heartlands of the Mongol empire. Any lands he took in the far west was to belong to him and his heirs. This bequest passed down in turn to Batu and provided him with the motivation to push onwards into the steppes of Russia. Here at least they established a base, whilst the lands of Russia further north were mainly seen as a source of revenue, or of soldiers in wartime. Whether Europe itself was ever a target for permanent habitation is much less clear.

If Europe was a distant priority for the Great Mongol Khans, lagging far behind China and even Persia and Syria in terms of importance, the same could not be said for the effect that the Mongols had on Europe. The Mongols would become, as one writer has described it, 'for a century or more Europe's most formidable and dangerous eastern neighbour'.[1] When they came careering into the continent in 1241, the shock-waves that rippled out from the east reverberated right across into regions as distant as Spain and the Netherlands. Whilst Louis IX of France was absent on Crusade, Blanche of Castile, his mother and regent, was convinced that all Europe would fall to the Mongols, who seemed to be irresistible. In part this was because their military record was indeed impressive, and the western forces that were deployed to meet them as they advanced into Europe were swept aside. Prospects of other European armies who might choose to fight them did not look good. Negative sentiments expressed at the time also reflected the apocalyptic mood that permeated Europe at this point in history – far from unique for the medieval period it must be said. In addition, it did not help that

Europe was singularly unprepared to resist the Mongols. Petty feuding, blatant opportunism, and the search for self-aggrandisement on the part of many of its rulers divided it, by increasing fragmentation within many regions, especially those in the path of the Mongol advance. All of these factors played right into the hands of the terrifying eastern hordes.

Even before the Mongols attacked, there were intimations right across Europe that awesome events were brewing. Rumours of their incursions were heard in Scotland in 1238 following the Mongol advances into Russia, and the port of Yarmouth was hit hard by the non-appearance of Baltic traders during the same year, due to their activities in the regions fringing that great sea. Added to this, Hungarian friars had been travelling into Russia in an attempt to convert the Cumans to Christianity for some time, and had experienced firsthand just how violent the Mongol attacks there had been. Graphic tales of the Mongols invincibility and savagery were soon being widely related around the hearths of Europe. The incursions that the Mongols made in the early years of the 1240s were the start of an ambivalent relationship between them and the West. At different stages, the Mongols were perceived as demons, or potential allies. At no time were they fully understood, though sometimes it became clear to better informed observers that they were truly set on world conquest, and that they believed without a shadow of a doubt that the great spirit who governed the universe had decreed that Genghis and his seed were destined to lord it over all of humanity.

The Mongols now made their preparations to move into Europe proper. Their invasion plan was simple in conception, but required a great deal of skill in its execution. To bring it off as they did required both discipline and coordination, qualities that the Mongols were to demonstrate that they possessed in abundance. In previous invasions, the Mongols had conquered through overwhelmingly coordinated attacks, which they launched simultaneously from a number of different directions. What they planned to do now was essentially the same but on a grander scale; to include a battlefront that was hundreds of miles wide. The idea was to launch a multi-pronged attack with the ultimate aim of overwhelming Hungary, their main initial objective. The country was rich and promised good plunder, but it was also a territory of sweeping grasslands which would provide excellent food for their vast horse herds. The plan involved attacking Hungary from several directions, sweeping up through the Transylvanian passes to the south-east of the country and also down from the north-east, through Poland and then on through the northerly Carpathians. It was a gigantic pincer movement, and a campaign that was as strategically brilliant as any ever devised. Its execution was not quite perfect, as the front was so extended that even the Mongols could not remain synchronised, but it was impressive nonetheless.

Hungary was ruled by King Bela IV, and unfortunately his position was perilously compromised by frictions between him and his barons, which were a source of constant difficulties. He cannot have been surprised to learn that an attack was coming. The large numbers of Cuman refugees who had sought sanctuary under his wing provided ample evidence for the ferocity and determination of the Mongols, and would have told terrifying tales of what had happened to them. The friars too had come back with lurid descriptions of the horrors of Mongol attacks, perhaps the first being the Hungarian Friar Julian who had been in Russia in 1237 when the invasion force had burst onto the scene.[2] The Mongols had sent emissaries anyway, to demand that Hungary should surrender to them, but they had been ignored. Batu sent an imperious final ultimatum to Bela setting out his demands:

> I, the Khan, the representative of the Heavenly King, the one to whom he has given power over the earth, to raise up those who submit to me and to cast down those who resist – I wonder why, oh king of Hungary, when I have now sent envoys to you on thirty occasions, you have sent none of them back to me: nor do you send me in return your own envoys or letter.[3]

Batu ordered Bela to stop giving shelter to the Cumans, whom he described as his slaves. He made a particular point that, if he attacked, the Cumans could easily run away, for they were skilled horsemen, but the Hungarians were a sedentary nation and therefore had no such luxury. It was a largely accurate assessment, though Bela would prove somewhat more adept at running away than Batu supposed him to be.

Just after Christmas 1240, alarming news began to come in that the Mongols were on the move, advancing towards Hungary. The lofty spiked Carpathians were the granite guardians of the kingdom to the south-east, and Bela hurried there to make sure the front-line defences were properly prepared. This should not have been a difficult front to defend, the passes were narrow and the cliffs either side of them precipitous. It looked like a perfect defensive position. Having visited the front, Bela returned to Buda (his capital) and called a council of war, which ordered a general call-up of the army. A strong show of unity was required to face up to the Mongol threat: exactly the opposite was to materialise. Many of the barons were hostile towards the Cumans. Some did not differentiate between them and the Mongols, and even felt that the former were traitors in their midst, who would betray them to the latter, a barbarian Fifth Column waiting to stab them in the back at the earliest opportunity. They noted that Cumans fought in the Mongol armies: a fact as it happened, though this was because many of them had been conscripted into it, and had no say in the matter. In particular, they did not trust the Cuman king, Kotian, despite the fact that the Mongols had persistently slaughtered his people for nearly twenty years now.

This intransigence backed Bela into a corner. Feeling that he needed to show his strength and keep his truculent barons onside, the king ordered Kotian to be placed under house arrest. This did not placate the barons, however: if anything, it had the opposite effect, for it seemed to admit that the king harboured doubts about Kotian too. Resentment against the Cumans simmered barely below the surface. For their part, the Cumans were far from happy about the actions taken against them and their sovereign lord. They had nothing to invite such actions and hated the Mongols more than most. These draconian measures were a rank injustice. News arrived at Buda on 10 March that the Mongols were attacking the Carpathian passes. Bela sent a letter to Duke Frederick of Austria asking for help. In itself this was an intimation of how seriously the Mongol threat was being taken, because Bela and Frederick had 'form'. At one stage Frederick had sought Bela's throne, but the latter had responded by raising a vast army, and advancing to the gates of Vienna itself. Frederick had been forced to step back into line but longed for revenge. There was an opportunity to gain it close at hand.

Just days later, on 14 March, a weary messenger made his way into the city of Buda. He was the bearer of grim tidings: the Carpathian passes had been forced. The news was shattering, as Bela must have been expecting that the front would hold for months. The speed of the advance of the Mongols was breathtaking: forty miles a day, a pace which no army in Europe could comprehend. This was war of a style, and at a place, that no one had previously witnessed. Bela sent his wife to Austria for safety's sake and moved his army from Buda to Pest on the east bank of the Danube. Ironically, given the suspicions against them, only the Cumans seemed prepared to fight the Mongols, no doubt ruminating on the fate that had befallen many of their friends and family back in the steppes not long before.

Details of what was happening followed. Subotai and Kuyuk had swept through Moldavia and Wallachia (two parts of modern Romania) in January and February. Their army had split into two, Kuyuk's army sweeping into the rugged woods and mountains of Transylvania whilst Subotai had gone further south. All were powerless to resist them. Kuyuk had fooled the defenders of Transylvania into thinking that the Mongols were more numerous than was actually the case, by placing dummies on horseback (an old Mongol trick, frequently employed). Rather than come out and fight, the Hungarian forces in Transylvania cowered behind the walls of Hermannstadt (now Sibiu in modern Romania).

The Mongols advanced on all fronts at a breathtaking pace. Batu descended like an avalanche from the Carpathians, decimating all who stood in his path, his army advancing at the rate, it was said, of sixty miles per day. Bela lost control of his army, and town after town began to fall, losses accompanied by great slaughter and destruction. The arrival of Duke Frederick of Austria soon after, ostensibly to help, only made things many times worse. Frederick was both a show-off and a troublemaker. He did everything he could to harm Hungary's defence: he in fact was the fifth columnist, not the Cumans. He stirred up feelings further against the Cumans, complaining of their presence in the Mongol armies. He then attempted to win hearts and minds by engaging in single combat with two captured Mongols, impaling one with his spear and chopping off the arm of the other with one violent swoop of his sword. This was a man of bluster and bravado, but no great intelligence; by failing to support Bela adequately, he was exposing his own country to their reign of terror, as it was next in the Mongol firing line if Hungary fell.

Faced with defeat after defeat, the Hungarians were about to collapse completely, as the barons now engaged in a near-suicidal betrayal of the Cumans, the people who had been doing the most to repel the Mongol invaders. Some of the barons' men descended on Kotian's house, meaning to kill him as a sacrificial and completely inappropriate scapegoat. He saved them the trouble, killing himself after slaying his family. The heads of the dead were cut off by the barons and thrown into the streets outside the house. It was an act of both brutality and stupidity and would have dreadful consequences. When news of this outrage reached the Cuman camp, there was an eruption of Vesuvian intensity. Incensed at this undeserved victimisation, they turned on the Hungarians close at hand, and slaughtered vast numbers of them. Then they got on their horses – they too were fearsome cavalrymen – and embarked on an orgy of destruction in the west of the country, eventually ending up in Bulgaria on the borders of the Byzantine Empire. Frederick had enacted a masterstroke. By stoking up anti-Cuman feeling, he had managed to engineer a situation whereby Bela's only reliable soldiers had ripped the west of Hungary apart, whilst the Mongols did the same in the east. With friends such as this, Bela was in no need of enemies.

Having done his worst, Frederick returned to Austria. However, for the time being, Bela was saved. The Mongols were on the wrong side of the Danube to attack Pest, and so instead they turned west. As they raided further in that direction, Bela assembled a large army by gathering together those troops who had not yet been decimated by the Mongols, and made ready to set off in pursuit of the enemy before they could devastate those parts of Hungary they had not yet touched.

In the meantime, the Mongols had descended on Poland too. The country was at this moment in time very fragmented, and about to become still more so. However, Bela had allies there, particularly in the form of the prince Baroslaw the Chaste. The armies of Baidar and Kadan, the Mongol generals sent to Poland, had two roles. Firstly they were to distract potential reinforcements amongst Bela's allies, and prevent them from coming to his aid. Then they were to move south and join the other Mongol armies in Hungary, as the northern sweep of a giant pincer movement. Poland was completely unprepared for the Mongol assault, though it should not have been, as accounts of what the Mongols had been doing in Russia, their next-door neighbour, must have reached them. The Mongol armies were not large, but swept into the country against limited resistance and quickly burned Lublin to the ground. Finding opposition cursory at best, Baidar and Kadan then gambled by splitting their small force in two, and setting off at breakneck speed on an orgy of pillaging and destruction, and succeeded in confusing the Poles.

Baidar moved towards the capital of Krakow. The Mongols approached the city, but then drew back. Inside its walls, Boleslaw's commander, Vladimir the Palatine of Sandomir and Krakow, believed the Mongols to be retreating, having lost their nerve. It was a foolish and fatal mistake. Baidar had laid a trap for him, which was sprung just eleven miles outside of the city, when Vladimir and his men chased after the supposedly fleeing barbarians. In the resultant ambush, Vladimir was killed alongside many of his men. The Polish survivors fled. Boleslaw abandoned the city of Krakow to its fate. Most of the people followed him. According to legend, a trumpeter sounded the alarm to the people from the bell tower of the cathedral, but just as he was about to finish it a Mongol arrow struck and killed him. In homage to the event, a trumpeter from Krakow's fire department still performs a ritual re-enactment of this event to this day. His distant predecessors would have been busy back on 24 March 1241 if they had been around, for on that day the Mongols entered the city and burned it to the ground.

The Mongols then moved on Breslau, which had already been burned by its own inhabitants to save the Mongols the trouble. They had then barricaded themselves in the citadel. But then Baidar, who laid siege to it, heard that Henry of Silesia was coming up with an army to relieve the siege, and also that King Wenceslas of Bohemia was en route to join forces with him. Baidar sent word of these tidings to Kadan and Batu, and then made haste to Leignitz to confront Henry, hopefully before Wenceslas met him and combined forces.

Henry, unfortunately, does not seem to have been a very capable commander. His men were unruly and untrained – little match for Baidar's battle-hardened veterans. A large number of them did not even have proper weapons, being conscripted miners, armed with the picks and other tools they used in their profession. Not all were amateurs though. Henry did have a well-armed personal retinue with him as well as some mercenaries. There was also a contingent from the Teutonic Knights, formed in the Holy Land half a century before to guard pilgrims on their way to Jerusalem, and increasingly influential in Prussia and the surrounding regions. But there were nowhere near enough of these to compensate for the deficiencies of the poorly equipped mass of the army. On 9 April 1241, Henry clashed with Baidar, now joined by Kadan. Wenceslas, with perhaps 50,000 men, was hurrying to join up with Henry and was only a day away, but no one in Henry's camp seemed to be aware of the fact. As Henry passed a church in Leignitz on his way to battle, a stone fell from the roof and nearly hit him: an evil omen indeed. Henry drew his men up for battle, around him a small and insignificant contingent of both Templar and Hospitaller knights.

The Mongols began the battle in typical fashion. A force of light horsemen charged Henry's ranks and then retreated in confusion when repulsed. Henry's cavalry charged after them, not realising that, of course, it was a trick. The Mongol cavalry force had been a *mangudai,* a group sent in specifically with the purpose of breaking the enemy's ranks by luring them into an ambush, a task that they performed splendidly. As Henry's cavalry charged recklessly after them, the Mongols fired smoke bombs to confuse them, and cut them off from the rest of their army. This move showed the Mongols flair for innovation and their ability to learn quickly off others who they conquered such as the Chin: the smoke screens were formed by simply setting reeds aflame. Then, when Henry's men could not see where they were in the cloud of acrid smoke, a force of heavily armed Mongols crashed into them, cutting them to ribbons.

The Polish cavalry were now widely separated from the infantry, who were vital to their defence. The armour of the knights was vulnerable to Mongol archers at close quarters. And even when knights were hard to shoot down, their horses made a much easier target, and a dismounted knight was next to useless. As a result, what was already turning into a defeat then became a slaughter, when archers were sent in to finish the job. Henry's army broke and fled. All that was left was for the Mongols to mop up, and number the enemy dead, a task which they did most efficiently.

Henry was killed trying to escape from the disastrous Battle of Leignitz. He was left with just four men in his bodyguard, and was shot by an arrow under his armpit. The Mongols charged forward and overwhelmed this puny force. Henry was decapitated and his head stuck on top of a lance, where it was paraded triumphantly around the citadel of Leignitz where a number of the inhabitants were doing their best to avoid being massacred, a macabre totem that the Mongols enthusiastically carried around with them. When the Mongols left, his wife devotedly went to look for his body. She found it only because Henry had six toes on one foot. The rest of the slain were each deprived of an ear, one of the ways in which the Mongols scored the numbers of the enemy dead. Allegedly, the number of ears filled up nine sacks. Wenceslas, when he heard the news of this disaster, retreated and regrouped. Significantly, his army was too strong to be attacked by the Mongols, but they had done their job by luring him away from Hungary, which was even now under attack. They were too light on their feet to be caught by him, and they easily evaded his slower force, galloped around his men and made their way post haste to Hungary to rejoin their comrades.

Shortly before, 500 miles away on the other side of Hungary, Hermannstadt was stormed, leaving the southeast of Hungary wide open. A noose was tightening around Hungary. Batu was about to jerk it violently tight around Bela's neck, in a decisive confrontation in the centre of the country. The spot he had chosen to fight on was a heath at Mohi, close to the river Sajo. There were many thickets, hills and vineyards in the area, which could be used to conceal the Mongol forces; a perfect position for them to employ their devastating tactics of ambush and surprise attack. On the evening of 10 April, the Hungarian vanguard of the army advancing to Mohi crossed a bridge. Their scouts reported no sign of the enemy. Bela ordered a vast laager to be formed, with hundreds of wagons in it. Although this was an understandable act of caution, it meant that his movement would be hampered if there were a battle, and he would be unable to react quickly if he needed to, a potentially catastrophic weakness in the light of the Mongols' renowned manoeuvrability.

Under cover of darkness, Subotai led 30,000 Mongol warriors into position for an attack. He would attack from the rear whilst Batu would do so from the front. It was just before dawn, a defending army's weakest moment (many of the men were dozing and off guard) that Batu unleashed the tempest. He attacked the bridge. At first its narrowness meant that his men made no headway. The bridge was defended heroically by just 1,000 men, led by the Duke of Slavonika.

This latter-day Horatio fought like a lion. A Mongol officer, who attempted to force his way across, was lifted up and thrown headlong into the river. However, the increasing severity of the Mongol arrow-storm forced the Duke to rush away and return with reinforcements. Eventually he was wounded and forced off the bridge. Then Batu brought up catapults to smash the Hungarian resistance. Firebombs bombarded them too, and they could not stand. They fled before what almost sounds like a precursor of a First World War 'creeping barrage'. The Hungarians still outnumbered Batu though, and, after several hours of fighting, began to push the Mongols back. However, Subotai had not yet made his move, waiting as he was for the ideal time to strike. He now did so, launching an irresistible surprise assault from the rear. The Hungarians, to their credit, did not panic, but retired calmly to the laager they had formed the night before. The battle was still in the balance, and even Batu began to doubt that his men would win the day. It was the wizened veteran, Subotai, who swung it the way of the Mongols. He looked on contemptuously when Batu talked of retreat, 'If the princes wish to retreat they may do so, but for my part I am resolved not to return until I have reached Pest and the Danube'.[4]

The Mongols assembled for one final mass attack. As they did so, a gap opened in their ranks. Seeing a chance to escape, some of the Hungarian nobility, who had lost the will to fight, made a bid for freedom. The Mongols smashed into those who were left, including a party of Templars who were heroically lost to a man, just as they had been at Leignitz. But amongst those who managed to extricate themselves from this death trap was Bela.

The survivors now found themselves on a ride of death. The familiar Mongol tactic of letting an enemy escape and then riding them down as if they were involved in a hunt was repeated yet again. Either side of the ever diminishing pack were hordes of Mongol light cavalry, shooting down Hungarian horsemen as easily as if they were chasing after deer back on the steppes. The fate of the Hungarian horsemen was not helped by the heavy rain that had fallen in the recent past, turning much of the surrounding terrain into a quagmire. The way back to Pest was littered with corpses. Bela, though, was not among the dead, having been saved by the devotion of his followers, who would give him a fresher horse each time his grew tired. By this expedient, he would outrun the Mongols, and live to fight another day. His tribulations were far from over though: the Mongols would ride half way across Europe trying to find him.

And so Mohi turned into a rout, ironically at virtually the same time that the Battle of Leignitz was going the same way in Poland. Pest was now defenceless against the Mongols, and soon fell. Buda, however, survived, saved for the time being by the watery walls of the Danube, which the Mongols could not cross. Instead they consolidated their hold on the east of Hungary. After their initial excesses in the moment of victory, they offered their protection to the peasants who worked the land; on this occasion they wished to ensure that they gained maximum economic advantage from their conquests, something that they could not do if every labourer and farmhand was dead.

Bela fled into Austria, where he met up with a kindred spirit in the same metaphorical boat, Baroslaw the Chaste from Poland. Bela was reunited with his family, but then foolishly accepted the proffered hospitality of Duke Frederick, his old adversary. If Bela had only studied the precedents, Richard I, King of England, could have told him to beware Austrian dukes offering gifts; but Bela appears not to have considered Richard's fate. Bela's ransom would involve the 'donation' of large chunks of his land to Frederick. It would also cost him the Hungarian crown jewels. Eventually, Bela managed to escape Frederick's clutches, and made his way to Zagreb. Even here he was not safe, for when the Mongols got word that he was there, they launched a raid against the city. In the meantime, Bela had sent pleas for help to Louis IX, King of France; the German Emperor, Frederick II; and the Pope. Unfortunately, Frederick and the Papacy were too busy fighting each other to come to the aid of the beleaguered king of Hungary. Whilst Hungary burned, Pope and Emperor fiddled. Nevertheless, the Pope did permit the preaching of a Crusade against the Mongols. There was a significant response, at least in terms of the money collected, and perhaps even the warring barons, bishops and kings of Europe had begun to understand the apocalyptic nature of the Mongol threat in a vague way. A reconnaissance force of Mongols had already crossed into Austria, though it had been forced back after a skirmish with some of the men of Duke Frederick.

Instead of joining the Crusade, Duke Frederick attempted to take lands in Hungary for himself. In the unoccupied western half of the country, Hungarian forces were still strong enough to drive this thoroughly unscrupulous opportunist back. In the east, though, the Mongols consolidated their gains. Later that year, Kuyuk and Buri returned to Karakorum. They had perhaps done their bit, and wanted to do no more, given their recent falling-out with Batu. Perhaps too they had caught a whiff of something in the wind: they would certainly be very conveniently placed when a drama was soon to unfold back in Mongolia.

As 1241 dragged on, and the Mongols did not attempt to push westwards; a sense of complacency crept in amongst those in Europe who had at first been startled by their appearance. The initial enthusiasm for the Crusade diminished, and the armies of the west started to dissolve. But then that old friend of the Mongols, brother Winter, returned. The Christians of medieval Europe saw the hand of God in everything, good and bad. If it were bad, then God was punishing them for some imagined wrongdoing. They must have seen the hand of God then in the unusual freezing of the Danube on Christmas day, holiest of all days. The ice acted as a road for the Mongol horses, and they were quick to take advantage of it. The Mongol army crossed over to Buda, burned the city and then marched on the rich town of Gram. Dozens of catapults poured their heavy loads onto the walls, shattering stone and bone as they plummeted down from the heavens. Prisoners were forced to fill in the ditches built as obstructions around the city, so that the Mongols could cross over.

Before long, a breach was made in the substantial walls. The Mongols poured through this in search of plunder. Many of the citizens had buried their treasures to preserve them from the enemy. Little good it did them, as they were slowly roasted over fires until they revealed the hiding places. Gram was a rich and welcome prize, but it was also another entry to write in the catalogue of Mongol atrocities. In the meantime, another group of Mongols made for Zagreb in search of Bela. Mongol scouts were even seen on the northern edges of Vienna. Some Mongol prisoners were taken, amongst them, extraordinarily, an Englishman, a knight who had been exiled from England. He said that he had previously been involved in delegations from Batu to Bela. Who he really was no one knows, which is a shame, for he must have had some story to tell.

Another party of Mongols appeared on the frontiers of Italy, just sixty miles from Venice. The position of the Doge's city was, not unusually for those days, somewhat ambivalent. Always quick to spot a good business opportunity, Venetian traders had, for some time, been swapping information with the Mongols, in return for commercial perks, and they at least were safe from attack. But no one was so sure about the rest of Italy.

The party that advanced on Zagreb was led by Kadan. They burned the city but Bela had gone. He had taken refuge on an island, and when the Mongols moved closer, he escaped by ship to the city of Spalatro. From here he moved to the nearby isle of Trogir – if necessary he could take flight to Italy from there by ship. The Mongols still pushed on after their prey, but they were now reaching their formidable limits. They had been badly cut up in battle with a Croat force, and their horses were finding it difficult to get enough grass in the relatively barren land. All were tired and far from home. Spalatro was left alone, and the Mongols moved to Dubrovnik. Soon after, they returned north, sacking the picturesque port of Kotor in modern Montenegro in the process. Never would the Mongols move so far west again, and Europe, though it did not yet know it, had been reprieved. Hungary had been singularly poorly prepared to resist the attack; many of its cities being without walls or adequate fortifications against the Mongol assault, but an accident of fate had saved them from worse punishment.

During the Mongol invasions, the areas of Europe that they attacked went into paroxysms. The continent was already volatile. The harsh conditions then pertaining meant that the peoples of many lands were already restless. The Mongols acted as a catalyst for mass movements of people. Peoples moved to and fro seeking safety in a gigantic game of musical chairs. When the music stopped, the shape of Europe was fundamentally different – certainly in the east, in areas such as Poland, Hungary and Romania.

Yet it was not ultimately through the actions of soldiers or diplomats that Europe was saved. No European army could have stood up to a full-size Mongol force. Instead, it was an extraordinary event in far-off Karakorum, that had been the source of deliverance; for Ögedei, the Great Khan, was dead. His end would have done the Romans of antiquity proud. Ögedei was inordinately fond of alcohol, and it was said that he had drunk himself to death. However, there were uncharitable souls who said that he had been poisoned by his wife, Töregene. Her eldest son was none other than Kuyuk, the general who had fallen out so badly with Batu and incurred his father's wrath. Töregene, not unnaturally, wished for Kuyuk to succeed Ögedei on his death, but the late *khan* did not wish it to be so. Instead, he nominated a grandson named Shiremun, but his wishes were to be ignored.

There was indeed strong circumstantial evidence of the hand of Töregene (or, it was rumoured, one of her sisters) in his death. Kuyuk's decision to return to Karakorum had, to say the least, been fortuitous. He was exactly where he needed to be. There would now be an election where all the chief notables of the Mongols would return to Mongolia to decide on Ögedei's successor. Kuyuk had been given (or perhaps manoeuvred for himself) a head start. Until a new Khan had been elected, Chagatai decreed that Töregene was the most suitable person to be regent until a *kuriltai* had been held to finalise the succession. She was, however, a very shrewd and manipulative woman. She detested some of the late *khan's* advisers, and tried to take advantage of the opportunity now given her to revenge herself on them. Several of them evaded her clutches. Some, uncomfortable with the way things appeared to be going, went not to Karakorum, but to the court of Batu, far to the west.

Töregene sent instructions to all the great men of the Mongol empire to present themselves at the *kuriltai*, at which the election would be held. All across the expanding Mongol empire, the chief men of the race turned their armies about and headed for Karakorum. Hungary was abandoned, though not before a final terrible reckoning by blood and fire when the Mongols slaughtered indiscriminately as they left. On the way back, Bulgaria chose to pay tribute to the Mongols rather than be pillaged. Another piece had been fitted into the jigsaw of empire, this time without much bloodletting. Amongst those who, in the end set out for Karakorum was Batu. Not every historian is convinced that the death of Ögedei was the event that caused him to withdraw, preferring the theory that it was the depletion of grazing-land in Hungary.[5] In support of this contention is the fact that Batu never actually made it back to Karakorum, though he may well have had other reasons for his non-appearance there. But there is another possible explanation, which is more in line with the belief that it was power politics that led to Batu's withdrawal from Europe. He would certainly have opposed the accession of Kuyuk, but as he travelled east, perhaps he sensed that matters had already gone too far for him to stop them. His very life might even be in danger if he went back to Karakorum. No matter, the empire was large and there were still lands to be conquered in the west. He opted to stay in the steppes and build a sub-empire there. And so was born the Golden Horde, the longest-lived part of the Mongol empire.

The shadow of a disgruntled Batu loomed over Europe. However, Batu did not return to the continent. It might of course be the case that a permanent occupation of any of the countries in Europe was not at this stage envisaged by the Mongols anyway. World conquest would take many years to achieve, and the vast Russian territories that Batu and his men had already occupied provided a substantial challenge to control as it was. It could be that Batu had never envisaged more than a heavy raid to teach Bela a lesson and, if this were indeed so, then he had more than adequately succeeded.

Although the events in Europe seared themselves into the imagination of the West during these years, the Mongols were far from inactive elsewhere. They were advancing into Asia Minor, into the Turkish sultanate known as Rum, and had handed out heavy defeats to their enemies there, especially at the Battle of Kose Dagh in 1243. By 1244, they were pushing on into Syria, where they demanded the submission of major cities such as Aleppo and Damascus. For the time being, they were bought off by the payment of tribute, though this, it transpired, would not prove to be a permanent solution.

That same year, the Crusader kingdoms of Outremer in the Holy land felt, second-hand, the impact of the Mongol invasions. The Khwarismians, who had been so badly beaten by the Mongols, had fled west and into the service of the sultan of Egypt. They swept down on the city of Jerusalem, briefly returned to western hands a few years before, and smashed through its frail defences, slaughtering or enslaving its inhabitants. Never again would it be in the possession of the Crusaders.

As the Mongols left Europe, at least for a while, the continent did not lose interest in them. The unexpected incursions from the east had shaken the confidence of Western Christendom, and some reasoned that it would only be a short time before they were back. After 1241, several delegations were despatched eastwards to gauge the Great Khan's intentions. As a result, new things were learned about Mongol paradigms, though whether this did much to put anyone's mind at rest is a moot point. It was a Pope, Innocent IV, who took the lead in these initiatives. When he first took up the role, his position was parlous. Frederick II, Emperor of Germany, was moving in on Rome, sensing the scent of victory in his ongoing battle with the Papacy for supremacy. Despite his vulnerability (or perhaps because of it, as it reminded Europe that it was in great danger, and should not be immolating itself just when it was most at risk) Innocent vigorously took control of the diplomatic situation vis-à-vis the Mongols, and sent several brave men eastwards in search of the Great Khan.

The fact was that few men had any idea where the Mongols had come from and what they wanted. It was almost as if Europe had been invaded by creatures from another planet. The impact that they had had though was huge, and the way in which powerful armies had been crushed in Poland and Hungary did not bode well for any other European army game enough (or foolish enough) to face up to them in battle in the future. Innocent therefore took the initiative and decided to find out as much about his potential enemy as he could. He was beholden to the far-sightedness of some of his recent predecessors who had supported the establishment of new preaching orders, the friars, just a few decades previously. The brothers of the orders of St Francis and St Dominic, the Franciscans and Dominicans, provided an antidote to some of the excesses of the conventional Church, who to some seemed to be far too complacent and wealthy. The friars eschewed worldly wealth, and embraced hardship as a way of finding the path to salvation. They were also adventurers, used to long journeys in trying conditions, and experienced in living off their wits. These hardy mendicants were ideal ambassadors to send into the far reaches of the world.

Their mission was a brave one, and the Mongols' lack of knowledge was demonstrated in the objectives of their mission, which included an offer of baptism to the Khan. Baptism of course meant nothing to him, and the chances of him meekly submitting to the Pope's spiritual authority, and accepting that he was inferior to his earthly power, were nil. Two Dominicans were chosen: Ascelinus of Lombardy and Andrew of Longjumeau. Two Franciscans were also picked: Lawrence of Portugal and Giovanni of Piano Carpini, an Italian. The first three were to travel to the Middle East with two messages, which they were to deliver to the first Mongol commander they met. One was addressed to the Mongol nation as a whole, the other to the Great Khan in person.

Giovanni of Piano Carpini was to take on the massive task of making his way to the Great Khan in person. In terms of personality, he was ideally suited for it, though physically this was not so much the case. A one-time confidante of no less a man than St Francis himself, he was a jovial, larger-than-life figure (a description that encompasses his physical characteristics too – it was said that he was too obese to travel on horseback, so he used a mule instead. One feels an innate sympathy for the latter). He was also in his sixties, and, to a man of his age and with his corpulence, the journey ahead would be an arduous ordeal. It was his personality, however, that set him apart. Self-deprecating and tactful, he was easily able to get on with the most difficult of people, including men such as the Great Khan, which was something that had distinguished him from his colleagues on the other mission. He was therefore able to inveigle his way into the good graces of some very powerful people amongst the Mongols. This was to prove invaluable, for as well as being a diplomat, he was something else much more sinister – a spy.

Carpini left Lyons on 16 April 1245, and made his way eastwards. As he passed through the territories in Eastern Europe (which were in the line of fire should the Mongols return) he was understandably enthusiastically received. Here, Carpini was joined by another friar,

Benedict the Pole, who would prove a real asset, being skilled in languages – a talent that Carpini lacked. Passing through the shattered remnants of Krakow, the delegation must have been all too aware of the extent of the challenge facing them, but they pushed on regardless, well stocked with presents (they chose beaver pelts) which they had been told would be needed to impress the Mongols.

They travelled further into Russia, through lands denuded of their people by the depredations of the Mongols, through a desolate landscape of smouldering ruins and depopulated wastelands (in fairness the Mongols were not the only danger – Carpini's mission was also under threat from marauding Lithuanian raiders). The Mongols had been and gone, like a rogue tide that washes up on the beach out of nowhere, and then recedes far out to sea again. It was not until they reached Kiev that Carpini found a Mongol garrison and passed under their protection. From here they moved further eastwards, into a world beyond their imagination, in a region that was unknown to the West. As they did so, they were gradually forced to give away many of their gifts to the local warlords that they came into contact with. They were now firmly in the heartlands of the Golden Horde, speeded on their way by a succession of horses, which formed part of the very efficient Mongol transportation service (perhaps Carpini's deprivations had by now led to a certain loss of weight on his part, making the horses' progress somewhat less burdensome).

They found their way to the court of Batu. From Carpini's account we get a flavour of just how imposing a figure Batu was. He may have been inferior in the Mongol hierarchy to Kuyuk, but he held audience like a king. Although he was only acting as he was entitled to do, it is hard to avoid the impression that Batu certainly saw himself as a first amongst equals:

> This Batu is quite magnificent, he levies taxes and has officials just as if he were emperor. Indeed he sits in the highest place, as on a throne, with one of his wives. All others, however, whether brothers or sons and other nobles, sit down in the middle of a bench. The other men sit beyond them on the ground, with the men on the right and the women on the left. He has great and beautiful tents which belonged to the king of Hungary.[6]

The latter, stolen booty from a once-proud European king, were a potent symbolic reminder of just how great the Mongol threat was.

Despite his outward confidence, Batu's position was an awkward one. The election that was due in Karakorum had not yet taken place

A distant view of Venice: the great Italian city-state was an unlikely ally of the Mongols as they expanded westwards.

2. The magnificent and sacred site of Saint Sophia, once at the heart of the Byzantine empire, – Byzantium was an ally of the Mongols of the Golden Horde as they fought for dominance with the Mongols of Persia.

Opposite:
3. The mountains of Transylvania were supposed to hold up the Mongols for months as they advanced on Hungary: in reality they were forced in days.

Opposite:
4. The central square of Sibiu in modern Romania: as Hermannstadt, its loss was a bitter blow to the defence of Hungary.

5. The relatively fertile plains of Northern Syria proved an insignificant barrier to the Mongols as they advanced towards Egypt.

6. The magnificent gatehouse to the fortress of Aleppo in Syria: this important city was stormed several times by the Mongols.

Below:
7. A medieval water wheel from Hama in Syria: the town was on the road to Damascus, and was sacked by the Mongols as they advanced south through Syria.

bove:

. The fertile lands of Moldova continued on
rom the Ukraine and provided the Mongols
ith a convenient back door into Europe.

. Tiananmen Square in Beijing, close to the site
f the ancient city sacked by Genghis Khan.

10. The confluence of the Savo and the Danube in Belgrade: another city attacked by the Mongols as they moved through Europe.

Below:
11. A giant Buddha looks out from the foothills around Ulan Bataar, capital of modern Mongolia: Buddhism became increasingly influential as the Mongol empire expanded.

Above:

2. A modern statue of Subotai, perhaps the greatest of all Mongol generals, which stands in the central square named after him in Ulan Bataar.

3. An *ovoo*, a sacred hilltop shrine, in Mongolia: such holy Buddhist sites dot the hills of the country.

14. The Adriatic Sea: this marked the westernmost point of Mongol expansion.

Below:
15. The walls of Kotor in Montenegro: the city was sacked by the Mongols as they retreated back towards the borders of Europe.

16. The harshness of the Syrian Desert which marks the east and south of the country: terrain such as this proved a major logistical challenge to the Mongols.

Below:
17. The interior of the great Umayyad mosque in Damascus sacked by Tamerlane despite its sacredness to Islam.

18. This stretch of wall in Damascus is one of the few obvious reminders of the city that was sacked by the Mongols: Damascus is now a sprawling, modern metropolis.

Below:
19. The walls of Bosra in the south of Syria: the city was close to the southern limits of Mongol expansion in the region.

20. Shot from a medieval catapult: the use of siege engines proved crucial in the success of the Mongols.

Below:
21. The Hospitaller super-fortress of Krak des Chevaliers: the Hospitallers allied themselves to the Mongols against Sultan Baibars but were overrun when the triumphant Egyptian Sultan attacked them after their allies retreated.

22. The harshness of a Mongolian winter: the toughness of the terrain played an important role in developing the toughness of the Mongol warriors.

Below:
23. The statue of Genghis Khan erected in Ulan Bataar in 2006 to mark the 800th anniversary of the founding of the Mongol state.

24. Tourists stroll along the Great Wall of China where once Chinese soldiers looked out for another Mongol raid.

25. The splendour of the Forbidden City in Beijing. It was erected by the Ming dynasty that conquered the Mongol Yuan dynasty and destroyed most of the city that they had constructed

when the friars arrived in Batu's camp. The letter they carried was explicitly for the eyes of the Great Khan only, and Batu would not presume to open it on his behalf. He therefore decided to send them on to Karakorum itself - they might even be able to witness the election of the new Great Khan first hand. Batu, though, obviously made an impression on the delegation, for Carpini later remarked that Batu was the richest and most powerful Mongol after the emperor.[7] Batu had done what he could to prevent the election of Kuyuk, but he would fail. Soon, Töregene was playing the part of the avenging matriarch to perfection, dominating events in striking fashion. Whenever a vacancy in a position of influence came up, she would do her utmost to ensure that one of her son's affiliates succeeded to it. Batu must do nothing to antagonise Kuyuk, so he sent the ambassadors on their way.

Though they had a vast distance to travel, they made rapid progress. Sometimes they had as many as seven fresh horses in a day. They crossed deserts where the sun beat down like a fiery hammer on an anvil, lands devoid of moisture and life. There were varied landscapes, myriad peoples who must have seemed strange indeed to these men from the West. Only one common sight greeted them as they moved from one unknown land to another; piles of bones bleached white by the flaming sun, shattered cities, heaps of battered rubble, everywhere a macabre fresco of death, destruction, devastation. Such was the price of resistance against the iron will of the Mongols.

As his eyes took in these awful sights, Carpini must have been learning some daunting lessons about the Mongols. He passed into Mongolia, where he was exposed to the ferocious, dust-driving winds that sweep the country. The diversity of the weather was something that the friar found quite overwhelming: great heat, fierce thunder and lightning, bitterly cold winds and heavy falls of snow all get a mention. After weeks of exhausting travel, they at last arrived on the edge of Karakorum itself. Here, they were given a *ger* along with hundreds of other ambassadors, and leading Mongol nobles who were gathered together to witness the enthronement of a new Great Khan. After a few days, they were allowed into the presence of Töregene, still acting as regent pending the election. This initial meeting was good-humoured, and may at least have served to relax the delegation to an extent.

It was noticeable that the Pope's envoys were given pride of place during the subsequent days (although they never in fact saw Karakorum). On 24 August 1245, the election of Kuyuk was confirmed amidst scenes of great pomp. He sat on a throne, sumptuously decked with jewels, itself a sign of just how far the Mongols had come from their austere beginnings on the steppes. They then returned to their roots somewhat, by indulging in days of dancing and drinking.

One great man was not there though: Chagatai, the keeper of the law, was gone. Following the death of Ögedei, many men came to his camp, as he was highly regarded for his wisdom and knowledge. Soon after, he fell ill. His vizier and a physician tried everything they knew to save him, but the disease was too far-gone. When he died, his distraught widow had both vizier and physician executed. This was, if Carpini but knew it, a time of great events and tensions. The accession of Kuyuk was fraught with difficulty. Not everyone was convinced that he was the right man for the role. Shortly before the *kuriltai* that elected him, Genghis' younger brother, Temüge, a man well in his seventies, had suggested that he should become *khan* without the inconvenience of an election. It was a bold move but was followed by an even bolder one; soon after, he was executed, an unbelievable turn of events given his connections.

This was followed by yet more signs that all was far from well in the Mongol camp. Töregene had a Muslim confidante, a woman called Fatima. She had wielded an undue amount of influence at court, and had made a number of enemies in the process. They longed for a chance for revenge. Their opportunity came when Kuyuk's brother was taken ill. People were quick to suggest that Fatima had bewitched him. The accusation stuck, and Kuyuk ordered that she should be executed. This was done by sewing up every orifice in her body and throwing her into a river. Carpini was quickly struck by the number and rank of foreign guests approaching Karakorum, for this was truly an international capital in significance, if not in scale. He observed that 'at the court of the emperor we saw the nobleman Ierozlai [Yaroslav], Great Duke of Russia, the son of the King and Queen of Georgia, many great sultans, and even the Emir of the Solangi'. However, they were left in no doubt that their rank won them any special treatment. In fact, the Mongols went out of their way to remind them that they were their subjects, for they failed 'to receive the honours due them, but they were very rude, walked in front of them and always took the first and highest place; in fact these nobles always had to sit behind them'.[8]

This came as a shock to Carpini apparently, but it epitomised the Mongols' view of the world. They were the dominant power, and those that came to see them, however mighty they might think themselves, had to accept their place in the pecking order. These demonstrations of apparent bad manners were in reality a statement of political domination.

The envoys entered Kuyuk's presence with a mixture of trepidation and hope; the latter stemming from the fact that Töregene was a Christian.

However, the Nestorian branch of the faith would have been regarded as little more than heresy by the Pope. The Nestorians did not regard the Catholic Church highly either. Kuyuk, despite his Christian roots, was not minded to be encouraging towards the papal representatives. The Nestorians could be traced back to fifth-century Antioch, and they disagreed fundamentally on the nature of Christ from the mainstream Catholic Church. This might appear an argument over detail to modern eyes, but to medieval theologians, the difference was fundamental, and marked the Nestorians out as no more than schismatics, as bad in some ways as pagans.

The lack of presents from the papal delegation annoyed Kuyuk, and it would be two months before he deigned to see them. The cold shoulder treatment was noted, but was a trifle unfair: most of the gifts that Carpini had bought with him had been filched by many of the Mongol officials whose lands they crossed en route to the capital. The point was noted by Carpini in his account, when he said that 'princes and other nobles and lesser men seek gifts from them, and if they do not give them, the Tartars insult the ambassadors as though they were unimportant'.[9] It sounds as if Carpini is speaking from bitter experience, as an under-resourced ambassador.

Kuyuk's response to Innocent's demands was curt to say the least. The Pope had admonished Kuyuk for his invasion of Hungary: the Great Khan replied with words to the effect that it served Bela right, as the Hungarians had killed the ambassadors that he had sent to him. Innocent had told Kuyuk he should be baptised, but Kuyuk did not see the point of this. Further, he told Innocent, he had been given authority by the Great Spirit who governed the universe, whoever he might be, to be ruler of the whole world, and it was wrong of Innocent to interfere with the will of the divine. Given this, it would behove Innocent well to make his way to Karakorum as soon as possible, and pay obeisance to Kuyuk as was his due.

One of the problems was that the Mongols equated 'submission' with 'peace': in Turkish, a widely used intermediary language, there was in fact just one word for the two. The effects of philology on history are perhaps underestimated. And so, when the delegation arrived seeking peace, Kuyuk misunderstood completely what was on offer. Carpini's good grace and tact ironically did not help, as he did pretty much as he was told, and gave the Great Khan every intimation that he himself was submissive and, as a vicarious extension of this, so too was the Pope. It is fair to say that the message that Carpini was going back with was not exactly the response that Innocent had been hoping for (it was translated into Persian as a common intermediary language between east and west, and it still exists in this form in the Vatican archives). In any event, it was now time for Carpini and his fellows to return to the West. Kuyuk's peremptory response was translated into Latin with the aid of a Russian knight as an interpreter, but a copy was also made into Persian as well, just in case.

They left Kuyuk's camp on 13 November 1246, after what was surely one of the most extraordinary journeys of the Middle Ages, though it was of course only half over as yet. They paid their respects to Töregene, who was as kind on their departure as she had been on their arrival. Although the letter to Innocent from Kuyuk had been far from friendly, fortunately for Europe the Great Khan had other distractions to worry about. Subotai had been sent into China to carry on the subjugation of the Song dynasty, Kuyuk was planning further incursions into Persia, and there was, perhaps most worryingly of all, Batu to worry about. The latter had dutifully paid homage to Kuyuk, but it was unlikely that either party was under any illusions about the uneasy and unofficial truce that existed for the time being.

The small Western delegation returned through a bitter winter, to an incredulous reception from the citizens of Kiev, who could not believe that they had survived. They reached Poland and then Hungary, where Bela was struggling manfully to restore his lost territories, an aspiration that was helped no end by the death in battle against him of Duke Frederick of Austria. The king of Hungary at last had his revenge. Arriving at Lyons, Carpini gave Kuyuk's message, and his own interpretation of events to Innocent. The Mongols spelt trouble for the West, he warned, though the ongoing tension between Kuyuk and Batu offered some hope.

Carpini's name went down in history, literally, because he wrote a detailed exposition of his journey, and as a result became something of a *cause célèbre*. For all that, the diplomatic results of the mission had been extremely disappointing, though they had at least succeeded in giving Innocent a very clear picture of what he was up against with the Mongols. Carpini's report back to the Pope reads most of all like the intelligence dossier that an observer might expect a well-educated and observant spy to prepare. However, it is in places just a little fanciful: amidst what appears to be a good deal of factual information there are a number of fantastical references to strange peoples with small stomachs and mouths, and men with only one arm, and a hand in the middle of the chest. The former qualities make it a valuable reference for the historian: the latter make it a ripping good read.

Above all he returned with a grim warning. The Mongols were set on global domination, as they believed was their right. Should they try to conquer Europe, then it was crucial that they were driven off. Carpini had seen how downtrodden subject peoples of the Mongol empire were, and the prospect of Christendom going the same way was unthinkable. The alarming message was that the Mongols planned to return. They would strike once more through Hungary and Poland, the side door to Europe. They reckoned that the conquest of the continent would take eighteen years.

Carpini believed that there was only one hope for the West: to unite its forces. This was a familiar cry at the time; successive Popes had been saying the same to the kings and barons of Europe for centuries in an attempt to drum up support for their Crusades. They had been voices in the wilderness, crying in vain for unity, when all that most of the lords of the West were interested in was furthering their own self-interest. Sadly, the recent wars in Hungary and Poland suggested that more of the same was on the menu. Weaponry, too, was important in the warrior friar's view. Crossbows were especially feared by the Mongols (as indeed they were by many enemies of the West). Arrows should be strengthened to be armour-piercing. Armies should be organised, like the Mongols, in units of tens, hundreds, thousands. Like the Mongols, too, the generals of the European armies should control the battle from a distance, coolly and clinically, rather than letting themselves get dragged into the thick of the fighting.

Discipline was to be strictly observed. Men who fled in battle should be punished. Open ground should be chosen where the generals would have an uninterrupted view of the battlefield. If the Mongols broke and fled, then the Europeans should not flee, for this was a trick. If caught in a city and besieged, then they must destroy the Mongols' catapults, for they would otherwise wreak havoc. It was all good advice. But if push came to shove then it probably would not be observed. And even if it were, the Mongols would almost certainly still have won. Fortunately for Europe, Carpini's ministrations would not be put to the test.

So Europe survived, living on by default. At the moment, the Continent was not on the Mongols' itinerary. There were other areas that needed their attention first, the Middle East especially. Although they had pushed far westwards during the Khwarismian campaign and afterwards, they had not made a permanent conquest of Syria. It was time to put that omission right. So the Mongols made their meticulous battle plans, carefully crafted as ever, and prepared to make their move. Ironically, by pushing on into Syria the Mongols would come into contact with the West once more, for both the Mongols and West–European powers had a common enemy in the Muslims who lived in the area. This was the time of the Crusades, and Europe sought to win back the Christian holy places in Palestine for their faith. The Mongols and the West were not yet finished with each other.

For the Muslim world that lay between these two, this was a time of dark omens and bitter portents. A cloud was coming from the east, presaging a wind that would blow away everything in its path. Its force would be so great that the earth would seem to tremble before it. Islam itself would totter on the edge of a precipice and its very survival would be in doubt (or at least so it seemed). The years that loomed before would be the Dark Age of Islam, a period of yet more terror, in which wise men either hid or fled. Catastrophe was coming, and death was in its train.

CHAPTER 7

The Black Day of Islam: The Sacking of Baghdad & the Invasion of Syria 1247-1260

The Mongols were about to come into contact with the west in another way. They were moving closer to the tiny Crusader kingdoms, which hung on precariously for their lives on the shores of the eastern Mediterranean. Ironically, the Mongols had already had a great impact on the Crusades, though it was achieved vicariously. When the Mongols shattered the fragile infrastructure of the Khwarismian empire, they unleashed a domino effect through the Middle East. Thousands of dispossessed Khwarismian warriors roamed west in search of gainful employment as mercenaries. A large number of them made their way to Syria, where they found service in the wars of the Sultan there, against both the Egyptians (fellow Muslims but traditional rivals) and the Christians (who precariously hung on to a West European enclave known as Outremer). In the campaigns that followed, the Khwarismians had swooped on Jerusalem (1244) like a hungry raptor homing in on its prey, and ejected them from the city. The Christians would never return.

In direct response to this loss, another Crusade had been sent to recover the city (the Seventh granted the status of the title 'Crusade' though many smaller expeditions were not given the same exulted recognition of a formal number), led by Louis IX of France. Louis had set sail from France in 1248 at the head of one of the greatest Crusades ever to make its way to the Holy Land. Whilst on his way out, he stopped off at Cyprus, and it was here that he received two envoys from the camp of Eljigidei, a prominent Mongol leader who was in search of allies. Eljigidei was planning an attack on Baghdad, and the idea that a Crusade might be persuaded to assault the Syrian coast and cause a distraction was an attractive proposition. To encourage Louis to support such a scheme, his messengers told the king that Kuyuk had now been baptised a Christian and others had followed suit. All this was a lie

– subterfuge was as much a part of the Mongol armoury as their cavalry charges were – but these sweet words proved to be of great comfort to Louis, a devout though sometimes naïve monarch.

What Louis singularly failed to understand was that the Mongols practised religious toleration, which made them much less inflexible about religion than he was. This was not through altruism but, at several levels, through expediency. By allowing conquered races to keep their faith, provided that it did not clash with the needs of the state, they helped to keep their loyalty. This was in stark contrast to the paradigms of Louis, a western king whose religiosity sometimes approached fanaticism, and who adopted a variety of measures, some of them extreme, to convert non-Christians to his faith. This extended across nearly all faiths. The Nestorian element in Mongol society encouraged them to be relaxed about Christianity, but Judaism and Islam too were treated well on the whole. The religions of the east were no less favoured. Many of the Mongols eventually became Buddhists, so adherents of this religion were also not persecuted. Confucianism benefited too. There was a law introduced in the Chinese territories, for example, that forbad making Confucian scholars into slaves. Only when religion imposed negatively in politics did the Mongols interfere, as, for example, when a dispute between Buddhism and Taoism in China did so, and the Mongols decided in favour of the former. And only when a number of Mongols eventually became Muslims did they take a dimmer view of other religions.

The Mongols, too, were fascinated by the beliefs of others: Genghis Khan held an audience with Changchun, the Taoist holy man, who supposedly held the secret of eternal life, not realising that he meant it in a spiritual rather than a literal sense. As Juvaini eloquently put it, Genghis was 'the adherent of no religion, and the follower of no creed, he eschewed bigotry, and the preference of one faith to another ...'[1] In fact, apart from the Nestorian Christians, the beliefs of the Mongols themselves were based on much older roots than those of Christianity. Carpini had said that 'the Tartars believe in one God whom they think is the creator of all things visible and invisible, and they believe he gives rewards and punishments in this world'.[2] He says further that they place idols of men at each side of the doorways of their *gers*, which they offered the first milk of their flocks to. This sounds like a very ancient fertility offering, which probably went back thousands of years.

The objects that they venerated are further evidence of the almost primeval roots of Mongol religion. They worshipped the sun and the moon, as well as the earth, and they made offerings to them regularly.

They began their military campaigns either at the time of a new or a full moon, regarding these times as especially auspicious.[3] They also believed that the sun was the mother of the moon, and their faith was promulgated by their shamans, the magic men who cast spells and performed strange (and to the uninitiated frightening) rituals. They were, in other words, a people who venerated a large number of gods (somewhat contradicting what Carpini said) although the most prominent of them all was Tengri, the God of the Sky. Also important was a spirit known as Nochigai (also named as Etügen or Itügen) who was responsible for the health of the grass, the crops and the herds. An image of her was venerated in most Mongol dwellings.

The Mongols did not force anyone to deny their own faith, with one recorded exception. Carpini relates how a visiting prince of Russia arrived at the Mongol camp and was told to bow south in the direction of Genghis Khan. The prince replied that he could not do so, as to bow to a dead man was against his religious beliefs. He was promptly killed for his refusal by a Mongol stamping on his chest until he was dead. Genghis, to some, had become a god.

When Louis received this embassy from the Mongols, he immediately informed Pope Innocent in Rome of Kuyuk's supposed conversion, and sent a delegation of his own east in return. Andrew of Longjumeau headed it, and he carried with him the gift of a sumptuous tent, which served as a chapel, a present that would prove to be surprisingly useful in the future. Louis's plan was clear enough. His confidante, the chronicler Jean de Joinville, noted that:

> To attract the Tartars to our faith he had ordered a set of figures to be placed in this chapel representing every point of our religion: the Annunciation of the Angel, the Nativity, the ceremony of our Lord's Baptism, all the stages of the Passion, the Ascension, and the coming of the Holy Ghost. With the chapel he had also sent cups, books, and everything necessary for the celebration of mass, and two predicant friars to chant the service before the Tartars.[4]

The West was unsure what to expect in the lands that lay to the east. These were the lands of Gog and Magog, mystical giants, and of Prester John, the saviour of Christianity who even now ruled over some of the Tartars in western lore. Prester John occupied a place of great importance to the West. It was widely believed that a Christian ruler by this name was governing vast territories in the unknown lands of the east, and that he would one day bring his forces to help the West gain final triumph in their battles against the Infidel. As a result, Christendom would be both united and universally victorious.

This was in the main a triumph of hope over expectation, though there was a grain of truth perhaps in it all. It is now widely supposed that 'Prester John' was a misinterpretation of Wang or 'Ong' Khan, the honorific title given to Genghis' mentor, Toghril, whose tribe was largely composed of Nestorian Christians.[5] There was trade between East and West at the time, though it took place through the mechanism of intermediaries. There is therefore a rational explanation which might underlie the tale of Prester John, though of course this is supposition rather than provable fact. Gossip might have travelled along the trade roads and got back to Western ears in a somewhat distorted fashion. But there was also an irony of the most painful kind in all this, since Wang Khan was no more, his life having been ended in effect (if not in fact) by Genghis.

Louis, though, was in great need of help if the Crusade he was engaged in was to succeed, and the Mongols might well be able to provide this if the terms were right. Equally – and even if he was pious, Louis was not stupid – the Mongols had already demonstrated what a threat they might be in Europe, and it would be useful to get further information on a potential threat. In any event, the delegation would provide valuable information, so it set off with his blessing. They went first to Antioch, and from there to the camp of Eljigidei, who was near Tabriz. As they progressed further into the areas that the Mongols had recently devastated, some shocking vistas opened up before them. It had:

> ... Taken them a full year's travel, riding ten leagues a day, to find the Great King of the Tartars. They had found all the lands they passed through subject to this monarch, and seen many cities the Tartars had destroyed, and great heaps of dead men's bones.[6]

This was an unpleasant eye-opener, but before Andrew went further, great upheavals once again hit the Mongol world. Batu had been summoned to Kuyuk's camp. There were rumours that he was to be executed on the Great Khan's orders when he arrived, but everything was overtaken by events when Kuyuk died (reputedly) of excessive drinking. Others though were not so sure. His death was, to say the least, convenient for Batu, who might himself have perished if Kuyuk were still alive. A *kuritai* was held to elect a successor. The election that followed went the way of Möngke, a friend of Batu. On 1 July 1251, he duly succeeded Kuyuk.

It was quite a coup, and it is probable that an amazing woman was behind it, Möngke's mother Sorkaktani. When Tolui had died twenty years before, she had been left as a very marketable widow. Ögedei had even suggested that she should marry Kuyuk, her nephew. But she had declined, citing as her reasons her devotion to the cause of her sons. At the time, it may have seemed nothing more than pious niceties uttered in order to protect her from an unattractive and possibly incestuous marriage, but over time it came to seem as if she was speaking the truth. She had bitten her tongue even when the power of Töregene, mother and champion of Kuyuk, had held sway, forced to stand idly by whilst a woman, whose influence she must have regarded as vile, appeared to be sweeping all before her. But even though she and her offspring now appeared to have finally triumphed, she and they could not rest on their laurels, for there were many who were unhappy at this turn of events. Genghis' dubious legacy in the form of an ill-defined succession was now coming home to roost with a vengeance.

There was soon a plot against Möngke from a group of dissatisfied Mongol warlords, but it was discovered and put down ruthlessly by the new Khan. Eljigidei's sons were implicated and brutally executed, by having stones forced down their throats until they choked. Even Eljigidei, who was probably not involved, was killed on the orders of Batu, who now felt much more secure. A night of the long knives followed. The wives of those implicated in the plot (some 300 prominent Mongols) were bought before Möngke, and forced to confess their involvement in the planned coup. They were whipped with burning brands until they admitted their guilt, and then they too were summarily executed. Even Shiremun, grandson of Ögedei, was implicated, it was alleged as a prodigy of Kuyuk's widow Oghul Ghaimish, and although he initially survived, Möngke eventually decided that he could not be allowed to live. An infant son of Kuyuk alone was left alive as he was too young to have knowledge of the plot. Even Kuyuk's widow, for some time after his death regent, was killed.

In the meantime, Andrew had reached the camp of the Mongols out in the great steppes, and the tent he carried with him as a gift had been treated as a prize present. His arrival was well timed. Möngke was receiving ambassadors from a number of peoples who had not yet submitted to Mongol rule. The Great Khan was about to spectacularly misinterpret the gift, which he presented to the various delegations there, as an inducement to them to submit to him as well. The chronicle written by Jean de Joinville, a close confidante of King Louis, described how:

> When they had come he [Möngke] had his new chapel pitched for all to see and addressed them as follows: 'My lords, the king of France has sued

for mercy and submitted himself to us. Here you can see the tribute he
has sent us. If you do not submit yourselves to us, we will send for him to
destroy you'.[7]

Möngke in other words interpreted the gift as an offering which
betokened Louis's submission to Mongol rule. Perhaps Louis had
overdone the extravagance. Plans for alliance had come to nothing. At
any event, Louis' world had been turned upside down by now, as he
had in the meantime been taken a prisoner after his Crusade had been
trapped and annihilated. There was little to be gained for the Mongols
in an alliance, at this point in time. Louis had no army left to send to
Möngke, even if he had wished to do so. And as ever the Mongols were
set on nothing save the king's submission – his embassy had failed. With
wonderful understatement, Louis' chronicler noted, 'His Majesty, I can
assure you, bitterly regretted that he had ever sent his envoys to the great
King of the Tartars'.[8]

Möngke had greater plans of his own to focus on. He would let Batu
do as he wished in the west, whilst he would concentrate his efforts in
the east. His brother Hülegü would lead a renewed invasion of Persia
and beyond into Syria and even, it was planned, into Egypt. The Russian
princes were now instructed to give their allegiance straight to Batu,
a tacit but crucial step towards dividing up the enormous Mongol
empire. This move, forged in bonds of amity and goodwill, presaged
a far more violent schism within the Mongol world, just a few short
years later. Möngke would leave both Hülegü and Batu essentially to
act as autonomous players. In so doing, he was removing the centralised
adhesive that had held the extended empire together. There were to
be further links between the West and the Mongols. In 1253, Friar
William of Rubruck, a Flemish Franciscan cleric, would make his
way to Mongolia, and be the first Westerner to set foot in Karakorum
(Carpini having only reached its periphery). His mission was essentially
of a humanitarian and evangelical nature, rather than an ambassadorial
effort. Louis IX in fact had been careful to ensure that it did not give
the appearance of being one, not wanting to encourage the Mongols in
further plans to make him their client.

Rubruck would go to the Mongols to try and convert them and, in the
process, to bring succour (and hopefully freedom) to the large number
of Western Christian slaves that had been seized by the Mongols during
their pillaging in Europe. From the start, Rubruck made clear that he
was acting independently, publicly declaiming this when he arrived in
Constantinople, writing to Louis that 'I was not an envoy, neither yours

nor anyone's, but was going among these unbelievers according to the rule of our order'.[9] In some ways, this made his task harder. The Mongols were usually scrupulous in treating ambassadors well; they were less bothered about meeting the needs of missionaries. This time, William made sure that he had plenty of gifts with him, carried in carts bought from Russians. He was struck, as Carpini had been, by the devastation that greeted his eyes as he moved further into what he called another world. He came to the plains where the Cumans had once lived,

> All of whom had fled to the shore of the sea [where] they ate one another, the living the dying ... the living devouring and tearing with their teeth the raw flesh of the dead, as dogs do corpses.[10]

He moved into the lands of Batu, where he was struck by the strange rituals that the Mongols practised. Before a gathering, a servant would proceed out of the *ger* and make offerings of drink to the spirits of the world. He would sprinkle it three times to the south, revering fire; the same to the east, reverencing air; the same to the west for water and then to the north and the harsh, cold lands that lay there, in honour of the dead. More references to the Mongols' propensity to have a good party, and consume copious amounts of alcohol, were included in his report back too, 'sometimes they do drink right shamefully and gluttonly. Then they all drink in turn, men and women alike, and at times compete with one another in quaffing in a thoroughly distasteful and greedy fashion'.[11]

William enthusiastically set about his task of converting the Mongols to his faith, but the task was far from easy. He was on the verge of converting one of those he met, but the potential proselyte was lost when he reasoned that he would have to give up excessive use of alcohol if he were to become a Christian – an act few self-respecting Mongols would contemplate. Like Carpini, William also made his way to the court of Batu, a man almost as powerful as the emperor himself, perhaps in these, his own lands, even more powerful. Batu again complied meticulously with protocol, commanding that the delegation should be sent on their way to the Great Khan, Möngke, at Karakorum.

As they progressed, dressed now in furs supplied by the Mongols to protect them from the winter temperatures that were so low that 'stones and trees are split by the cold',[12] alien sights assailed their senses. There were idolaters dressed in saffron robes with shaven heads, Buddhists as we would now know them to be, chanting constantly as they moved the mantra *on mani baccam*. These people cremated their dead and left their ashes in large pyramids, a practice that was anathema to Catholic

Christians. William enthusiastically entered into theological debate with them, enjoying the cut and thrust of the intellectual challenge that this gave him. Sadly the conversation was cut short when the interpreter tired of his task, and refused to work any longer. He also met Christians, Nestorians. However, they did not meet with William's approval. The priests ate fish on Fridays, adopted pagan customs and, worst of all, were allowed to marry. All these were of course habits that were abhorrent to the Catholic Church. The delegation moved on into the land of the Naimans. Strange tales reached their ears; that Batu had been behind the election of Möngke, that he had arranged for Kuyuk to be poisoned, that he was then kingmaker and unseen power behind the throne.

Further strange sights continued to materialise. William came across a tent topped with a cross. On entering, a wondrous vista unfolded. There was an altar, encased in embroidery of cloth of gold, and a great silver cross, encrusted in precious jewels. It was clearly a Christian place of worship. This most pleasing sight encouraged the friar, and gave him fresh heart as he continued to make his way towards the court of Möngke. The encouragement was timely. The harshness of the steppes' winter was having a terrible effect on the friar. He noted that it was so cold that the animals were dying off in their thousands, that even in May there was frost in the mornings, though the sun later melted it. One has to experience the gnawing intensity of the Mongolian winter to understand how intensely painful it can be, for its energy-sapping effect is almost beyond the power of description.

Like Carpini's, the real significance of William's account is in the insight it gives us into the Mongol way of life. William also noted the international nature of the court that he was now approaching. There were, for example, delegations from John Vatatzes, Emperor of Nicaea and rival to the West European dynasty that had seized Constantinople half a century before. John was a client king of the Mongols, recognising that when they had burst into Asia Minor he was powerless to resist them, and that submission was the only way to survive. Then at last, after months of travelling, they arrived at the court of Möngke, who was camped about ten days from Karakorum. The keenly anticipated moment when they would present their case before the Great Khan was at hand. The formalities were complied with, they were searched for knives and then they entered into the presence of the most powerful man in the world. Möngke was seated on a couch, a man of medium height William noted, about forty-five years of age. The audience began, not helped by the fact that by the time it started, the interpreter was already drunk.

William played his part well, being appropriately obsequious to

Möngke. His mission he explained was an evangelical one. They had neither gold nor silver (the gifts had presumably been lost to rapacious Mongol officials through whose lands they had journeyed so his good intentions had come to nothing). After that, the conversation became vague. It appeared to William that the interpreter was now completely intoxicated, and that even Möngke was tipsy. It was presumably not quite the kind of royal audience that William was used to.

Soon, tremendous news reached William. It was said that Möngke was to be baptised. A monk told him that Möngke preferred the Christians to all other men. Presumably, at the time, William's hopes soared, but they were to be quickly dashed, as William caustically remarked in his account that he (Möngke) 'believes in none ... and they all follow his court as flies do honey, and he gives to all, and they all believe that they are his favourites, and they all prophesy blessings to him'.[13] Shortly afterwards, William became the first westerner to set eyes on Karakorum, capital of the world, the seat of power, the Washington of its day. He was not impressed. He reckoned that the Parisian suburb of St Denis was larger and that its monastery was ten times bigger than Möngke's palace. Karakorum was surrounded by a mud wall and had four gates. It was a city of all faiths, with mosques, Christian churches, Buddhist temples. It was all very incongruous, just as the sight of Western slaves must have been; they had been captured during the Mongols' recent European incursions (one from Belgrade, another a Norman bishop from Rouen in France).

Unknown to William, he had arrived at a turning point in Mongol history. There was, at the time, in Persia and Syria, a Muslim sect known as the 'Assassins', a group who were renowned for their skills in assassination. William remarked that there were reputed to be 400 of them homing in on Karakorum with Möngke as their target. The repercussions of these alleged plans were to be enormous.

William indulged in religious debates with the representatives of other faiths but, apart from its success as an intelligence-gathering exercise, his mission must be regarded as a failure. Soon after, Möngke ordered him to go back to the West. There would be no argument, no appeal. What Möngke said, went. Möngke gave his own views of religion to the friar before he left. There was but one God he said, but there were a number of ways to him. That was the Mongol way, and it went without saying that it was in stark contrast to European Christian paradigms of the world. Before William left, he noted the presence of representatives from the Abbasid Caliph, who was based in Baghdad. It was said that Möngke would not have peace with his people, unless they destroyed all their fortresses and recognised his suzerainty. There were also delegations from India with leopards and greyhounds, which bizarrely had been taught how to stay on horseback. Envoys from Turkey were present as well.

Möngke commanded William to take a letter back to Louis IX with him. The opening phrase gave the gist of what was to follow, 'the commandment of the eternal God is, in Heaven there is only one eternal God, and on earth there is only one lord, Chingis Chan. This is a word of the Son of God, Demugin, 'sound of iron'.[14] So, as the heavens above belonged to God, so did the earth belong to Genghis, his son (a claim that would surely, with its blasphemous bluster, have made the Pope and devout Christians like Louis IX apoplectic). Apart from anything else, it is also a strong clue as to the impact that Genghis' legacy was continuing to have on his successors. The letter bristled with threat to Louis, lord of 'the great realm of the French'. He should send ambassadors to Möngke to decide whether they would have peace or war with the Mongols. As previously mentioned, peace equated to submission in the Mongol language, so it is clear what Möngke had in mind when he sent this message – surrender or fight. Although there might be vast distances between them, endless lands and towering mountains, nothing would save the French, if they refused to submit to God's injunction that the world belonged to the Mongols.

So William returned to the West, a disappointed man, back through the lands of Batu and the Iron Gate in Central Asia, where Alexander the Macedonian had built a city 1,500 years before. He had acquired some interesting Mongol tastes, preferring fermented mare's milk to wine by now. It was an incredible journey, preceding that of Marco Polo by several decades, but being much less well known. This is less than the friar deserves for his Herculean efforts. However, the French and the other peoples of Europe were to be safe for now, for Möngke's attention had alighted elsewhere, having decided that the Mongol war machine should start rumbling again, and that it would head off in two opposite directions. As for all Mongol Khans, China continued to exercise a hypnotic fascination, and plans were afoot to put further pressure on the Song dynasty there. Korea was on the itinerary too, with an expedition due to go there under Genghis' nephew, Jochi Khasar.

As Möngke considered the campaigns that lay ahead, he did not just look at the military options, but also gave a lot of thought to developing a more sophisticated tax system to fund these expensive enterprises. Censuses were carried out to better establish who was a subject of the empire, and what wealth they might own. Head taxes were placed on subjects across the empire, agricultural taxes on farmers and commercial taxes on businesses. All of this was to help finance further expansionism, in both east and west.

The invasion of Korea duly went ahead in 1254. It would prove to be a devastating campaign, with the Mongols taking 200,000 prisoners it was said.[15] However, the country proved notoriously stubborn. It remained defiantly unconquered despite the widespread damage that the Mongols caused. It was governed in effect by its generals and not by its king, who was a titular monarch only, and at the mercy of the generals' whim. But then, in 1258, he saw an opportunity to escape from their clutches. He staged his own coup, killed the leaders of the military junta, and offered his kingdom to Kublai, who was the nearest prominent Mongol in the absence of Möngke. Soon after, the king died, and was replaced by a Mongol nominee, a very convenient resolution to the Korean problem indeed.

The Middle East was another area where expansion was targeted. The Mongols, despite Genghis' conquest in Khwarezm, had not really pushed on into the west, as they had once threatened to do. Now it was decided to put that particular omission right. An army was assembled which would be led by Hülegü, Möngke's brother. There is some doubt about the specific objectives of this expedition, though it has been suggested that, after Persia had been subdued, Syria, Egypt and possibly even the lands beyond were the target. Whatever the truth of this, the move on the Middle East would have massive consequences for the Mongol empire, though perhaps not exactly in the way anticipated. There were two definite objectives, which are clear even after all this time. First of all was the destruction of the radical Islamic group widely known as the 'Assassins' (though members of the sect called themselves Nizaris). They were well-known for two particular traits. Firstly was their supposed liking for hashish (from which their well-known nickname is derived – 'Assassin' being a mistranslation of 'hashish taker'). This suggestion is unlikely to have much basis in fact, but was rather a term of abuse from the many enemies of the sect. Secondly, and more based in certain fact, was their propensity for removing political opponents by means of assassination.

The Nizaris had been around for several hundred years. The number of victims that they claimed over this time was surprisingly low given their renown. They were an extreme Islamic sect from the Ismaili branch of the faith with many bitter enemies, most of them other Muslims. Although they were not prolific killers, they were nevertheless widely feared, most of all because their 'assassins' had no fear of death, and indeed welcomed it, as it gave the killer a passport into paradise. It was this latter trait that allegedly attracted Möngke's unwelcome attentions. The presence of supposed assassins at Karakorum was noted by William of Rubruck, and, there being no reason for him to make up such a story, it is easy to accept his account at face value. What is less clear is why the Nizaris would embark on such a reckless venture, which must have inevitably called down the wrath of an avenging Mongol army on their heads. There were, however, rumours that the current master of the sect, Ala ad-Din, had as his mistress the wife of a man who was once a prisoner of the Mongols. This cuckolded husband appears at times to have had some influence over Ala ad-Din in a strange *ménage a trois*, and it may be that there were acutely personal factors behind any move against the Mongol *khan*.

Another source says that a Persian leader had asked for the Mongols' help in removing the Nizari threat. It was a request that Möngke was pleased to respond to. There were other objectives which the *khan* had in mind as well. The nominal head of the Muslim faith (the Sunni branch of it at least) was the Abbasid Caliph, based in Baghdad. For several hundred years he had been little more than a symbolic totem, given protection by Turkish adventurers in return for the credibility that this religiously important, though otherwise powerless, figure gave them.

There were rumours that the Nizaris had been looking abroad for allies. There is an intriguing story, related by the lively English chronicler Matthew Paris, that a delegation from the Nizaris' leader (the semi-legendary 'Old Man of the Mountains') had made its way to the court of the English king Henry III, looking for support against Mongol threats as long ago as 1238. Many historians are sceptical about this claim, but if it did in fact happen, then it would suggest that the Nizaris had been feeling exposed to Mongol attack for a considerable time.[16]

A massive Mongol host prepared to set out on a campaign that would change the course of history. Composed of Mongols and large numbers of Turks, supplemented by contingents from Armenia and Georgia, this was probably the greatest army ever to set out from the steppes. However, after this magnificent force advanced, it seemed Hülegü was in no hurry to fulfil his aims, provoking Möngke to admonish him for his dilatory progress. In part this may have been because of the very size of the Mongol horde. Not only were there the soldiers, perhaps 100,000 of them, but many had their families with them, perhaps tripling the size of this force, which was more like a mass migration than an army. Provisioning this city on the move must have been an enormous logistical nightmare.

In 1256 Hülegü at last stormed into Persia. The Nizaris were the first to feel the wrath of the Mongols. They were led by a young imam, Rukn al-Din Khurshah, who had recently engineered the removal of Ala ad-Din. His first response was to dissimulate, something the Nizaris were rather good at. Not only were they accomplished assassins, they were skilled political players too, and Rukn al-Din sought to prevent the catastrophe that now loomed, by peaceful means. The Mongols, however, were also astute politicians (when it suited them) and they would not start a fight if they could achieve the same ends through other means. They in their turn dissimulated. Rukn al-Din's approaches were welcome, they responded, but to prove his sincerity, he should surrender himself in person. The young *imam* justifiably smelt a rat and sent his brother Shahanshah in his stead. The Mongols, saying that Rukn ad-Din had failed to comply with their demands, used this as a pretext to attack the Nizari heartlands.

However, they had sprung their trap too soon. The Nizaris had castles perched high in the mountains, granite eyries that only the eagles could approach easily. The Mongols found that these were harder to subdue than expected, and this initial rapier thrust was repulsed. As a result of this unsatisfactory outcome, Hülegü changed tack and entered into negotiations once more. To show good faith, Rukn al-Din dismantled a number of his castles. However, he was careful not to significantly diminish the defensive capacity of his major castles, especially the major Nizari base at Alamut. And he was equally cautious in ensuring that he kept himself safely out of the clutches of Hülegü, for now at least.

But time was running out. Hülegü was increasingly frustrated that Rukn al-Din refused to give himself up and now, at last, grabbed the bull by the horns. In what was a surprising burst of activity – his performance so far had been almost lackadaisical – he led his army on towards Alamut. Realising that the crisis point had been reached, Rukn al-Din sent frantic messages to Hülegü, trying to delay the inevitable. Hülegü sensed the desperation that Rukn al-Din, liked a trapped animal, now felt. He replied with an ultimatum. The castle of Maymundiz, a crucial citadel, was to be destroyed, and Rukn al-Din was to stop playing for time and come at once to Hülegü. In such a case, then, the Mongols would accept this as an satisfactory act of submission, but for the time being Rukn al-Din still refused to go along with the Mongols' demands.

So the Mongols advanced on Maymundiz from all directions, tightening their noose round the neck of Rukn al-Din. In a passage as vivid as any he ever wrote, Juvaini described the scene:

The valleys and mountains billowed with the great masses of men. The hills
which had held their heads so high and had such strong hearts now lay trampled with broken necks under the hooves of horses and camels. And from the
din of the braying of those camels and the noise of pipe and kettle-drum the
ears of the world were deafened, and from the neighing of the horses and the
flashing of the lances the hearts and eyes of the foe were blinded.[17]

The siege was undertaken with brutal efficiency. The trees around
the castle – which had been planted by the Nizaris for the fruit they
provided – were torn down, and transformed into mangonels and
catapults, from which huge stones were flung at the castle walls. Seeing
that further resistance was only prolonging the inevitable, Rukn al-Din
gave himself up.

Hülegü was generous in victory, or so it seemed, giving extravagant
presents to his captive. He even gave him a wife, a Mongol girl who had
caught his eye. Gifts of a hundred camels followed. But this was mere
opportunism on Hülegü's part. Although the *imam* had surrendered,
his people had not. Rukn ad-Din could be used as a tool to manipulate
those who had not yet given up the fight, and was therefore still useful.

Alamut itself still held out, but not for long. The Mongols used powerful
catapults to hammer away at the lofty citadel, and then persuaded Rukn
al-Din to intercede with the garrison to capitulate. The plan worked, and
Alamut was handed over to the Mongols. It was a major coup. The castle
was an immensely tough nut to crack. It was perched thousands of feet
up in the mountains, and could only be approached by the narrowest
of passes. Huge cisterns of water provided the garrison with months of
potential sustenance, yet the castle was gone with barely a fight. Alamut
was the Nizaris seat of power, not only a massively impressive fortification,
but also a seat of learning. Within its walls was housed a great library,
stocked with the religious treasures of the sect, as well as a number of
advanced scientific works. It had a massive psychological significance to
Nizaris everywhere. It was essentially the Vatican of the movement.

Juvaini, who became Hülegü's vizier in Persia as well as an important
chronicler, was given permission to tour the library and save any works
that he wished to keep. He made sure that the copies of the sacred Koran
were saved, as well as some astronomical instruments. The rest of the
items in the building were torched. Juvaini particularly delighted in the
destruction of documents containing the Nizaris' religious doctrines.
Like many orthodox Muslims, he detested the sect.

Before long, the library, its precious manuscripts and the soul of the
Nizari faith were lost forever in a vast pall of smoke. The rest of the

castle followed suit. The castle was too strong to be demolished stone by stone, so torches were set to it, and was soon blazing fiercely as a result. The heartbeat of the Nizaris ceased, and the movement to all intents and purposes died, consumed by a cloud of fire. This must have been a crushing blow for Rukn al-Din. He asked for permission to journey to Karakorum where he hoped to have an audience with Möngke in person, to try and save the life of the movement for which that he had been responsible for for such a short time. He was allowed to go there but Möngke refused to see him, possibly angry that some Nizari outposts still held out against the Mongols. On his way back to Persia, his Mongol guard turned on Rukn al-Din and kicked him to death. This must have been on Möngke's direct orders, given the Mongols' aversion to the execution of the leaders of any nation.

There then followed an act that was as cynical and cruel as any in the history of the Mongols. The Nizari population that remained was told to present itself to the nearest Mongol garrison for a census where they would be registered. This was a front. Möngke had sent secret instructions to Persia, allegedly based on the commands of Genghis Khan himself. The message was as chilling as it was clear. In the words again of Juvaini:

> It had been laid down in the original yasa [law] of Chingiz-Khan and also in the decree of Mengu Qa'an, that none of the people should be spared, not even the babe in its cradle ... [The order went out that] Rukn al-Din's sons and daughters, brothers and sisters and all of his seed and family should be laid on the fire of annihilation.[18]

It was little short of an instruction to initiate genocide, and the order was followed with ruthless efficiency. All Nizaris who gave themselves up were despatched without pity or second thought. No mercy was shown on account of sex or age. There was a merciless equality in the slaughter that followed. The Nizaris had attracted a bitter hatred from the Mongols, and they could not be allowed to live. Juvaini for one was convinced that this was a just punishment for the wrongs that had been committed over the years. In his words, 'so was the world cleansed which had been polluted by their evil'.[19]

The Nizaris had attracted widespread hatred from their enemies, who were determined to wipe them from the face of the earth. The point was proved in striking fashion by the Nizari stronghold of Girdkuh. Rukn ad-Din had instructed the castle to surrender, or at least that was what he stated publicly, though it was said that he secretly sent instructions for the garrison to carry on the fight. In any event, Girdkuh fought on. In a heroic action, the men there held out against the Mongols for thirteen years, only eventually surrendering when the clothes were literally falling off them. No mercy was shown even to this gallant group – they were promptly killed on the spot as soon as they gave themselves up.

The removal of the Nizaris from the political scene in Persia (though a branch of the sect lived on in Syria) would have caused barely a tear amongst Muslims across the Middle East who were not of their persuasion. However, the same could not be said of what happened next, namely when the Mongols moved in on Baghdad. The Caliph, al-Mustasim, was a weak and easily led man, who did not know how to respond to the Mongol threat. He had, in fact, been economising in recent times, and cutting back expenditure on the army (hardly the best way to prepare for a confrontation with the greatest military power in the world.) The chronicler Juzjani alleged that this was at the instigation of his chief minister, who was a Shi-ite, secretly desiring the fall of the Sunni Caliphate. Suspiciously, he was re-installed in his position by Hülegü after Baghdad fell. The Caliph in any event responded initially with bluster but his apparent confidence was not based on realism, and he sent an army out to face the Mongols. Some of the Mongols had crossed the River Tigris at Mosul and were making their way down the west bank. Kitbuqa, one of the Mongol generals, led his men in from the east, whilst Hülegü led his army in the centre between the two. The Caliph's army under Aibeg met another force about thirty miles to the west of Baghdad. The Mongol commander of this particular force, Baichu, was as well versed in military tactics as one would expect a man in such a position to be. Adopting time-honoured measures, he retreated before the Caliph's army. It was of course a trick, as he had lured his enemy on into a low marshy area. Then, when they were exactly where he wanted them to be, he had the dykes which were used to help irrigate the area broken. The waters flooded onto the plains, cutting off any retreat that the Muslim force might be thinking of making.

The next day, the Mongols went on the offensive. The Muslims were no match for them, and they were driven back into the flooded fields. Those who were not killed in battle, drowned. Only a few men escaped, though Aibeg was one of the handful of survivors. Those who did survive fled into the desert rather than try and make their way back to Baghdad, which was now a doomed city. The Mongols reassembled at the ancient site of Ctesiphon, once the home of a magnificent ancient Persian civilisation, whose glories were now long gone. It was a poignant place at which to discuss the final move on Baghdad, home of another great civilisation that was about to die.

The Mongols moved in for the kill, surrounding the city and putting a wall of boats both above and below it on the Tigris. There was no escape from this snare. Al-Mustasim was by now in abject despair. He waited for the Muslim princes of the Middle East to rush to his aid, but he had been a poor and uninspiring figurehead, and no one moved to help him. The spiritual authority of the Abbasids over the Muslim world had been surrendered long ago. He despatched the Nestorian Patriarch of Baghdad to Hülegü's camp, to intercede on his behalf. Hülegü's wife Doquz was a Nestorian herself, and she used what intercessory powers she had with him, to persuade him to show mercy. Hülegü noted his wife's interventions, though in the end it was only the small Christian community in Baghdad that would benefit from them. They were advised to make their way to the nearest Christian church should the Mongols break in. Hülegü demanded that the Caliph should give himself up in person, along with his family, and he should tell his people to surrender too. Of course, this was exactly what Rukn ad-Din had done, and little good it had done him.

On the other hand, Al-Mustasim was in no position to fight on, and so he did as he was told. Baghdad was abandoned to its fate. It was a huge prize, packed with worldly wealth so vast that it was almost beyond counting. For 500 years, the fate of the Abbasid Caliphate, and this vast metropolis, had been intertwined. It was both appropriate and poignant that as they had lived together, they were now about to die together as well.

There could be little doubt as regards Hülegü's determination to exact a heavy toll from the city or the Caliph. He had sent an imperious letter to him containing the following chilling words:

> When I lead my army against Baghdad in anger, whether you hide in heaven or on earth, I will bring you down from the spinning spheres; I will toss you in the air like a lion. I will leave no one alive in your realm; I will burn your city, your land, your self.[20]

Baghdad, for so long the jewel in the crown of Islam (though perhaps past its best by now) was now naked before a cruel foe. Letters were attached to arrows and shot into the city, declaring that only non-combatants would be spared when the Mongols took it. In a colourful, though dubious, account by the chronicler Ibn Kathir, it is said that one of these message-carrying arrows struck and killed one of the Caliph's concubines whilst she was dancing in front of him, as the last moments of the city approached. The walls had been battered by Mongol artillery, and breaches were appearing in them at frequent intervals. 10 February 1258 marked the lowest point for Islam since its founding six centuries before. This was its Black Day. As the Mongols poured into the city, the streets ran with blood. The population was slaughtered pitilessly, although a group of Christians, who sheltered in their church as directed, were spared.

Horror stories about the sack proliferated. It was said that one Mongol warrior slaughtered forty orphaned babies, though this was reputedly done as an act of kindness as they would not survive without a parent to look after them. The Mongols were accompanied by Georgian allies, Christians who were particularly enthusiastic in destroying their Muslim enemies. It was ironic that the Georgians, who would suffer so often at Mongol hands, were so quick to mete out violence to a conquered foe. The numbers of the dead were immense. Not long after, Hülegü would send a letter to Louis IX in France, in which he claimed 200,000 had died.

The Mongols themselves abandoned Baghdad in March, driven out by the stench emanating from thousands of putrefying corpses. Before they did so, a cruel scene was played out in the palace of the now deposed Caliph. He was summoned into this magnificent building and mocked. He was 'invited' to a banquet, where he was made to reveal all the places that treasure could be found. Once he had told his captors where the most obvious places were, he was then instructed to tell them where all of the secret hiding places that he had omitted to mention might be. Terrified, he then told them the location of these too. His usefulness now exhausted, the Caliph soon met a bitter end. Once he had revealed the secret hiding places in which his vast wealth had been stored, he no longer served a purpose. Some said that he was locked up in a tower and starved to death, as a salutary reminder that his well-known love of riches could have been better used, if his money had been employed to build a credible army. More commonly he is supposed to have been wrapped up in a felt carpet, and either ridden over by Mongol horses or kicked to death.

The former vizier, Muwaiyad, was installed as governor of Baghdad by the Mongols. This was in line with similar cases elsewhere, when they sought to control the local population by installing familiar figures into positions of power. But he was a Quisling-like figure, a marionette with Mongol puppet-masters pulling the strings. Baghdad would eventually be rebuilt and cleaned up, but it was a pale shadow of its former self.

The city that existed forty years later was a tenth of the size of the one that the Mongols had destroyed.[21]

On 18 December 1259 Hülegü moved on into Syria itself, crossing over the great River Euphrates to do so. Aleppo was placed under siege on 18 January 1260. The Sultan an-Nasir Yusuf was in Damascus, and reacted to the Mongol threat by offering to pay homage to the Mamelukes in Egypt, traditional enemies in the divided Islamic world, if they would come to his aid. Whilst he waited for their response, he gathered an army. At the most inopportune moment possible, he uncovered a plot against him, but the conspirators realised in time that the game was up, and fled to Egypt. After a bitter fight of six days, Aleppo fell. Again, mass slaughter followed, with the Christians the only party spared (except for the Orthodox, whose church was accidentally overlooked in the chaos that followed the fall of the city, and was duly sacked). This benevolent pro-Christian attitude reflected the prominence in Mongol ranks of Nestorians, who recognised a connection of sorts with Christians from other groups. Only the vast citadel held out under the gallant command of the old governor of the city, Turanshah. When that fell four weeks later, he was unusually spared as a mark of respect for his venerability and bravery.

As the Mongols pushed on, they found themselves on the borders of Christian territory in the shape of the Crusader Principality of Antioch. The Prince of Antioch, named Bohemond (as Princes of Antioch invariably were) came to the camp of Hülegü and paid him homage. It was an act of both prudence and opportunism. In return for this, several towns that had been lost to the Muslims for years were returned to Antioch. Hülegü, however, atypically involved himself in Church politics when he ordered that the Roman Catholic Patriarch of Antioch should be replaced by a Greek Orthodox one. Bohemond received little credit elsewhere in Christendom for this act of alliance. In fact, the same year that Damascus fell, Pope Alexander IV was sending an appeal for unity to all the leaders of Christendom, in the light of the Mongol threat. The dramatic language he used in his bull *Clamat in auribus* told eloquently of the threat he felt that the Mongols posed to the well-being of the Christian world:

There rings in the ears of all, and rouses to vigilant alertness those who are not befuddled by mental torpor, a terrible trumpet of dire forewarning which, collaborated by the evidence of events, proclaims with so unmistakable a sound the wars of universal destruction, wherewith the scourge of Heaven's wrath in the hands of the inhuman Tartars, erupting as were from the secret confines of Hell, oppresses and crushes the earth ... [22]

Alexander's view of the Mongols as the scourge of God is chillingly similar to that which Genghis himself had held towards the Mongols as their leader. Bohemond received an excommunication for his pains, signifying Church disapproval for submitting to a regime that had caused so much devastation in other Christian lands. But when, shortly after, Damascus fell without a fight, Bohemond and Hethoum, King of Armenia, were at the head of the procession that marched through the city gates. Alongside them rode Kitbuqa, a great general and a Christian to boot (a fact that may have played a significant part in the enhanced life expectancies of Christian communities in the cities that had fallen to the Mongols.) He soon indulged himself in a rather un-Christian act by personally beheading the city's governor.

These Christian generals reputedly forced Muslims in the city to bow to the Cross, whilst the conquerors drank openly and conspicuously during Ramadan. When Bohemond entered Damascus, it was the only time that a Crusader leader had entered the place in triumph, though his part in the campaign was, in fairness, small. However, it was not all good news. Apart from the fact that Bohemond was excommunicated, the city of Antioch would later pay a heavy price for its support of the Mongols, when the Muslims in the region grew stronger. Retribution for his part in these shocking events would be brutal. Shortly afterwards, an-Nasir, who had tried to flee to Egypt, but had then rather foolishly changed his mind, was captured. There was one hope left for Islam: the Mamelukes of Egypt, the slave dynasty renowned for their fighting skills (Mameluke means 'he who is owned'). There was something of an irony in this, as the Mamelukes were recruited from the Central Asian steppes, and were therefore of a similar background to the Mongols. The representatives of two groups of warriors from the far reaches of Asia were about to fight it out for supremacy on the shores of the Mediterranean. The Mamelukes would pose a serious threat to the Mongols, but few doubted what the outcome of a battle would be, for the armies from the east had so far proved invincible for the best part of half a century.

The next place to feel the lash of the Mongol whip was Mayyafaraqin, whose ruler had rather unwisely crucified a Christian priest who was under Hülegü's protection. Early in 1260, the city fell with Hülegü's Armenian and Georgian allies again prominent in the attack. The Christians were once more spared, and the Muslims massacred. Kamil, the foolish ruler of this place, was tortured to death, being force-fed with chunks of his own flesh. Next his head was cut off and carried in triumph on to Aleppo, then to Damascus, carried on a pole and preceded by women playing tambourines in a macabre celebration of his death. Other places followed, at the time renowned but whose significance has, over the centuries, waned. One such was Bosra in the south of Syria, once a great Roman city and then an important stopping-off point for those on the *hajj* from Damascus to Mecca. The city, like others in Syria, was overwhelmed by the Mongol invasion force. Bosra was past its peak, but was defended by a strong citadel, newly built, ingeniously hugging the superb remains of a Roman theatre. Once overcome, Bosra suffered a blow from which it never recovered.

The Mongols now had possession of the three great Muslim cities of western Asia outside of Arabia: Aleppo, Damascus and Baghdad. They had even probed into Palestine, raiding parties taking possession of both Nablus and Gaza. Ascalon, Hebron and Jerusalem were raided. The Mongols now abutted onto the Crusader kingdom of Outremer but, given relatively good relations with the Crusaders, they showed no desire to subjugate them. However, there was one particular foolish Christian lord, Julian of Sidon and Beaufort, who sought to take advantage of the chaos that the Mongols had caused by launching a raid into newly-captured Mongol territory. Kitbuqa sent a small party under his nephew to admonish Julian, but he was killed when the Crusader lord attacked it. This was guaranteed to call down a terrible vengeance on Julian's head. Kitbuqa sent a much larger force which sacked Sidon. Julian's rash actions had proved to be a very expensive mistake.

Islam tottered on the brink of irreversible disaster, standing precariously close to the edge of an abyss into which the Mongol hurricane threatened to blow them. At this seminal moment, fate intervened as it had done when the Mongols had been bursting into Europe over a decade before. Back then, the death of the Great Khan Ögedei had resulted in the Mongol army turning round and heading back east. Now, the situation was repeated when news arrived that Möngke was dead, passing away on 11 August 1159. The timing of this was crucial. Hülegü had no desire to be away from Karakorum when the jostling and manoeuvring for position took place there. So he headed back towards Mongolia for what would, in the event, be a particularly messy succession dispute. His army was left in the hands of his experienced and trusted general, Kitbuqa (not a Mongol but a Naiman), but it was denuded of many of its men.

Just as the army was weakened it was about to face its greatest trial of strength for many a year. An ultimatum had been sent to Cairo demanding that Qutuz, Sultan of the country, surrender to the

Mongols. His reply was, if nothing else, unambiguous. The unfortunate messengers carrying the demand were cut in half. Qutuz then led his army into Palestine to face up to the now inevitable battle. By going onto the offensive and moving into Syria to face the Mongols rather than wait for them in Egypt, Qutuz had decided that defence was the best form of attack. They made their way up along the Mediterranean coast, where they entered into discussions with the Crusader lords of the port of Acre, who decided that they would stay neutral and not hinder the Egyptian army as it passed close to the city. Their support was encouraged by offers from the Egyptians that they would be sold captured Mongol horses at reduced prices (good horses were always at a premium in the Crusader kingdoms.)

The Mongols and the Mamelukes moved closer together. The advance guard of either army met near Gaza on 26 August 1260. The Mamelukes had an emerging genius of their own on display. His name was Baibars, and he would later become one of the greatest of all medieval Muslim leaders. Baibars forced the Mongols to flee. As they did so, they were tirelessly harried by him. The Mongols were already struggling in Syria and, even as Kitbuqa moved forward, he also had to watch his back as Damascus was now in revolt. The two armies met at a place called Ain Jalut on 3 September. It was close to the place where David had met Goliath, an apposite omen for the battle that loomed (Ain Jalut was also known as 'The Springs of Goliath'), except that the supposedly invincible Mongols had lost much of their strength, and the Mamelukes were in the ascendancy.

Although Kitbuqa had taken up a strong defensive position, he was in fact very vulnerable, and Qutuz had a numerical advantage over the depleted Mongol army. There were perhaps 20,000 men in the Mameluke army against 12,000 in that of Kitbuqa.[23] Qutuz hid the bulk of his army in the hills and sent Baibars in to provoke the Mongols. In the initial fighting, a Mongol reconnaissance force was wiped out by Baibars. In the light of what followed, this seemingly subsidiary event may have had enormous consequences, as the Mongols do not appear to have realised how large the enemy's army was. Kitbuqa was about to have a nasty taste of his own medicine. Baibars continued to forge forward relentlessly. When he was driven back and hurried into the hills, ecstatic Mongol warriors followed him. At the perfect moment, the trap was sprung. Thousands of Mameluke warriors, hidden in the folds of the hills, suddenly swarmed out of their hiding places and enveloped the Mongol army. Lured into a trap and ambushed, the Mongols were undone by failing to recognise their own tactics.

Relying themselves on mounted archers, they were met by men who fought with the same weapons. Supremely disciplined, they were up against Mamelukes who themselves were used to drill and rigid obedience and who received and acted on orders even in the heat of battle. The Mongols were being out-thought and out-fought by an army in their own image. The situation was made worse by the fact that this Mongol army was more hotchpotch than most, with many of its most experienced Mongol warriors away with Hülegü.

Even at this point, though, the result was in doubt. Qutuz too proved himself a worthy warrior in the battle, at one stage removing his helmet to show his men that he was still alive and to encourage them to even greater efforts. By all accounts Kitbuqa fought heroically but inexorably as the tide turned against him. His fate was sealed when a contingent from Homs that had been recruited, deserted him at a crucial moment. Some of his men escaped, but he scorned flight. When he was at last captured, so the chroniclers say, he was almost alone. Kitbuqa, loyal servant of the *khans*, now a captive, remained defiant to the end. When told to submit to Qutuz, he looked him squarely in the eye and told him that he would not pay homage to a man who would soon be removed. His courage did him little good, as he was promptly executed.[24]

Many of his men died with him. A number sought refuge in some reeds nearby, but they were burned on the orders of Qutuz, and those who were found slaughtered. Prince Said, a Muslim fighting on the side of the Mongols, knelt before Qutuz and motioned to kiss his hand. The Sultan was having none of it, and kicked him violently in the mouth, ordering that he be beheaded at once. Ain Jalut was not quite the turning point it might have seemed. The Mongols would continue to expand for a time yet, and they were still a force in Syria, where they were able to hang onto some of their gains, even though it never became confidently assimilated into the Mongol empire. They returned there again in 1300, and it was conquered in its totality once more. Elsewhere, the conquests would continue. Further east in China, that most important of lands to Mongol khans, expansion would carry on unabated.

However, Ain Jalut did have an enormous symbolic significance. The Mongols could, after all, be beaten. The Mamelukes were clearly in the ascendancy in the Muslim world, and their rise would continue. Qutuz would, as Kitbuqa had allegedly predicted, lose his throne, and Baibars would rise to power in his place. Baibars had a long memory and took note of the fact that Christian Antioch had supported the Mongols. Years later, in 1268, he descended on the city, which was, after Jerusalem, the most crucial part of the Crusader kingdoms for nearly 200 years, and devastated it. It would be nowhere near as long before Damascus was restored to Islam, the city being entered by Qutuz within five days of the battle. The Mongol commanders there knew what was coming, and had already taken the opportunity to escape. The Muslims in the city, who hated their conquerors, rose up in a mob which destroyed Christian churches and property, for the part adherents of that faith had taken in the fall of the city. Collaborators were lynched and when soon after Qutuz made his triumphal entry into Damascus, yet more were hanged at his command. For Baibars in particular, the moment must have been sweet; he had started his life as a slave by being sold in the market at Damascus. Aleppo was taken back a month later.

Hülegü was incensed at the loss of Syria, and so, soon after it had been taken, sent back a force to retake Aleppo in December 1260. The Mameluke garrison that had been installed there abandoned it, and they retreated to join compatriots at Homs. The Mongols drew their army up for battle there, in the plain to the north of the great citadel. The field was cloaked in a blanket of fog. With the help of nature, the Mamelukes won another stunning victory. The Mongols withdrew back to Aleppo, which they themselves abandoned a few months later. It was said that they had received communications from the Crusaders of Outremer that a large Mameluke army was on its way to attack the city, and they fled rather than face slaughter.

The Mongol story was about to start a new chapter. The empire had started to weaken, not as the result of any external attacks against it, but because of a bitter internal division that resulted in its being split into several factions. Just like Rome, nearly a thousand years before, the once united empire was beginning to fragment, having grown too big for itself. The bigger the prize, the greater the temptation for powerful men to seize even more power, and the more desperate the gambles that men were prepared to take in return for such high stakes. Although territorial expansion might continue for some time yet, in actuality the Mongol empire had already reached high-water mark.

CHAPTER 8

A Family at War:
The Mongol Civil War
& the Division of the Empire
1261-1267

The greatest achievement of Genghis Khan and his immediate successors was not necessarily the conquest of the world, but rather the suppression of dynastic disputes that so marred many Central Asian steppe societies. It was this that gave the Mongol empire its relative longevity. This factor, so easily overlooked, ensured a continuity that was far from the norm. Genghis was certainly aware of the risks of internal divisions, and it was significant factor behind his decision to nominate the tactful and mild Ögedei as his successor. However, it was inevitable that a succession dispute would eventually arrive once the empire was so dispersed. The maxim that power corrupts is well known, and was certainly proved by the events that were about to hit the Mongol world. For so long they had seemed invincible, but now they were faced with the greatest enemy of all – themselves.

It was Möngke's death that precipitated a crisis. In the struggle for power that followed, two men fought for the ultimate award of the *khanate*, in other words, the whole Mongol empire. Meanwhile, two others fought for supremacy in the western part of it. The two men who tried to gain the *khanate* were Kublai and Arik-Böke, both brothers of Möngke. Kublai had long been marked for greatness by his grandfather Genghis, if Mongol propagandists are to be believed, and it was no surprise that he sought to take his late brother's place. However, Arik-Böke also desired the supreme prize. It is worth dwelling briefly on the nature of the succession process on the steppes. For one thing, strength of character in an erstwhile *khan* was important. Warrior races like the Mongols require warlords to lead them, men of vigour, leaders, men most of all tried and tested in the art of war. Mongol warriors valued plunder above most other things, and were therefore likely to gravitate towards those who appeared to offer the greatest opportunities of getting it. Perhaps because of this, it was by no means inevitable, or even likely, that succession would pass from father to son. It had of course done so in Genghis and Ögedei's case but Genghis had lived, by the standards of the time, to a reasonable old age. As a result, when he died his sons were tried and tested quantities. However, later successions tended to be 'brother to brother' and this was more in line with what happened in other steppe societies.[1] The very vagueness of the line of succession became the bane of Mongol constitutional issues. To have a claim to be *khan*, one need only be a prominent member of Genghis' immediate bloodline, the so-called Golden Kin. Such flaws were to prove one of the greatest challenges to the Mongol empire, and one that it never fully coped with.

Kublai, after Genghis the most famous of *khans*, was not born to be great. As a secondary son of Tolui, himself the fourth and youngest of Genghis' sons, he appeared to be far distant from the throne when he was born. Perhaps this explains his exaggerated interest in China above all other parts of the Mongol world. As he was given estates here when he was a young man, it would be understandable if he chose to develop his interests exclusively in the region, given the fact that he cannot have expected to play a wider part in the Mongol empire. Now, however, accidents of fate had changed all this for the better. Kublai and China had long been acquainted with each other. As long ago as 1236, Kublai had been given estates in the country. He then began a life-long love affair with the region. Unlike some of his predecessors, he was keenly interested in education, and was seduced by the knowledge of eastern philosophers and scientists. In 1242, he had even converted to Buddhism. Thereafter he became well acquainted with the tenets and principles of a number of different religions. Like most Mongol *khans* he would practise religious toleration.

It was in China that he came into contact with some important men, who were to shape his philosophy and his future career. One of the most influential was a Buddhist monk by the name of Liu Ping-chung, who became a regular adviser as to how he should govern his Chinese lands. He was a man of many talents, and someone who, in the West a couple of centuries later, might have been termed a 'Renaissance Man'. He was a calligrapher, poet, artist, mathematician and astronomer. He even helped set up a new calendar for the Mongols. He was also versed in the beliefs of Confucianism, Buddhism and Taoism, and was a key adviser to Kublai for decades.

As early as 1253, Kublai had been given a prominent role by Möngke in the invasion of independent territory in China called Ta-li. It was strategically important, being astride the trade routes to Burma and

South-East Asia, now on the Mongols' horizon. Ambassadors were sent by the Mongols, demanding that Ta-li surrender. They were promptly executed. The campaign that had followed then had exhibited much that was typical of Mongol warfare. It had been a three-pronged approach and, at one stage, Kublai had ordered his soldiers to cross a river using blown-up sacks as makeshift rafts. The campaign had ended in success. The main town of Ta-li was the last to fall. Although the campaign had been hard-fought, even bloody (a factor that might have been expected to whip up Mongol bloodlust) there would be no major massacre once the town was taken. Only the unfortunate officials who had ordered the death of the Mongol ambassadors at the start of the campaign had been executed, an unavoidable consequence of their blunt and rather foolish actions. But as a result of both his military success and his prudent actions in the aftermath, Kublai's stock was on the way up.

Later, in 1258, he had led troops in campaigns against the Song in the south as the Mongols sought to continue their subjugation of China. This was a fertile area on which much of the region depended for its food. Its loss to the ruling dynasty would have enormous repercussions for the local population. The Song also held the biggest city in the world at the time, Linan (now Hangzhou) which had a population of one and a half million people. This would be a sedentary campaign, where the Mongols' cavalry strength would be of little use. Instead, Kublai would rely on Chinese infantry from the north turned against their enemies in the south, frequent opponents in the past. Möngke had divided the invasion force into three, once more following the traditional Mongol tactic of a multi-pronged assault. One of these was led by Kublai, who had his base in the fabled city of Xanadu, later immortalised by the nineteenth-century poet Samuel Taylor Coleridge.[2] At one time, Möngke had suggested that Kublai should not go on the expedition: Kublai suffered from gout for much of his life and his health was unsound. Kublai was indignant and would have none of this.

Möngke himself had led the expedition as a whole on what would be his last expedition. After it was launched in 1259, the campaign turned into a painful, hard slog. The great fortress of Chongqing held the Mongols up for weeks. That age-old enemy of armies – disease – struck down Mongol soldiers in their thousands. The heat of the sun was scorching and, to escape it, Möngke had moved into the hills. Whilst he was there, he probably over-indulged himself with alcohol, a natural Mongol reaction to escaping the trials and tribulations of war for a time. Shortly after, he was taken ill. It was probably cholera, though some writers said he had been wounded by an arrow. For a few days he lingered on in agony, gripped by unbearable cramps. Then, mercifully, he died. His body was taken back to Karakorum where it lay in state, then across the rolling hills of Mongolia back to the sacred mountain, Bhurkan Khaldun, where he was buried somewhere close to Genghis and other family members. Great care was taken as always to ensure that his resting place was kept a secret.

Kublai was surprisingly slow in his reaction to the news. Recent Mongol successions had been messy. On Genghis' death there had been a division of the empire, albeit on amicable terms as far as anyone could see. But then, on the death of Ögedei, it had taken years for Kuyuk to be elected. It was widely believed that Kuyuk and Batu, the *khan* of the Golden Horde, were on the verge of coming to blows. When Kuyuk died, many were convinced that Batu was behind his demise. And then, when Möngke was elected, there had soon after been a coup that had been put down with the spilling of much blood. There had, then, been an ongoing deterioration in the straightforwardness of the succession process, with each roll of the generational dice. Despite this, Kublai stayed in China, carrying on his campaign in the region which he loved the most. For several weeks he hesitated whilst those opposed to his succession planned their next move. It has been suggested that he perhaps felt that he needed to win a victory in China, to emphasise his credentials for the major role that he sought, but this does not ring true. He already had major victories in China to his credit. It appears rather that he underestimated the level of opposition to his succession.

It was now winter, time to rest up and recoup depleted reserves of strength. No time to hold a *kuriltai* to discuss a successor, Kublai reasoned. That would have to wait until the spring, a delay that would give rival claimants time to manoeuvre for position. Möngke's death left Kublai in a difficult position, as news of it would soon spread amongst the Song, and they would be encouraged to make greater efforts to resist the invaders. For the time being, he decided to push on with the campaign, and pretend that the news of Möngke's demise was gossip.

Kublai then pushed on to the mighty Yellow River, vast and seemingly endless. Here he was faced by the great Song fortress of Wuchang. He laid siege to it, but seemingly not closely enough, as Song reinforcements managed to evade the normally iron grip of the Mongols and push on into the city. The commander of Wuchang, a well known warrior by the name of Jia Sidao, made a secret approach to Kublai offering to agree terms. The conditions he suggested were that Kublai should leave Wuchang in peace and that, in the future, the border of the Song lands should be on the Yellow River. This was a rash act on Jia Sidao's part, as he had far exceeded his authority in making the offer. Nor did it do any immediate good, for Kublai rejected the terms in peremptory fashion. However, he did withdraw, for there were greater immediate issues to be resolved. He had no desire to agree to a boundary for the Song lands, as he wished to return to conquer them in the future. But for now he had to turn his eyes westwards if he wanted to secure his position, as there were clearly problems with his planned succession.

Fortunately for Kublai he had a spy in the Mongol camp further west in the form of his wife. She had sent him word that his younger brother Arik-Böke had been collecting troops, and was even now moving towards China. It did not take a genius to work out why. Arik-Böke was an ambitious and traditional Mongol, with lands back in the Mongolian homeland. Kublai meanwhile had become much more interested in China. Whilst his back was turned, Arik-Böke attempted to take the *khanate* for himself. Soon after, Arik-Böke sent messengers to Kublai in an attempt to reassure him. The effect that they had was precisely the opposite of that which was desired. They were shifty and uncomfortable when Kublai questioned them on Arik-Böke's plans. Their protestations that he was not after the throne for himself were so stumbling that they confirmed to Kublai that this was exactly what he was up to. It also confirmed that China was no place for Kublai to be at this delicate time. It was time to head back to Mongolia to assert his rights.

Messengers sped to and fro between the brothers. Arik-Böke tried to call a *kuriltai* without Kublai being present. It was so obviously an attempt to ensure that he was elected with Kublai *in absentia* that several important figures refused to attend, denying that the proposed meeting had any kind of legitimacy. Then Arik-Böke asked Kublai to join him so that they could mourn Möngke together. Kublai smelt a rat and refused to comply. Instead he started to look for Möngke's army. It was staying safely out of the way in Hsi-Hsia, looking to see how events would pan out before committing itself. Arik-Böke now saw that he could vacillate no longer. Throwing off all pretence, he declared himself *khan*. He had the support, so he said, of the Mongol leaders in Persia and Russia as well as Chagatai's *khanate* in Central Asia. He bluntly declared that Kublai's claims to succede were not recognised by anyone of importance and should therefore be ignored.

The old adage states that fortune favours the brave, but that is not always the case if courageous moves lack wisdom. Arik-Böke had been both rash and presumptuous. The thing that grated most with many Mongols was his complete overturning of Mongol tradition. In many ways a conventional and conservative people, a number of Mongols were turned against Arik-Böke by the fact that he was rewriting the rules of election in his own interests. As Arik-Böke claimed to be a traditionalist, this made him look even more duplicitous. Neither was he factually correct in his statements regarding those he claimed to have supporting him. Relationships between the Mongols in Persia, led by Hülegü, and those of the Golden Horde were becoming increasingly tense. It was not likely that the leaders of both factions would support Arik-Böke in his claims. Hülegü, as we have seen, had already moved himself back from Syria to better intervene in events as necessary. These rash acts by Arik-Böke forced Kublai's hand. He declared himself *khan* in opposition to Arik-Böke though he had to do this at Xanadu rather than Karakorum. War between the two was now inevitable.

The setting was appropriate. Xanadu was Kublai's creation. Over time, the Chinese influence over him had become increasingly significant. He felt that to be considered a real player in Chinese politics, a man must live in a city, not a *ger*. Karakorum was far away, it was not his anyway and it was small. Something greater was needed. Not all Mongols had been happy when he first started to build his city at the site he had identified at Xanadu in 1256. Traditionalists tutted to themselves at this most un-Mongol development. Even Möngke had initially been suspicious; he probably interpreted Kublai's plan to build a city as excessively ambitious, though he was talked round before he died.

The city was undeniably based on a Chinese model, which fuelled the angst felt by Mongol traditionalists. It was divided up into several parts. The outer portion was in the shape of a square surrounded by a wall of earth up to eighteen feet high. There were six gates in total and six towers on each side of the wall. The population, which was perhaps 100,000 in total,[3] lived in this section in the main. Then came the inner city, the more prestigious area, where Kublai and his entourage lived. This was surrounded by brick walls with four towers on each side. The Imperial Palace of Kublai was built here, erected on a platform of earth to lift it out of the marshes that were found in the area. The walls were decorated with lavish paintings of birds and beasts, an artistic reminder of the wildness that the Mongols were once so close to. Around it were government buildings, the workplace of Kublai's officials who ran his domains for him.

The buildings, although perhaps not the grandest in China, were certainly luxuriant when matched against the trappings of a Mongol *ger*. The palace walls were generously dotted with marble, there were coloured tiles and exotic decorations on the roof. Near to the city Kublai had ordered a hunting park to be set up enclosed by another wall of earth. Here, like a true Mongol, Kublai could engage in his favourite pastime. If this was not built as an emperor's city, it was certainly a fitting place of residence for such a man.

The *kuriltai* that considered Kublai's claims was held at Xanadu on 5 May, 1260. The formalities were scrupulously observed. As tradition demanded, Kublai was offered the *khanate* twice and refused, but at the third time of asking he accepted the nomination. Given the fact that the meeting was held in the heart of China, Kublai's strongest powerbase, the result was inevitable, but it was not truly decisive as the vote was only attended by a small fraction of the Mongol world. Kublai sent news of his election further afield. The self-proclaimed Great Khan sent out a proclamation in a style that a modern politician would recognise as part of an election manifesto. He promised that he would rule his people wisely and that he would reduce taxes. It was his target audience though that was of greatest note, for it was an unmistakable plea for the Chinese to support him as the provider of law and order in their troubled lands. It was not addressed to any great extent to Mongol traditionalists and this led to a problem that was to dog him throughout his reign: was he more interested in the Chinese than the Mongols? Some conservative Mongols believed it to be so, a perception that was to continue to cause Kublai difficulties for years to come.

An ambassador was sent to the Song in China telling them of the result of the *kuriltai*. As soon as he set foot in Song territory he was thrown into prison. He was to stay there for sixteen years. It showed how little Kublai counted, for at the time he was outside of his immediate environs, and he must have been infuriated to know that there was nothing he could do to punish the Song for their failure to recognise him, given distractions elsewhere. However, it did not stop him from sending a scathing warning to them in 1261 promising them retribution in the future. It would be some time in coming but Kublai, like any good Mongol *khan,* would not forget.

A period of phoney war followed within the Mongol territories, with neither man seemingly wanting to be held responsible for striking the first blow against his brother. Rather then erupting, matters simmered slowly to a head. Arik-Böke moved on Karakorum and took it over – an important symbolic move even though true power no longer vested in Mongolia itself. In response, Kublai sent a small force under Abishqa, a distant relative, to ensure the support of the Chagataids in Central Asia. Unfortunately for Kublai, Abishqa's party was captured by Arik-Böke's men. When shortly afterwards the first skirmish of the war took place – a low-level affair that ended in a minor victory for Kublai – the men captured en route to the Chagataids were summarily executed. The gloves were now off.

Kublai held the upper hand in a strategic sense. Karakorum and Mongolia relied on supplies from China to a large extent. This was Kublai's backyard, so he could strangle Arik-Böke's supply lines from that direction. He further strengthened his hand by winning influence on the borders of the Chagataid lands to the west of Mongolia. Unable to support itself from its own internal provisioning, Mongolia turned to Siberia to scratch around for supplies from there. This gave Kublai a substantial advantage, which he was able to obtain great benefit from. Arik-Böke soon found himself cut off and, in desperation, went through the motions of paying homage to Kublai. He apologised for his presumption in seizing the khanate, but even as he did so, he carried on the fight. Kublai, anyhow, was not fooled. He continued to build up his armies in preparation for the battle that he knew must now come. Large numbers of men were added to his forces and substantial volumes of supplies were built up in China. Arik-Böke came off worse in two major battles that followed, in which there was a large loss of life. Defeated, he retreated towards the thick forests and jagged hills of Siberia.

Arik-Böke had also been let down badly by Alghu, the ruler of the Chagataid lands, who had been collecting taxes in his territories to hand over to Arik-Böke, whom he had supported in his claim to be Great Khan and had therefore recognised as his lord. However, he then refused to hand the taxes collected over, realising that the authority of Arik-Böke was weak and that he was in danger of backing the wrong horse. When envoys were sent to Alghu by Arik-Böke to convince him to forward the taxes, he first of all prevaricated, and then had them executed.

Whilst Kublai and Arik-Böke fought for supremacy, two other Mongols far to the west took their sides, in the hope of gaining maximum personal benefit from doing so. Batu was now dead, the arch-schemer having been unable to outwit the greatest enemy, death himself, who had finally caught up with him in 1255. However, his brother Berke took on his role as leader of the Golden Horde (after two short reigns by Sartaq and Ulaghchi which jointly only lasted about a year) and inherited his fighting spirit. He was soon in conflict with Hülegü, fresh from his triumphs in Persia and Syria. Berke took the side of Arik-Böke and Hülegü that of Kublai and the Mongol empire began to implode. In the course of his victories so far, Hülegü had taken parts of Georgia, Azerbaijan and Rum (modern Turkey) and in doing so, he was getting dangerously close to the patrimony of Berke. Genghis had bequeathed very specific instructions to Jochi, his first-born, that he was to head as far to the west as he was able, and conquer as many lands as he could take. Once territories there were conquered, they would be his, and would, on his death, pass down through his immediate bloodline. As Jochi's grandson, the lands in the west, so Berke felt, were his and not Hülegü's. His definition of the west included the lands that Hülegü had recently acquired. Unsurprisingly, Hülegü's did not. The two men were on a collision course.

There were other reasons why Hülegü and Berke were at each other's throats. Berke was a Muslim and he had been far from pleased when the fabled Islamic city of Baghdad had been put to the torch, and the Caliph had had the life trampled out of him by Mongol horses. It was an outrage against his faith. He was far from happy that Hülegü seemed to favour Christians. It is ironic that the Mongols, rather than subduing those civilisations that they came into contact with, were being subsumed into those self-same cultures.

Histories of the Mongols tend to concentrate on major campaigns and big events, but there were other processes of long-term assimilation taking place. Nowhere is this better illustrated than with the story of the Golden Horde, the Mongols' greatest success story in terms of longevity. After the dramatic events that had seen the fall of Russia (or much if it anyway) some twenty years before, the process of enforcing Mongol rule continued, though often in more subtle, non-military ways. Russian warlords were encouraged to act as clients of the Mongols, the most famous of these being Alexander Nevskii of Vladimir. He had received his position as a gift from the Mongols, in return for which he offered his loyal service. Alexander was able to use the security this brought him to fight successful military campaigns against the Teutonic Knights and the Swedes. Some might view this as opportunistic collaboration, but a more generous – and realistic – interpretation is that this was merely making the most of the inevitable. The inherent weakness of the alternative approach was graphically illustrated by the fate of his brother, who rebelled against the so-called 'Tartar Yoke' and suffered exile as a result, though this could have been worse: a co-conspirator Mikhail of Chernigov paid for his actions with his life.

The 'Tartar Yoke' has become part of the Mongol myth, and an oft-repeated phrase in any history of the Mongols in Russia. What is less well known, is that the phrase has a literal interpretation attached to it. Russian princes were summoned regularly to the camp of the *khan* of the Golden Horde. Here, they had to go through humiliating ceremonies of obeisance. They would have to walk through two lines of fire, a symbol in Mongol lore of purification. Then they would have to walk underneath a yoke held up in the air and prostrate themselves before the *khan*. Most of Russia was powerless to do much about this humiliation, other than to manipulate personal advantage from it. Recognising the need to protect itself – as much against Alexander Nevskii as against the Mongols – the great city of Novgorod volunteered tribute to the Mongols. Unlike China and Persia, where annexation was the name of the game, the Mongols were prepared to exploit large parts of Russia by the imposition of taxes and tributes on individual principalities, especially in forested areas which were of limited use to the Mongols in terms of pasturage for their herds. The power of the Golden Horde, now headed by Berke, continued to expand.

Because of his religious sensibilities Berke had come into contact with an unlikely ally. Baibars, the great Mameluke warrior, had already shown himself to be an astute warrior; now he proved himself to be equally as adept an opportunist. After his part in the crucial victory of Ain Jalut he sought after the governorship of Aleppo, as a reward for his endeavours, but unwisely Qutuz chose not to give it to him. It was a fatal mistake. Baibars, as well as being a first-class military tactician, was also an ambitious man who would stop at nothing to fulfil his objectives. On October 1260, Baibars went out riding with Qutuz, his nominal lord, when, at a prearranged signal, the Sultan was struck down by would-be assassins. Baibars quickly showed what part he had played in the scheme by finishing off the wounded Qutuz with an arrow.

For centuries the throne of Egypt had been the plaything of ambitious men, and Baibars now followed in the footsteps of tradition. He made himself Sultan and soon began to plot to protect the security of his kingdom. He saw great potential in an unexpected direction. He sought to take advantage of Mongol disunity by contacting Berke with a view to entering into an alliance with him. The Mamelukes in Egypt were in great need of allies. Hülegü had been seeking closer ties with the Crusaders in Palestine and that, Baibars felt, could upset the balance of power in this strategically critical region. Although the Muslims of the Levant had proved themselves more than a match for the Crusaders for decades, they still had respect for their fighting skills, and a match with the Mongols presented a worrying prospect for Egypt. An alliance with disaffected Mongols would help no end in terms of counterbalancing such a move.

Baibars still had large parts of Syria to re-conquer, but before he set off to do so, he sent a message to Berke urging him to seek revenge against those who had stained the reputation of Islam so heinously amongst his brothers. His approaches met with rapprochement. By early 1262 Baibars and Berke were exchanging ambassadors, through an unexpected third party – the recently restored Byzantine emperor in Constantinople – Michael Paleologus. These arrangements demonstrate the complexity of thirteenth-century power politics perfectly. On the one hand, a Muslim Sultan allied himself with an Islamic Mongol, ably assisted by a Christian power in Byzantium. On the other, there was another large grouping of Mongols seeking friendly relations with powers from other parts of Christendom. The medieval world was not black and white: it was coloured in with liberal doses of grey. Just to prove the point, Venice allied itself with the Golden Horde and their allies, whilst Genoa threw in its lot with the Mongols in Persia.

These shenanigans encouraged Baibars to move into Iraq, though he himself did not lead the expedition that advanced towards the country. A small army moved towards Baghdad accompanying a would-be new Caliph to be installed in the city. The Mongols in Iraq set out with 5,000 cavalry to face them, but first of all they moved on the city of Anbar, which they suspected might rise in support of this enterprise from Egypt. They broke into the city and slew indiscriminately. Then they moved on to face up to the Egyptian force that had had the temerity to move against them. The battle that followed was little short of a rout, with the Mongols winning an easy victory. In the chaos the Caliph was lost, never to be seen again. It was easy to think after Ain Jalut that the war would now go irrevocably against the Mongols, but such was clearly not the case.

Berke had to ensure that he demonstrated due cause for going to war with other Mongols. This was no easy step for any man to take, and he had to resort to traditional Mongol reasoning to gain legitimacy for his planned coup against Hülegü. Two of his senior generals had been serving under Hülegü, and mysteriously disappeared whilst they were there. Berke asserted that they had been murdered on Hülegü's orders, and he vowed to avenge them. A force was gathered together to bring Hülegü to book: command of this was conferred by Berke on his nephew Nogai. Berke could not allocate as many resources as he would have liked to for the enterprise, as he was forced to put down a rebellion from Suzdalia, one of the Mongol-held territories in Russia. This uprising had come at an inopportune moment, but Nogai nevertheless crossed the mountain barrier of the Caucasus towards Persia, initially winning a battle against Hülegü's armies on 11 November, 1262. Nogai then advanced towards Shirvan, but Hülegü moved up to meet him. Hülegü's force on this occasion outnumbered that of Nogai, and forced the invading army back over the mountains where they continued to chase in hot pursuit, led by Hülegü's son, Abaka.

However, Abaka's men were overconfident of their success. Berke had put down the revolt in Suzdalia, which meant that he now had more men available to reinforce his efforts against Abaka. The news clearly did not reach Abaka's ears. His men were busy enjoying themselves in Nogai's recently deserted camp when they were attacked by Berke. Abaka's army was caught off guard, quite likely because they had over-indulged on the alcohol and women they had found in the camp. A terrifying rout ensued. Many of those under attack in the camp hurried as fast as their mounts would take them to the nearby River Terek. It was frozen over by the winter ice but not strongly enough to take the weight of the panic-stricken Mongols. The ice shattered like thin plate glass beneath them, and many of the army were drowned in the frigid waters. Abaka was one of the few to make good his escape, and he made his way back post haste to Hülegü. So great was the defeat that Hülegü withdrew his men back to Tabriz.

Hülegü had in the meantime been seeking new allies of his own. Baibars had been advancing into Palestine, burning the church in the sacred town of Nazareth whilst he was there, and destroying the farms that provided much of the food supply – for the major city of the Crusader kingdom at Acre. Hülegü hoped that this would encourage the Christians to enter into an alliance with him, and had sent envoys off to Rome to plead his case with the Papacy. It was interesting how the times were changing. Previous communications from the Mongols to the West had been couched in the most peremptory and patronising terms. They had demanded that the kings and popes of the West surrender themselves to the Mongols and become their subjects. The message that Hülegü now sent was far more conciliatory, almost an approach seeking an alliance amongst equals, something unthinkable under previous regimes. However, this new approach was no more successful than the former, merely leading to a non-committed response from the Pope, who congratulated Hülegü on the diplomatic nature of his overtures.

Despite the battles between Mongols and their kinsmen, the war to conquer Iraq led by Hülegü still continued apace. The Mongols assaulted the important city of Mosul, defended by its emir Salih. A fierce battle followed, with the Mongols increasingly frustrated in their attempts to take it. At one stage eighty Mongol warriors managed to break onto the battlements, but they were overwhelmed, decapitated and their heads were shot back over the walls with catapults. The fury of the defence guaranteed a shocking fate for the city, should it be taken. As time passed, Mosul's position became desperate. A carrier pigeon, the favoured method of communication for Islamic armies, was despatched with a message from a would-be relieving army that was coming to its rescue. However, when it had the poor judgment to land on a Mongol siege engine, it was seized along with its information. This meant that when the relieving army drew near, it was attacked by Mongol forces waiting in ambush and virtually annihilated. The Mongols then used subterfuge to try to take the city, dressing up in the clothes of their slain Muslim enemies. Many inside the city were caught out. Rushing out from the city to greet them as liberators, they were slaughtered by the Mongols.

The city still held out, but it was now without hope of relief. Accordingly, the defenders sought terms. The Mongol commander offered to send Salih on to Hülegü, where he would be granted a full pardon if the city surrendered. When Salih left the city on 25 June 1262, he was led into the Mongol camp preceded by dancers and musicians. The mood was festive, even exuberant, but it was an inappropriate greeting, for on arriving in the camp he was seized.

The duplicity of the Mongols outside the city was then revealed for all to see. They moved into Mosul, now off its guard, and slaughtered everyone they found there. Salih was sent off to Hülegü where his fate would be decided. It would undoubtedly be a terrible one, as the Mongols once more found an innovatively savage way of killing a detested enemy. Salih was stripped naked and tied in the skin of a newly-slaughtered sheep. As it rotted around him, so too did he decay. It took him a month to die. His son, a three year old boy, was taken back to Mosul where he was cut in half, a portion of his tiny body being hung either side of the Tigris as a grim and terrifying warning to anyone who dared resist the Mongols.

In the meantime, further east, Kublai had suffered a setback. Things had initially gone well for him. When Arik-Böke fled to Siberia he left Mongolia open for Kublai to move in, which he duly did. By taking the symbolic and traditional heartlands of the Mongol people, Kublai would greatly strengthen his grip on the *khanate*. However, when he was seemingly on the verge of decisive and ultimate triumph in the war against Arik-Böke, victory was pulled from his grasp by rebellion in China. Kublai had an ally – or so he thought – in China, in the form of a powerful warlord called Li Tan, but he now proceeded to betray his lord. Li Tan had been an ally of Kublai for several years. Kublai had recently sent him money to fund actions against recalcitrant Song enemies. However, these were campaigns of a defensive nature, as Kublai did not want to encourage Li Tan to get too powerful by going onto the offensive. Kublai realised, as a Chinese warlord, that Li Tan's loyalty could not necessarily be relied upon, but he had so far proved himself a trustworthy partner. Throughout 1261, regular reports had been received from Li Tan of his victories over the Song, seemingly confirming that he was a man who could be trusted.

Whilst Kublai was diverted by his battles against Arik-Böke, Li Tan seized the moment to rebel with the help of Song soldiers. There were several warning signals that called Kublai's attention to the fact that something was wrong. Li Tan had been required to send Kublai horses in his campaign against Arik-Böke, but failed to do so. His son had been in Kublai's camp, essentially a hostage for his good behaviour, and he had slipped away, the clearest sign possible that trouble was brewing. These events collectively presaged open rebellion against Mongol rule. Mongols around the Chinese lands controlled by Li Tan were slaughtered and their goods taken. Kublai had no option but to turn east in early 1262 and put down the rebellion, being forced in the process to leave Arik-Böke and give him time to recover for the time being. The rebellion was crushed with relative ease. The outcomes of initial battles against Li Tan were decisively in favour of Kublai's army. Li Tan was forced to retreat. His generals, believing him beaten, approached Kublai and pleaded for their lives, saying that they had been duped by Li Tan. Atypically their pleas were accepted – in the past, most such treason would have been punished with death as the men had proved themselves unreliable – and their lives were safe.

By August 1262, the war was over. Li Tan, seeing that he had lost and was without hope of redemption, tried to drown himself, but was saved from death by Mongols who pulled him out so that they should not be deprived of the pleasure of killing him themselves. Li Tan suffered the fate of other great men by being sewn up in a sack and trampled to death by Mongol horses. But the distraction did buy Arik-Böke some valuable time as he garnered his strength. In the meantime, Kublai pondered on the lessons he had learned in China. He had emerged from the rebellion fairly well, but believed that he needed to set up a ministry solely responsible for the prosecution of war and separate from the civil administration. This Ministry was accordingly set up, an important development in Mongol bureaucracy. Underpinning this move was the fact that Kublai no longer believed that he could trust the Chinese to support him, and he therefore needed Mongols in positions of authority in his absence.

Kublai demonstrated that he was uncomfortable with being forced to rely on the Chinese by several key policy decisions. Society was to be divided into four estates. The paramount estate, naturally enough, was reserved for the Mongols themselves, but the next lowest was composed of Central Asians whom Kublai felt could be trusted more than the

Chinese could. The northern Chinese were in the next group and the southern in the lowest. Key positions in the administration would be barred to the peoples in the two lowest estates, that is those of Chinese descent. It was an interesting but not unique approach: not that different to that adopted by the British in the Indian Raj centuries later, when a small foreign ruling class ruled over a much more numerous group of indigenous subjects. Although understandable given Kublai's position as the head of an invading army, it did nothing to win the hearts and minds of the Chinese. It also contrasted with the Mongol approach elsewhere, for example in Persia, where local officials had been retained to provide an element of continuity.

Kublai's enforced return to China left the way open for Arik-Böke to punish Alghu for his treachery whilst his rival was distracted. He sent an army under one of his leading commanders, Khara Bhuka, to deal with him, but it was routed in battle against the untrustworthy *khan*. Delighted in their victory, the forces of Alghu celebrated too soon, as they themselves were soundly beaten soon after and Alghu was forced to flee for his life. However, this did not really improve Arik-Böke's position at all. He continued to advance against the retreating armies of Alghu, meaning that his supply lines were more extended than ever, as he was pulled further from his base. Although Alghu was beaten, he was not crushed, and his men still blocked access to supplies to the south as firmly as they had ever done. Kublai's grip on China was solid too. Arik-Böke managed to make his position still worse by cruelly punishing enemy captives, even some who were not proven supporters of Alghu. This alienated much needed support from him. His position deteriorated so markedly that Alghu built up his strength again and prepared to drive Arik-Böke out of the areas he had conquered.

The war was now running towards its unavoidable conclusion. Kublai's strategic advantages had given him an overwhelming edge. Arik-Böke and his men were desperately short of provisions and even lower on hope. He had gambled all on the toss of a dice and lost. Key supporters deserted him, and in the end he decided that he had no alternative but to sue for peace. And so, in Kublai's tent, one day in 1264 a moving scene was played out. Arik-Böke crossed his brother's threshold with great humility. The writer Rashid al-Din, not a fan of Arik-Böke, has Kublai wistfully asking with a tear in his eye, which of these two brothers had been in the wrong in this protracted dispute. Arik-Böke answered that he had been in the right at the first but that Kublai was now. The two men then gave the appearance that they had been reconciled. That may have appeared to have been the end of the matter but it was not. A civil war in which thousands had died was no minor matter, and great blame rested on the shoulders of those responsible for it. There were men in the camp, some of them powerful, whose kin had been killed at the command of Arik-Böke. The following day, Arik-Böke was placed under arrest. An inquisition followed. Ten of Arik-Böke's key advisers were executed for their part in the war. For the time being, Arik-Böke himself survived, Kublai unable to bring himself to order the death of one of his own bloodline.

Kublai felt the weight of the decision that loomed greatly. He asked Hülegü and Berke to come and advise him on the matter, as well as Alghu, ruler of the Chagataid lands. None of them came. The first two were too busy fighting each other, whilst the third still felt insecure. It was a strange situation. Everyone knew that Berke was known to support Arik-Böke, and Alghu had too at one time. Kublai was on his own in making this particular decision.

Soon after, the decision was made for him. Arik-Böke was suddenly taken ill and succumbed to his illness quickly. Of course the exertions of the past few years must have taken their toll on a man now in middle age, but the timing of all this was, to say the least, fortunate as far as Kublai was concerned. Arik-Böke was, by all accounts, a man in good health with no known previous serious illness. The evidence is entirely circumstantial, but it is impossible to avoid the suspicion that Arik-Böke was murdered on Kublai's command, saving the *khan* the agony and embarrassment of a public trial and execution.

This was a time for the deaths of great men. Hülegü was still severely stretched in Persia and the surrounding lands, trying to tighten his grip there. A rebellion in Mosul diverted his attention. Hülegü could have done with help, but Kublai still had problems of his own to contend with. Kublai's defeat of Arik-Böke in 1264 had merely meant that another man, Kaidu, had taken his place. Kublai could not afford any reinforcements for Hülegü at the current time, so the war in the west went on without outside support. The exertions of Hülegü had worn him out. On 8 February 1265, Hülegü died. He was buried soon after on an island in a lake, along with beautiful young maidens who were interred alive with him to look after his needs in the next world. Hülegü might have been a friend of the Christians, but personally it was clear that he held age-old pagan beliefs. Just four months later, his Nestorian wife, Doquz Khatan, expired too. This was a significant death for she, as a Christian, had encouraged him to support members of that faith during her life, and the loss of her influence would harm their cause.

Hülegü's army lived on, now under the command of his son Abaka.

News of Hülegü's death reached Berke and he decided to take advantage of the situation and go onto the offensive. He invaded Georgia with an army allegedly 200,000 strong.[4] Abaka moved up to meet him, and there was an initial skirmish after which Abaka withdrew. The two armies stared at each other on either side of a river, seeking to gain an advantage, catch the enemy off guard and strike. However, the gods intervened once more, for Berke died in the middle of the campaign. His place was taken by Batu's grandson, Möngke-Timür. He was far more conciliatory than Berke, and was a supporter of Kublai in the ongoing war, as was Abaka. Although the alliance with Baibars was continued, Mongkë-Timür did not have territorial ambitions in Persia, and so the war between the Golden Horde and the supporters of Hülegü therefore came to an end. The two opposing Mongol powers there had fought themselves to a standstill, and the war ended as much as anything through exhaustion.

To complete the circle, Alghu too died soon after. His position was an odd one, having initially been installed by Arik-Böke but then changing sides and throwing his lot in with Kublai. Kublai was the only man left standing, and was able at last to cement his position. These deaths, even those of allies, wiped the slate clean for Kublai, and he could build new alliances to strengthen his once shaky hold over the empire. He would turn his eyes to the east once more, to China where he held great estates and where his interests truly lay. Greatness was ahead of him; however, it would be some time in coming, and he would have his hands full keeping Kaidu in check. What is more, he had still not been confirmed as the Great Khan by a *kuriltai* of all the Mongol people, a question mark over his legitimacy that would be hard to erase.

Despite Kublai's rise to power, which continued on an upwards plane, the days of the Mongol empire were already numbered. The internal divisions of these years of bitter intra-family dispute had weakened its structure irretrievably. They were, though, not the cause of the decline, but a symptom of it. Steppe society had always been faced with the danger of internal dispute and dynastic division. Genghis had managed to stop the trend for a while, but he could not reverse it anymore than Canute could turn back the tides of the ocean. In fact, the new source of tension, Kaidu, proved to have the tenacity of the most stubborn of limpets. At the time of the civil war he was a young man, less than thirty years old. He was grandson of Ögedei and therefore from a different branch of the dynasty: no doubt Kaidu's supporters argued that as an older brother of Tolui, Ögedi came from the more senior branch of the family. In his earlier years he had enjoyed the kind of success teenagers can usually only dream about. By the time that he was sixteen years old he had his own landholding 1,500 miles away from Karakorum. In later life he became a major thorn in the flesh of Kublai.

He also had a larger-than-life daughter (apparently literally). Her name was Aiyurek and it was said that this Amazon was stronger than any man in the kingdom. Kaidu gave her permission to choose any man she wanted as a husband. She said that she would have none unless she could find a man who could out-wrestle her. None could, and defeat would prove expensive, for she insisted that if any suitor wanted to fight for her hand then he would have to wager 100 horses as his forfeit if he should lose. Apparently she collected 10,000 horses as prizes in these fights. She must have taken after her father, for Kaidu was possessed of both ruthless determination and fierce ambition. When Kublai had made his bid for the throne, Kaidu threw in his lot with Arik-Böke. When Kublai commanded him to attend the *kuriltai* that elected him *khan*, Kaidu made the feeblest of excuses for his non-attendance. From then on, Kublai marked his card.

But Kaidu was no fool. He knew that Kublai's real interests lay in the east and therefore he headed in the other direction. In the greatest of ironies, he used traditional Mongol tactics, raids from out of nowhere in supremely organised fashion, to discomfort his fellow Mongols. Year after year he nibbled away at lands in Central Asia and Persia, the patrimonies of the successors of Chagatai and Hülegü. Eventually Kublai sent one of his advisors, Baraq, to bring order to the Chagataid lands. Central Asia was crucial: it controlled the vital trade routes from east to west and back again, and was therefore vital in controlling a significant chunk of the empire's wealth. Kaidu was having none of this attempt to bring him to book. He led an army against Baraq and won a stunning victory. Then, knowing his limitations, he proposed peace to Kublai.

From now on, the empire was increasingly divided amongst four different segments; China, Chagataid Central Asia, Persia and the lands of the Golden Horde. In actuality it was even more divided than this, with the emergence of Kaidu who had won lands from the Chagataids but was also at war with the Mongols in Persia. The lands of the Golden Horde too would become increasingly fragmented. In 1269, Kaidu came up against Arghun, the son of Abaka. The two armies came face to face just to the north of Herat in modern Afghanistan. The outcome after a fierce fight was a victory for Arghun. Nevertheless, Kaidu was proving himself to be a major headache. As a successor to Ögedei, and also a figurehead for more traditionalist Mongols, he had a wide pool of support. Kublai tried to prove his Mongol credentials by honouring his roots. For example he would later have a patch of steppe grass planted in the garden of his palace; but many were unconvinced. When Marco Polo passed through Samarkand a few years after the civil war had died down (it never actually stopped completely) he noted that the people were 'subject to the nephew of the Great Khan who is no friend of his but is often at enmity with him'.[5]

Yet for all that, Kaidu was not an arbitrary destroyer. He was an opportunist for sure, but he was hardly unique amongst the Mongols in that respect. He was, it seems, a man who genuinely felt uncomfortable with the way that core values were being eroded. As a result, the glue that bonded the empire together weakened irrevocably, and the great schism accelerated. Increasingly it was meaningless to talk of a Mongol empire and more relevant to talk of the Mongol lands in Persia, Central Asia, China and the regions inhabited by the Golden Horde. Even inside these arbitrary classifications there would be further localised schisms, for example there was also the so-called White Horde in the far north, of which little is known. Now the great unified Mongol empire had gone forever, as dead as Genghis in his long-lost earth-bound tomb. No longer was it one coherent entity and no longer could the Great Khan assume that the days of conquest would continue forever until all the world fell under the spell of the Mongols.

CHAPTER 9

The Chinese *Khan*:
Kublai Becomes Emperor of China
1268-1277

As titular emperor of much of the known world, Kublai had interests which covered a huge geographical area, but there was no doubting which portion of his territories interested him the most. His greatest attraction had always been to China, a region whose civilisations went back for millennia. Great cities dotted the Chinese landscape, scientists had provided some of the world's most advanced inventions and scholars worked unceasingly in their quest for knowledge. It was all a long way from the steppes.

Soon after his troubled accession to the *khanate,* Kublai decided that his empire lacked something, namely a capital that befitted its status. He decided that this omission must be corrected as a matter of urgency. He did not consider Karakorum to be an appropriate spot for a major city, stuck out on the rolling plains of Mongolia, miles away from the great civilisations that formed part of the great empire that Kublai was responsible for. Rather, he felt, the capital must be in China. It did not take him long to find the place that best suited his purpose. Zhongdu, sacked by the Mongols in 1215, was selected. That city had been small, just 3.5 kilometres on each of its sides. Nothing of it now remains, but it was in an area not far from Tiananmen Square, where the portrait of a later twentieth-century absolute ruler still watches on sternly as millions of Chinese pass on their everyday journeys in a city that was to be rebuilt by Kublai. It was his decision to create a new capital there in 1263 which made Beijing, the successor to Zhongdu, the capital of modern China, though most of the city that was erected on his orders was incinerated when the Mongols were ejected from China, a century or so after it was built.

It took several years for work to begin in earnest. In 1266, work began on building the walls and major palaces of this new metropolis. Showing how much the Mongol world owed to the peoples that they had conquered, the brains behind this enterprise belonged to an Arab architect, Ikhtiyar al-Din. Kublai's palace was built on top of a hill which was itself man-made, the original site not being impressive enough. It was important that the palace spoke eloquently of the power and prestige of the *khan* who was to live there. Although nothing of the edifice now remains, the site that he chose lives on in the form of the Forbidden City, one of the most famous of all China's monuments. The palace was surrounded by four walls, a mile long on each side. It was whitewashed and battlemented. There was a great gate through which the *khan* was to enter and exit, and subsidiary gates for lesser mortals. Inside the palace, the walls were covered with gold and pictures of dragons and other exotic beasts. Marco Polo estimated that the hall was so large that up to 6,000 people could feast in it at any one time.

There was of course still much of China still left to conquer in the Song south of the country. However, before turning his mind to that outstanding task, Kublai found himself involved in affairs elsewhere. Some of the greatest driving forces in the global impact of Buddhism had come from Tibet, and, as an adherent to that faith (an allegiance which owed something to his supposedly beautiful wife, Chabi) Kublai was very interested in what happened there. The role of Chabi is an under-rated one. Behind every great *khan*, to inaccurately paraphrase a modern saying, there was a great woman. Genghis had Boerte, Kublai had Chabi. She was not his first wife but his second. They were married in about 1240. But she became his dominant wife. Kublai had four major wives, each with a court of their own in which minor wives and concubines also lived – there was no room for marital jealousy in Mongol society. But of all of them, it was Chabi who had the easiest access to Kublai's ear.

Kublai was not the first Mongol to have an interest in Buddhism. The second son of Ögedei, Kōten, had sent a rather brusque demand to Tibet in 1244 asking that one of the country's foremost holy men be sent to his court to act as his spiritual adviser. In case he thought that was an invitation rather than an order, it was made transparently clear that if he did not come, a Mongol army would shortly be despatched to persuade him to change his mind.

Kōten died shortly afterwards, though not before he had arranged to marry his daughter to the leading Tibetan lama of the day. This gave the Mongols an excuse to interfere more proactively in Tibetan affairs. The emperor Kuyuk had despatched troops to the terretory to further his claims on the country. One of the chief Mongols, who became more actively involved in Tibetan affairs as a result of the devastation that followed, was none other than Kublai, who took the son of an important lama under his wing. Although only a teenager at the time, he was an adolescent of great promise. He moved to Kublai's court, learned Mongol ways, and grew into a man of great influence in Tibetan affairs. He would become known as *the noble guru*: Phags-Pa. Despite his relative youth, he became a powerful influence over Kublai, a fact demonstrated by his consecration of Kublai into the mysteries of Lamaism when he was just eighteen years old. In 1258, when still only twenty-three, Phags-Pa became a fully-fledged Buddhist monk and found himself Kublai's *guru*.

Whilst Kublai had been involved in civil war, as part of his successful attempt to become *khan*, he believed that there were some in Tibet who were siding with his rival. By 1264, Phags-Pa was officially the head of Buddhist religion in Kublai's Chinese lands. Soon after, the religion was granted special privileges including exemption from taxation. Then Phags-Pa went home to Tibet where, it was hoped, he would unify the country and persuade its citizens to unequivocally accept Mongol rule. The young mentor of Kublai and his supposed master had not always enjoyed a straightforward relationship. As a man who believed that the spiritual took precedence over the secular, Phags-Pa believed that he was superior to Kublai, a claim that no self-respecting *khan* could countenance. Kublai unsurprisingly rejected the claim. In the end, a most un-Mongol like compromise was agreed. Phags-Pa took precedence when the men were discussing spiritual affairs, and Kublai was the superior when secular matters were being considered. This agreement was evidenced by overt symbolic statements: when spiritual matters were being discussed, Phags-Pa sat on a dais that was higher than Kublai's and vice-versa.

Phags-Pa though did not limit his involvement to spiritual affairs. In doing so, he was inheriting a strong Buddhist tradition. Modern perceptions of lamas tend to see them as otherworldly holy men, with no interest in secular matters, but at that time exactly the opposite was the case. The lamas of Tibet were, like many religious leaders before and since, astute political operators. Kublai clearly hoped that Phags-Pa would prove to be a capable political as well as a spiritual operator. In reality, Kublai was probably attracted to the Tibetan form of Buddhism because it sought to be politically effective and not just some ethereal form of mysticism. Kublai hoped that the Tibetans would meekly submit to one of their own, but it was not quite that easy. Many of the Tibetans saw Phags-Pa as a traitor, and there was widespread dissatisfaction and unrest when he returned. In the end, a Mongol army was sent into Tibet in 1267 to conquer it, and bring it firmly under Kublai's rule: a precursor of similar actions by Communist Chinese troops half a millennium later.

The country was administered by a so-called Pacification Bureau (something else that sounds horribly resonant of twentieth-century China). It is a supreme, and, to many, a sad irony, that the Chinese claim to Tibet is derived from the country's conquest by Kublai, who was of course a Mongol. It was only the fact that Kublai later established a Chinese dynasty that gives the claim any legitimacy at all.

That same year, 1267, Phags-Pa was required to provide his greatest service yet to the Mongol empire. It was his mental abilities that Kublai desired to use, for he had a difficult problem to solve. As the Mongol empire grew, so too did the number of languages in use across it. This was a major problem, especially as one of them was Chinese, a complex linguistic challenge with a vast number of characters available. Phags Pa's challenge was simple to understand, extraordinarily difficult to deliver. It was nothing less than to provide a universal language for use across the empire. Just two years later he did it, which for him proved to be the gateway to great riches as a reward from a delighted *khan*. Family problems, however, continued to nag away at Kublai. Kaidu has proved extremely difficult to bring to book. In 1269, a peace convention was held in Central Asia. Baraq and Kaidu agreed to a division of lands in the region between them. Abaka, successor to Hülegü, was also allocated more lands. This was an interesting turn of events. Bovaq had gone to the region to bring Kaidu into line – now both of them were acting as autonomous rulers. Genghis must have been turning in his secret grave. The convention solved nothing, which cannot really have surprised anyone. The region quickly became a complete mess. Abaka's men were soon involved in a fierce battle against those of Baraq, who was killed. Baraq's men then took Kaidu's part. By 1271 Kaidu was being crowned *khan* of his own large state in Central Asia.

Even though he was, as we shall see, heavily engrossed to the east by this time, Kublai – who showed a toleration of the wayward Kaidu that his grandfather Genghis would never have contemplated – saw this as a step too far. He sent a large delegation composed of some prominent princes of the blood, to persuade Kaidu to present himself before him at either Xanadu or Beijing. Kaidu, as elusive as an eel, moved out of their way, avoiding a fight – the princes did not have a large enough army to start a battle anyway – and proving impossible to catch. The problem of Kaidu just would not go away. Given this intransigence, why then did Kublai not seek a decisive confrontation? The answer is simple – he was by now deeply enmeshed in China. A Mongol lord was expected to go forth and conquer, to fulfil the destiny handed down to him by Genghis.

There was no doubt whatsoever where the focus of Kublai's drive for conquest would be. He inherited the north of China when he became *khan*, but there was still a large slab of Song territory in the south to add to the empire. The conquest of such a prize would be a magnificent ornament to any *khan's* reign.

Kublai had not forgotten the rejection of his proposals to the Song before he had become involved in the civil war with his younger brother. He had been forced to wait for a few years before attempting to make good his claim to the Song kingdom. It would prove a tough nut to crack. The country was divided by major rivers, and large cities were liberally dotted across it, far more so than was the case in the north. This meant that it will be ill-suited to Mongol cavalry, the key to their success so far. New tactics would be needed. However, there was no doubt that the prize was an enormous one. The Song territories were very wealthy. Great cities were dotted along the coastline, ports which gave access to South-East Asia, India and the Middle East. Descriptions of its great city, Hangzhou, speak of a cultured, elegant place with restaurants and tea houses dotted liberally around. It was a city of luxury and opulence.

Yet it contrasted with other parts of the country. The Song kingdom's terrain was very different from the Mongol homeland. Forests blanketed the region, hot and sultry, humid and tropical, which not only made it poorly suited to Mongol cavalry trained on the steppes, but also meant that it was home to strange viruses and diseases to deplete an invading army. Where it was clear of forest, there was an agricultural area: the widespread use of land to cultivate crops meant that there was little of the fodder that the horse herds needed. But these problems were countermanded to an extent by other considerations. The Song kingdom was financially weak, and prone to dissension: in short, it was exposed and vulnerable before the Mongol threat. Kublai was wise to the political divisions and sought to take advantage of them; his offer of 1260 had proposed a degree of self-rule for the Song if they would accept Kublai's suzerainty. 'Divide and rule' was his approach, so much so that he was angry when two captured Song generals were executed as he wished to adopt a 'softly, softly' approach to winning the people of the south over.

The key to taking the Song territories was the mighty Yangtze River. The river, known to the Chinese as Ch'ang Chiang, is the longest in China, and the third longest in the world. Rising far across China on the borders of Tibet, it was the major artery flowing across the country and into the Yellow Sea, close to modern Shanghai. But the key to it as far as the Mongols were concerned was the River Han, which merged into it from the north. The strategic importance of the Han was so obvious to everyone, however, that the Song had built a massive set of fortifications there at Xiangyang. It was surrounded by a huge moat, and was a major trading centre with perhaps 200,000 inhabitants. Opposite it on the other side of the river, a smaller reflection of this massive place, was Fancheng. A makeshift bridge linked the two, built of small boats tethered to posts driven into the riverbed. Xiangyang could not be left untaken. It dominated the river, and the river was the key to the Yangtze. There was no alternative but to attack it for as long as was needed to eliminate it.

This daunting challenge was given to a young commander called Aju. His bloodline was imperious. His grandfather had been none other than the renowned Subotai. His father too, had enjoyed an impressive career. His name was Uriyang-kadai and he had won great victories in China fifteen years before. These men were tough acts to follow, but Aju was to prove himself a worthy successor to his illustrious predecessors. Yet it should also be noted that this was far from an exclusively Mongol enterprise. Kublai recruited leading military thinkers from elsewhere, Muslims, Central Asians, even other Chinese to participate in the campaign.

Aju began his attack early in 1268. He was equipped with some of the most modern weapons of his day. He was well provided with traction trebuchets, the traditional rock-throwing engine of choice at the time. However, they would not prove sufficient to batter down the massive walls of Xiangyang; something more powerful was needed. It was found in the form of counterweight trebuchets, massive constructions that operated by means of heavy weights attached to them which, when released in the appropriate fashion, hurled huge chunks of rock hundreds of feet through the air. These monsters were relatively recent inventions. No one is even sure where the machine were first developed, though the consensus of expert opinion seems to be that they probably came from the Muslim world. They had been around in Europe too for a while: Edward I of England had used one called the Warwolf in his siege of Stirling Castle, whilst other massive machines proved their worth in the Albigensian Crusade in the south of France in 1210. At any rate, they had been around since some time in the twelfth century, and by the beginning of the thirteenth, they had reached China.[1]

The siege of Xiangyang was to last for five years. It would be a test of perseverance, as much as military genius. Before it could start, Kublai needed something that most Mongols knew little about – boats. Kublai realised that this would be a battle that the Mongols could not win on their own, so he encouraged Song generals and officials to defect to him. One man who had done so was a man named Liu Cheng. He was made admiral of the fleet, which was probably a great honour, but might have meant more if a fleet actually existed. Liu Cheng was told to go and assemble one, and accordingly got on with the task of building 500 craft to use in the siege of Xiangyang.

In the meantime, the Mongols did all that they could to ensure that no supplies could get into the city. Fortifications were built on either side of the river from which brave but exposed supply vessels making their way to Xiangyang could be bombarded and destroyed. Aju decided that it was not enough just to attack Xiangyang, he should also attack her little sister Fancheng too. He met with some success, particularly when a group of impulsive defenders broke out and tried to drive the Mongols away. They were overwhelmed and beheaded. The fighting was characterised by the use of 'thunder crash bombs', primitive explosive devices that blew up on impact. Both sides had access to these weapons, but they caused limited damage. The siege went on for months, a desultory, slow-moving affair. This was a period when, although both sides were at war, there were long moments of inactivity, the odd foray here, the occasional rock lobbed at the city there. However, in August 1269 the Song launched a massive attempted counterattack with 3,000 boats. Despite the huge size of this force it was driven back, incurring significant losses in the process.

Despite this tactical victory, the Mongols were nowhere close to breaking through the immense walls of Xiangyang. The city was still regularly re-supplied by river with paddleboats powered by men driving treadmills (a rather unorthodox mode of transport). Stalemate was the order of the day; the Mongols were tired and Kublai was frustrated. Then an Uighur adviser spoke to Kublai and advised him to seek out the best siege engineer in the empire to provide him with one of these immense counterweight trebuchets that had proved so powerful. Kublai knew exactly where to look. The Mongols in Persia had access to some of the greatest engineers in the world, and he sent a message 4,000 miles to Abaka, to ask him to send the best men he had to help him solve what seemed to be an insoluble problem.

Abaka did his job splendidly. He sent an engineer by the name of Ismail and his assistant Ala ad-Din. They arrived at the court of Kublai late in 1271. By early next year they found themselves in front of the walls of Xiangyang ready to start on the business in hand. There was much to be done. Wood was needed to build the engines, large boulders had to be shaped by hand by stonemasons. It would all take time. But the Mongols were patient people, and Ismail was given all the time he needed to perfect his creation. He created a masterpiece (or a beast depending on one's perspective) that was soon hurling massive rocks against the walls and smashing large holes in them. The shock of these weapons cannot be understated. They hurled missiles ten times larger than any seen to date. The projectiles were several feet wide, and left an impact crater feet deep. One of them thundered into a great drum tower and brought it crashing to the ground. The ground shook as the massive projectiles unleashed by the trebuchets hurtled into the city.

It was not, however, Xiangyang that bore the brunt of this terrifying monster's assaults, but its neighbour opposite at Fancheng. It was all done in a clinically organised fashion. The bridge that connected the two places was destroyed by the Mongols, as if the umbilical cord of Fancheng was being surgically removed. This was done by the use of mechanical saws operated from the boats. Then the trebuchets did their bestial work. Fancheng was overwhelmed and taken. Kublai was faced with a conundrum. He was not like the *khans* of old who would massacre the population of any place that dared resist the will of Heaven. Surrounded as he was by more pacific Chinese advisers, he had learned from them that magnanimity in victory could be a useful asset. But the defence of Fancheng had been frustratingly stubborn. Further, events there could be witnessed from across the river in Xiangyang.

Kublai pondered whether or not he should mete out stern punishment to the inhabitants of Fancheng. Although he was inclined to show mercy in many cases, this time he decided that exemplary punishment should be meted out. Accordingly all the captured populace were slaughtered, regardless of age or sex. They had their throats cut in full view of the defenders of Xiangyang, who must have been devastated at their inability to intervene.

This was a big blow for those in Xiangyang. It appeared that a final terrifying assault on the city was now imminent. A bloodbath would inevitably follow. However, there were those who advocated other tactics. The Mongol general, Ariq-khaya, made a direct approach to the commander of Xiangyang, Lü Wen-huan. He gave his word that if the city surrendered no one need die. Eloquently he told the Song general that:

> You have held the city with an isolated army for many years but now the approaches are cut off even from the birds of the air. My master the emperor admires your loyalty and if you surrender he will give you an honourable post and a generous reward.[2]

The Song commander did not believe him at first, but the Mongol was insistent. Eventually, seeing that the alternative to taking the risk of throwing himself on Kublai's mercy was ultimate annihilation, he decided to hand the city over, which he duly did on 17 March, 1273. Kublai was true to Ariq-khaya's promises. There was no gratuitous slaughter, despite the extended siege and attendant loss of Mongol life. Kublai wanted to rule in the Song kingdom, and the people of Xiangyang were now his subjects. They should be treated as such, with mercy and tolerance. This was a crushing blow for the Song. It left their capital Hangzhou open to the Mongols. Panic set in, closely followed by disaster. The Song emperor Duzong died soon after, leaving behind a four-year old heir. The kingdom was about to be inherited by a child, a turn of events that could not have come at a worse time. The future looked ominous.

Aju was rewarded for his successful prosecution of the siege by a demotion. This was not a slap in the face, but instead a realisation that Hangzhou would be the last and most crucial battle in the war that caused this to happen. Another general, Bayan, would be given the daunting task of taking the city, and, with it, securing the Song kingdom for Kublai. He was only, in fact, a couple of years older than Aju, but he had a reputation for being an excellent administrator as well as a good warrior. He was also an educated man who spoke Chinese. To cap it all he had a reputation for clear thinking when under pressure, a commodity to be highly valued in a pressure-cooker situation such as this. Over the years, he would become Kublai's most trusted general and advisor. The choice of Bayan is interesting, as it demonstrates once more that what concerned Kublai was not racial origin, but talent, for Bayan was not a Mongol but a Turk. Some have argued that he was perhaps the greatest talent of his generation.[3] He was greatly experienced, having accompanied Hülegü in his campaigns in Persia. It would prove to be a wise choice on Kublai's part.

The army that was assembled for this great confrontation was vast. It was also multi-faceted, as befitted the nature of the operation before them. There were 200,000 infantrymen for a start, half of them recruited from northern China where the Chin had once held sway. 800 new warships and 5,000 smaller boats were also part of the force, reflecting the fact that this was to be an amphibious assault.[4] Kublai instructed Bayan to be careful and to show mercy when the city was taken. It was the jewel in the Song crown now, but it would be the jewel in his once it was taken. He needed to be magnanimous to his subjects if he were to win their respect.

A large army blocked the progress of Bayan as he moved down towards the Yangtze, and he attempted to neutralise the force by moving round it. Obviously it was a military risk leaving a large number of the enemy to his rear, but he was confident that he could cope with this problem. The boats were carried Viking-fashion across country on bamboo poles, and then put back in the water once the enemy's blocking force was safely at a distance. Another great fortress stood in Bayan's way, at Yang-lo. The approaches to it were guarded by a fleet much bigger than his. Its strength argued against a head-on attack; a more subtle approach was needed. So he sent some of his troops to attack the fort, which worried its commander and persuaded him to draw in reinforcements from his outlying defences. This of course weakened the defensive position outside of Yang-lo. Then Bayan sent the remainder of the army downstream, taking some of the boats with them.

It was January and the water was icy cold. This did not dissuade the Mongols from wading into the river and erecting a makeshift bridge across it. By the time that the watery rays of the morning sun were starting to shed their pale orange glow in the east, the Mongols were firmly established on the far side of the river. A fleet which came to drive them off was beaten. In a war of attrition such as this, the most fragile weapon is morale, and that of the Song defenders of Yang-lo was now shattered. The fortress surrendered, and another difficult obstacle had been eliminated. As the march of conquest continued, its progress was helped no end by Song defectors, who had allied themselves to the Mongols and now persuaded many of their former comrades in arms to surrender the towns and forts they held rather than fight. Hangzhou was losing the will to carry on its resistance against what seemed to be an invincible enemy. In the absence of a meaningful emperor, resistance centred around the Prime Minister, Jia Sidao. A man who loved luxury and ostentation, he was possibly not the best character to inspire a dispirited people.

Just then, in one of the blackest hours of Song history, a rallying-point emerged. As many people who have lived in a monarchy at a time of war over the ages can testify, a royal family that is revered and respected can have a massive influence over morale. Now the Dowager Xie, widow of the late emperor, spoke out. She was not a glamorous figure, having a cataract in one eye, and very dark skin. But she was admired by her people and now, at this critical moment, she spoke out, and so became a beacon of hope. She initiated what was essentially a recruiting drive, a Chinese equivalent of a 'your country needs you' campaign. Many of her people were moved intensely by it. By March 1275, over 200,000 of them had presented themselves for military service. In the meantime, the far less popular Jia had moved his army up to face up to Bayan on the Yangtze. However, his troops were badly battered by Mongol artillery, and retreated in disorder, allowing their enemy to capture thousands of boats in the process. Jia was banished for this disgrace, though Xie intervened decisively when some suggested he should be executed. Whatever his faults, he had worked hard for the Song, as well as for himself for decades, and was deserving of leniency. His reputation, however, was less fortunate, and he was vilified by future generations for his ignominious part in the last days of the Song. Even as he was marched off into exile, he was taunted by his guards for his failure.

City after city continued to fall before the cock-a-hoop soldiers in Bayan's army. At Nanjing, a major Song metropolis, Bayan perhaps showed why he had been chosen by Kublai. Here, once the city fell, he took months to establish a local administration that could rule it for the benefit of Kublai. He also halted for another reason, for he now sent envoys on to Hangzhou asking for the city to surrender. They were promptly killed. The local population, despite the fact that they were exploited by their rulers like all dispossessed classes of the time, showed a marked reluctance to submit to Mongol rule. Perhaps the Mongols' reputation for wholesale butchery was inspiring resistance rather than suppressing it. At any event, guerrilla warfare kicked off on a large scale.

Something of a Song fight-back ensued. Aju was forced to beat off a heavy counterattack at Yangzhou. The Song blocked the river with large boats but it did little good. Adopting tactics that resonate of Sir Francis Drake, the Mongols set small boats ablaze and set them adrift in the direction of the cumbersome Song vessels, which went up in a cloud of smoke and flame. However, this was the last huzzah of the Song. Their counterattack ran out of momentum and stalled. Only Hangzhou remained to be dealt with. By September 1275, Bayan was ready. He had adopted a three-pronged plan of attack, converging on the city from both land and water. The Mongols met stern resistance at the outlying town of Changzhou. Bayan gave due warning that the town and its people would be wiped out if they persisted in their stubbornness. Its people did not heed this dire threat, and carried on with their valiant, if ill-starred, resistance. Changzhou fell and Bayan made good on his warning to it. Everyone was killed. Kublai's injunctions to show mercy seemed to have had a limited impact on Bayan. Perhaps old habits really do die hard.

Bayan of course may have been calculating that his stern judgment at Changzhou would encourage Hangzhou to capitulate. The Mongols really did employ terror as an instrument of strategy, and, to an extent, it seems to have worked on this occasion. There was widespread panic in the capital, mutiny amongst their soldiery, unmistakable diminution in the will to fight. As a short-term tactic, perhaps terror can be a successful strategy. Its problem of course is that it breeds hatred and resentment, a simmering fuse hidden beneath the surface when the party perpetrating it takes power. In the longer term, the fuse will set off a major explosion with cataclysmic effect for the would-be rulers – as the Mongols would eventually find out in China.

Xie, trapped in Hangzhou, now saw that the unthinkable must be considered. Militarily the Song were outmatched and in order to survive she, as effective if not titular head of this centuries-old dynasty, would have to negotiate. Envoys were sent to the Mongols and a scheme to divide the country up with them was floated. The problem, which was obvious to everyone, was that she was negotiating from a position of terminal weakness. The Mongols did not need to negotiate as they were clearly going to win. They could take what they wanted, so it can have come as no surprise when Bayan refused to countenance anything other than total surrender. However, he did offer to magnanimity in victory. There would be no slaughter if the city surrendered, he promised. Xie would be treated with honour, and the respect that befitted someone of her exulted status. He even sent her a copy of a written statement from Kublai himself to this effect. Hangzhou was by now surrounded and cut off from hope. Although some of her advisers advocated a battle to the last man, she saw that this would result in nothing save thousands of avoidable deaths. Surrender, then, it would be.

On 26 January, 1276 she sent a note to Bayan, as Kublai's representative in the field. The opening phrase said, in reverential tones, all that needed to be said. 'I respectfully bow a hundred times to Your Majesty, the Benevolent, Brilliant, Spiritual and Martial Emperor of the Great Yuan'. Empresses did not bow to emperors (except for their husbands) unless they wished to acknowledge their subservient status. The use of the word 'Yuan' in her statement in fact said it all. Perhaps the greatest accolade that can be given to any group of rulers in any country is being accorded the status of a dynasty. Just as Ancient Egypt recognised the virtues of such an approach, so too did China. There were of course famous dynasties such as the Ming (yet to come in Chinese history) and now the Mongols too had been awarded dynastic status. Kublai's dynasty had been referred to as the Yuan since he started to conquer in the north. It means 'first' or 'principal', even 'great' (direct translations from Chinese into English whilst keeping the meaning are difficult). Now the empress of the Song also recognised that the time of a new dynasty had come. The old ways had passed away, never to return. The Mongols were a recognised dynasty in China, seat of some of the world's greatest and oldest civilisations. It was a long way from the Gobi.

The surrender was duly accepted. Bayan entered Hangzhou soon after in triumphant procession. The seal of the nation, that great symbolic store of a nation's identity, was handed over to him. A memorandum accompanied it, recognising Kublai's right to rule over the Song. A hundred beautiful women drowned themselves rather than be seized by lascivious Mongol soldiers. It all ended formally on 21 February, 1276 when a five year old boy emperor, Zhao Xian, knelt before Bayan and accepted Kublai as his master. Bayan observed that 'the south and the north have become one family'. Bayan observed the terms of the surrender scrupulously. There would be no blood-bath. The Song currency continued uninterrupted, and there was no attempt to ban Song clothing. Officials were of course replaced by Mongols, and their allies and militias were disbanded, but the Song world on the whole continued as if nothing had really happened.

A few days later, the surrender document was despatched to Kublai, accompanied by copious amounts of booty. Then, a month after, Bayan himself set out, along with the Song royal entourage, on its way to an uncertain new life many miles to the north, in the shadow of a man who perhaps they still felt to be little better than a barbarian. Only Xie stayed behind as she was too ill to travel. She would follow on later. It took them three months to make their slow journey to Beijing. There was no hurry now, and every reason for the Mongols to bask in the reflected glory of victory. When Bayan entered Beijing and came into the presence of his lord and master, Kublai lavished gifts on him. He had done all that had been asked of him. It was traditional to hand out robes of a single colour, as a sign of the greatest respect when a man was to be honoured. Kublai now rewarded him with twenty sets.

Xie eventually reached Beijing too. She was given a rent-free property and lived for another six years in comfortable conditions, albeit much reduced from the absolute power that she had been used to. Chabi, Kublai's wife, took a personal interest in her wellbeing and comfort. At one stage she even berated her all-powerful husband for not treating the Dowager Empress with due deference. The Mongols may have terminated the life of the Song, but they were still deserving of honour and respect.

Although this marked the end of the dynasty, it did not yet represent the end of the drama. Across Song territories hundreds of people, deprived of the traditional rulers that they had become used to and feeling that their way of life was at end, decided to take their lives rather than live on under Mongol rule. Over one hundred prominent officials decided to end it all rather than live on in obscure ignominy.

This phenomenon started even before Hangzhou fell. In January 1276 the Mongols moved on Tanzhou for example. The commander of the town, Li Fu, decided that, when defeat was inevitable, he would not be taken alive. All his family and servants drunk themselves into a stupor. Then one of his assistants went around putting them all to the sword. The adviser, in a final dramatic act, killed his wife and then slit his throat in a veritable Bacchanalia of death. Others threw themselves down wells, hanged themselves, anything that would relieve them of the shame of living with defeat. Two young princes of the blood also escaped south and headed for Vietnam. They took to the sea with an immense force, allegedly 200,000 strong, shipped in 1,000 vessels. But there was a storm, and one of the princes then died. The fleet limped on up the coast, still looking to act as the catalyst for a resurgence in Song fortunes. Their final battle took place close to Guangzhou, long known as Canton. Here the Mongols, with a much smaller navy, moved in for the kill against a Song fleet that had anchored itself in the shallows just offshore.

However, here they were sitting ducks. To return to Spanish Armada analogies, this was a classic case of large, immobile ships faced by much smaller and manoeuvrable craft. Although the Mongols were at a great numerical disadvantage in terms of the number of ships they had, they were able to blockade the Song fleet which was blocked in a narrow harbour with limited room to move. Occasionally one of the Mongol ships might nip in and out with the speed of a whippet and strike one of the enemies, but basically all the Mongols had to do was to ride at anchor and let the Song run out of water. However, the Mongols wanted a decisive win in battle rather than the slightly mundane victory that offered itself. After two weeks, they split their fleet into two, and descended on the demoralised Song navy.

It was a rout, and the chroniclers say that the sea ran red with blood. Tens of thousands of Song warriors and sailors perished. Some committed suicide by throwing themselves into the water attached to weights. The most poignant death of all was that of a six-year-old prince, the last of the Song line to live in freedom. His advisor Lu Xiufu was one of those who jumped into the water. To his robes were attached the royal seals of the Song dynasty, and on his back he carried a small boy, no doubt terrified and wondering what had happened to the world he had once known, a world once full of luxury and security, now just a vast wasteland of death and destruction. There are many poignant images from history, but this is perhaps one of the most haunting of them all; a child, born to riches, now seeing the world that he thought to be eternal, falling apart around him.

This dramatic end contrasted with that of Zhao Xian, the boy emperor captured by the Mongols. His fate was not to die at once, as Kublai had promised he would not, and he intended to honour that vow. He was instead consigned to a long, lingering death, forced to become a Buddhist monk in distant Tibet. Here he lived out his days in obscurity, far away from the gaze of the public eye. It is said, though no one knows for sure as he was lost to view for decades, that here amidst the towering mountains and the harsh terrain of that faraway land, he lived a life that could not have been more different to the one which he had seemed destined for. Here, decades after the fall of Hangzhou and the death of his way of life, the Last Emperor of his day decided that he could take no more and killed himself, unnoticed by the world to whom he had long become an irrelevance.

The final conquest of China was the fulfilment of a dream for Kublai. It cemented his place in a position of greatness that no Mongol before Genghis would have dared dream possible. However, the trouble with a would-be world conqueror was that his job was never done. There was still a large chunk of the world left to add to Kublai's patrimony. The conquest of the Song kingdom was a massive success story, but it was not the end of the tale. It was time to move on to the next stepping stone that led to world conquest.

Just where would the Mongols strike next was the key question. The Mongols were about to take the next step towards fulfilling Genghis' as yet unfulfilled legacy, and in so doing were to move closer to ultimate failure. Already internal division has started to nibble away at Mongol unity, undermining the foundations on which their success was predicated. Now they were to embark on an adventure which would also contribute to their decline, for the Mongols had built a reputation which was founded upon a virtually unbroken stream of triumph. It had already been tarnished against the Mamelukes. Now, that reputation was about to be seriously challenged again.

Across the sea from China was an island nation which, to all intents and purposes, had developed remarkably free of external interference. This was Japan, peopled by a mix of entrepreneurial traders and a warrior Samurai class that were to become the stuff of legend. Kublai decided that Japan too should be added to his extended domains. Some have suggested that this intervention was because Kublai was afraid that the Song would get help from the Japanese, as links between the two had become closer in recent decades, but this does not ring true.[5] It is unclear why the Japanese, who had stayed out of Chinese affairs for centuries, should interfere in Chinese affairs, particularly when they would have invited down the wrath of the strongest warrior nation in the world on their heads as a result.

A far more likely explanation is that Kublai believed that heaven's decree that the Mongol *khan* should rule the world should be taken literally. After all, Mongol *khans* had been arguing for decades that this was the case, and why should Kublai be any different? Japan should submit itself to the will of heaven, and accept that it too belonged to the Mongols. Japan just happened to be next on his shopping list. Advisors told him that the task should not be difficult. Of course the Samurai had a great reputation as individual warriors, but their code did not encourage them to fight as part of a large army capable of beating back the Mongols. Death with honour might be a proud code to live a life by, but it is no guarantee that it would lead to success in an extended campaign against a great power (as the Japanese would find out later in the twentieth century). In addition, the emperor of Japan appeared to be a mere cipher at the head of the nation. One blow from the Mongol hurricane, and the whole pack of cards would come tumbling down.

But Kublai underestimated an obvious challenge. Between his satellite kingdom in Korea and Japan, the sea stretched across for about 150 miles. It might look a narrow gap, but it might as well have been the width of an ocean. After all, the twenty-two mile gap that separates Britain from France has proved a so-far unbreachable drawbridge for almost a millennium. And the Mongols of course had no naval heritage to speak of that they could call upon. Kublai had a solution to this problem. If his own people did not have naval skills, his clients, the Koreans, did. The king that Kublai had appointed twenty years before was a suppliant soul by the name of Wonjong, who had at one stage been a hostage of the Mongols. Dutifully, his shipyards churned out large numbers of ships to make the crossing to Japan, thereby allowing the ocean gap to be crossed. Of course he was doing as he was told, but the Koreans resented the Mongols fiercely, and some even tried to convince Kublai to change his plans.

Whatever Kublai had done to ingratiate himself to the Koreans, he was on a hiding to nothing. No nation takes kindly to an invader. It was a situation uncannily similar to that in Manchuria in the 1930s, when the Japanese had set up a Chinese client state where the emperor was their puppet. Except in this case, the precise roles were different; for Manchuria read Korea, for the Japanese read Mongols. The Koreans though would have to go along with the *khan's* demands. Might, in this case, equated to right. The invasion of Japan would go ahead. Kublai had marked the Japanese card as far back as 1266. An embassy was sent, demanding that the emperor submit to Mongol rule. Discussions went on for months: the emperor wanted to negotiate but the real power, the head of the military known as the *shogun*, would have none of it, and sent the embassy packing. He would have known that the Mongols were still heavily embroiled in the Song kingdom at this stage, and were in no position to threaten Japan.

He hoped the problem would go away. It didn't. In September 1271 a Korean diplomat arrived with a message from Kublai. It repeated the demand that Japan accept Mongol rule, with the thinly veiled threat that if these instructions were ignored this time, then military action would follow. Japan again refused the order, and set about improving its meagre stock of coastal defences, which were in a poor state of repair. Another ambassador was sent in 1272 with the same response, a blank refusal to submit. Towards the end of 1274, the Mongols were ready to strike. The last embers of Song resistance had been beaten out, and there were plenty of ships to ferry the army across to Japan. A fleet of nearly 1,000 ships set out from Pusan with their first stop meant to be the strategically crucial island of Tsushima, the gateway to 'mainland' Japan, where an emerging Japanese navy obliterated a large Russian fleet at the beginning of the twentieth century. The island sits in an absolutely crucial position halfway between Korea and Japan, a giant stepping-stone from the former to the latter.

The addition of Korea to the Mongol empire gave Kublai an important launch pad for the invasion. For decades, the Mongols had been involving themselves in Korean affairs. When Wonjong had become king of Korea in 1258 he had approached the Mongols to seek a peace with them. Several rebels within the country were determined not to submit, and fighting had lasted until 1270. In 1273, the alliance was sealed when the crown prince of Korea was married to Kublai's daughter. The Mongols gave the impression of being temperate overlords at first, but this did not last long, for the next year the Mongols conscripted large numbers of soldiers and sailors for the invasion of Japan.

When the fleet set out that year, the Mongols duly landed on Tsushima on a sandy beach, which was perfect for amphibious operations in this era, though the land behind, a gnarled tangle of rocky hills and suffocating forest, was less so. Sure enough, the Japanese forces that had been drawn up to fight off the Mongols were swatted off as easily as the trunk of a mighty elephant would brush off the attentions of a fly. The invaders then advanced to a hill, Mount Sohara, which dominated the island. The Japanese bravely launched a counter-attack. This was repulsed with 'thundercrash bombs', crude artillery devices propelled by traction trebuchets. It was a heroic attack by the Japanese, consistent with their proud Samurai traditions, but all these brave warriors did was to deliver a series of pinpricks into the thick hide of the Mongol elephant, barely enough to be noticed.

The Mongols then moved onto the mainland of Kyushu, where they anchored in Hakata Bay. Here battle was joined once more. The 'thundercrash bombs' made a particular impact on the Japanese, perhaps as much for their noise as for the damage that they caused. A Japanese observer noted their effect in the following way:

> The commanding general kept his position on high ground, and directed the various detachments as need be with signals from hand drums. But whenever the Mongol soldiers took to flight, they sent iron bombshells flying against us, which made our side dizzy and confused. Our soldiers were frightened out of their wits by the thundering explosions, their eyes were blinded, their ears deafened, so that they could hardly distinguish east from west.[6]

In this land-based environment the Mongols held the tactical advantage, but the venue for the battle was about to change, which would swing things the other way. Out in the bay, worried Mongol sailors (more likely Koreans actually) cast nervous glances towards the horizon. Dark clouds were gathering, menacing, drawing closer by the minute. The weather was on the turn and they did not like the look of things.

Then, the sudden hint of problems closer to hand; hundreds of tiny craft moving towards the Mongol fleet, each of them with only a dozen or so warriors on board. They were light, nimble, easy to manoeuvre. The Mongol ships, by comparison, were hulks, and so the flies swarmed in and out of the herd of Mongol elephants, darting hither and thither, dodging out of the way of the missiles that the Mongols were hurling at them with impunity. Perhaps the analogy works better if one thinks of the Japanese as fireflies, for the task of these small craft was to set as many of the enemy ablaze as possible, a task they achieved with a considerable degree of success.

A cloud of acrid smoke filled the air around the bay. Overnight the sky was filled by another kind of cloud, blown in by winds that tossed the Mongol ships around as easily as if they were corks in a barrel. The next day broke, looking down on a scene of complete confusion. Mongol ships were everywhere, the fleet was scattered and the will of the Mongols to fight, broken. The survivors of the battle and the storm limped back to Korea. The Mongols had spent just one day in mainland

Japan and had lost a third of their men. They were humbled, though not finally beaten. They would return.

It was said in Japan, a very religious country, that this was the work of the gods: the gods blew and the fleet scattered. Japan must be the chosen land of great deities who would protect the sacred islands. Easy to say of course, but in our cynical age hard to understand. But men believed it in Japan, for sure, and morale soared as a result. In fact, reading the accounts of this campaign which have survived the passing of centuries, the tenacity of the Japanese defence also makes an impression, and played a crucial role in rebuffing the Mongols. In any event, when Kublai sent more ambassadors soon after, repeating his demands, there was no softly-softly response; they were executed.

The Japanese were not naïve, though, taking the view as later ages would that the gods helped those who helped themselves. The Hakozaki Shrine, particularly sacred to the Japanese, had been destroyed by the Mongols, but was now rebuilt. Economies were made in the national budget and the money saved poured into the improvement of fortifications. A wall was built, just six feet high in many places. It does not seem tall enough until one realises its purpose: six feet is higher than most horses can jump. The building of the wall neutralised the Mongols' greatest weapon. The Japanese clearly recognised that this initial foray from Kublai was merely a statement of intent; there would be bigger challenges to follow. They even apparently considered a pre-emptive strike against Korea, though it was a threat they never carried out.

Defeat was something that the Mongols were unused to, and Kublai would not have taken to the news from Japan well. Nor was it the only item of unwelcome news to be received at this time. As long ago as 1271, Kublai had sent his son Nomukhan to subdue dissentient elements in the far west. For years Kublai had been trying to do so, without success. Nomukhan was not helped by his entourage, which included a grandson of Tolui named Togh Timür, two sons of Arik-Böke and a son of Möngke. Unity between them proved impossible, and they eventually betrayed Nomukhan to the Golden Horde. Kaidu surprisingly proved reluctant to involve himself in these affairs, but Nomukhan would not be released until 1284 after eight years in captivity, even the efforts of Bayan proving powerless to free him earlier.

Despite these setbacks, Kublai had the compensation of a great empire to run, and in particular the challenge of administering his newly annexed Song dominions. He surrounded himself with the cream of the administrative class from across his bloated empire: Uighurs, Turks, the best from the Chinese lands that he had conquered. Racial origin mattered not a great deal, though it should of course be recognised that the main beneficiaries of his government of China were the Mongols themselves. There were privileges accorded to the Mongols that were not available to the rest of the population, for example lower punishments for equivalent crimes. Higher positions in the hierarchy were occupied by Mongols. Not all was repression though. Kublai was clever enough to realise that the Song kingdom was a breadbasket for millions of his subjects, and so he ordered that prime arable land was not to be used for grazing for Mongol horse herds.

Government departments were set up to administer the region, though he was very careful to ensure that only Mongols worked in the Bureau of Military Affairs, the body responsible for troop movements. Knowledge of these was to be kept from the Chinese for obvious reasons. The bureau would be at the heart of government, for this was effectively a military administration, with the army running the country. Trade continued unabated. Kublai improved things economically by ensuring the use of paper money was backed up by suitable economic policies. Paper money was not new to China, but it had not always functioned effectively. Kublai made it work; however, when the Mongols were eventually ousted from China, the paper money went with them and did not reappear for hundreds of years. They clearly made an impact though: not for nothing is the modern Chinese currency known as the 'yuan'.

He even reformed the criminal code. Given normal paradigms about Mongol brutality, it may be a surprise to find that he made them more lenient in some ways, though in others they were still barbaric. Standard methods of execution before the Mongols had been either strangulation or beheading. Mongol traditionalists did not approve of the former, as it avoided the shedding of blood, a 'kindness' reserved by Mongol convention to the higher echelons of society. A savage punishment was introduced for treason, to the Mongols as to others – the most heinous of crimes. Cuts would be made in eight different points of the body, from the head to the feet. The trick was for those who were particularly reviled to die slowly, so they might be cut in these places dozen of times before expiring. But on the other hand, the number of crimes for which death was the punishment, was reduced by half under the Mongols, and during the course of over forty years only 2,743 executions took place, which compares rather favourably with the rate of such punishments in modern-day China.[7]

Despite the reverses in Japan, Kublai appeared to be carrying on the great tradition of Genghis. The empire was expanding, and the addition of new territories had continued at a formidable pace. All, it seemed, was well with the Mongol world. Global conquest might take longer than expected but it would come.

But all great empires end. During Kublai's reign there were some alarming developments that presaged the destruction of the Mongol world. There were the internal divisions: Kublai's world was China but elsewhere Kaidu nibbled away at Mongolia, the Chagataids governed virtually autonomously and Persia and the lands of the Golden Horde were, to all intents and purposes, separate kingdoms. In addition, like all great imperialists, the Mongols became complacent, unaware of the challenges looming that would overwhelm them. It happened to others too. Rome, the British Empire and the empire of Alexander all shared one thing in common; they overreached themselves. Those subjected rose up against them, and the unity that has underwritten expansion weakens and then collapses. The Mongols may have believed that they were the people destined to buck the trend. If they truly believed this, then they were wrong. Allegedly, they were at the height of their powers, in reality the Mongols were already on a downhill slope.

CHAPTER 10

The Slippery Slope:
Kublai Raids Japan Again & the Overstretching of the Mongol Empire 1278-1294

It is difficult to see from a modern perspective what constructive impact the Mongols had on the world, because their violence and destructive prowess have made it hard to see any positive outcomes from their expansionism. But scratch the surface and it is clear how profoundly they shaped the world in which we live. Their impact resonated down history for centuries, and continues to do so. Kublai changed the world in which he ruled perhaps more than any other Mongol *khan*. He also became a fascinating figure to the West, for during his reign a young traveller from Europe by the name of Marco Polo made his way to his court. He was not, for sure, the first westerner to do so, but his narrative made a huge impact on the West.

Marco's book had often been regarded as a mixture of historical narrative and a fantastical make-believe account, which owed much to his imagination. He wrote less than a decade after he returned from his long sojourn with Kublai, whilst a prisoner of the Genovese (he himself being a Venetian). He was not the first Polo to visit Kublai. Marco's father Niccolo and his uncle Maffeo had been trading in the regions owned by Hülegü in 1262 when they found themselves caught up as innocent bystanders in the civil war. Rather than make the risky journey home through a war-zone, they instead made their way to Kublai's court, where they were well received. En route they stopped for three years in Bokhara. Eventually returning to the west, the Polos decided to launch another mission in 1271. Kublai had asked them to return carrying a vial of oil from the most sacred church in Christendom, the Holy Sepulchre in Jerusalem. They left from the Crusader port of Acre, this time with Papal support from Pope Gregory X. They planned to take a couple of missionaries with them, but the men chosen lacked the stamina for the task (they were put off by war in Armenia) so they went on alone, this time accompanied by

Niccolo's seventeen-year old son Marco.

The journey was excruciating. According to Marco's account 'they were hard put to it to complete the journey in three and a half years, because of snow and rain and flooded rivers'.[1] Their journey took them past many wonders: Noah's Ark in Armenia, and the tombs of the Three Magi who had worshipped Christ in Persia for example. They eventually reached Kublai in Xanadu where they were well received. They would stay in Mongol territory for the next twenty years. Marco's account of these journeys, essentially a travelogue, became one of the most famous books of the medieval period. It was also one of the most influential, in that it gave the West an insight into a strange new world that excited the imaginer of explorers like Columbus as well as, equally importantly, merchants, who drooled over the riches on offer in the Orient. Given its impact, it is important to spell out the strengths and weaknesses of this extraordinary narrative.

One of the book's weaknesses is its tendency to be fanciful in some of its descriptions. There are accounts of soothsayers, of people who could cast spells on wrongdoers, of men who protected themselves with lucky charms. Sometimes too, Marco is repetitive, particularly in his battle scenes. The following is a brief extract from a stock account of a battle that he trotted out with monotonous regularity:

> What more shall I say? This was the start of a bitter and bloody battle. Now you might see arrows flying like pelting rain, for the whole air was full of them. Now you might see horsemen and horses tumbling dead upon the ground. So loud was the shouting and the clash of armies that you could not have heard the thunder of heaven.[2]

This is a description of Nayan's fight with Kublai, but it could just as easily be lifted direct from Malory's *Morte D'Arthur*. All good poetic stuff, but Marco uses pretty much the same description in each battle scene that he talks about. This is more than just a criticism of literary style; it is symptomatic of something deeper. Marco is talking about events that he did not witness firsthand, though he may of course have got information from those who did.

The style is indicative of what Marco is trying to achieve; he is not trying to write an account which is historically accurate in every detail, he is attempting to talk about events in a way that would excite his readers. That inevitably has repercussions for his accuracy. In this he is no different than every other medieval chronicler who comes to mind. However, if we accept these deficiencies, there is much to commend him too. Some of the information about this new world must have stunned his readers. There were descriptions of ships from India, a little known world, carrying up to 6,000 baskets of pepper, vessels with watertight compartments that could keep a ship afloat if it was holed. Then there was Japan, a land not known at all. Marco describes how there were palaces roofed with gold and how pearls were so plentiful that when a man died, he was buried with one in his mouth. So wealthy were the islands that they had attracted the envy of Kublai himself. The book was full of strange, exotic, sometimes frightening tales, of cannibals on Java and the Andaman Islands. The modern equivalent would be if an astronaut returned from a space mission carrying word of some previously undiscovered planet, with an impressively advanced civilisation living on it.

From Marco we also have a description of Kublai. He described him as being neither tall nor short, but of medium height. His limbs were well fleshed out. His eyes were black and handsome, the nose set squarely in place. His face was ruddy like a red rose. He tells of his four main wives, and his many concubines. By his four wives, he had sired twenty-two male children. There were twenty-five other sons from his concubines. Think of the Mongols and one thinks of battles, conquests and massacres. It is less common to consider what motivated the Mongols. But great riches and other privileges came to the victor. Every year, Kublai sent officials around his empire looking for the most beautiful women for his harem. An extraordinary ritual then followed:

> After inspecting every girl feature by feature, her hair, her face, her eye-brows, her mouth, her lips and every other feature, to see whether they are well-formed and in harmony with her person, the valuers award to some a score of sixteen marks, to others seventeen, eighteen or twenty, or more or less according to the degree of their beauty.[3]

Kublai would then order the top scoring girls in this beauty parade to be brought to him. The valuers would then have a second look and the top thirty or forty would be brought to his chamber for his enjoyment. It was obviously not all hard work being a Mongol *khan*.

Marco Polo inspired men with tales of great cities and incredible riches. Returning from the East in 1292, he put quill to parchment in 1298. The impact was explosive: men who could read were fascinated by the tale and the world of which he spoke. One such, an adventurer by the name of Christopher Columbus, tried to sail west across the ocean, and bumped into America by accident. It was the successor to Kublai's China, real or imagined, that he was trying to find.

There were impacts on the world elsewhere too; for example, China itself. For centuries it had been divided, its greatness diluted by internal rifts. Kublai stuck it back together again. In the process he laid the foundations of modern China, the world's newest and fastest rising power. This was not all good. He gave it dubious claims to Tibet and possibly to Mongolia too (the Chinese have conquered it in the past: at the moment they are not claiming it for themselves, but who knows what the future might hold?). It was as if Kublai really did become Chinese, and in the process, gave China the rights to the empire once ruled by him.

Other consequences of the Mongols' expansionism were powerful too. One in particular came about in an indirect way, but was nonetheless real for all that. As the Second World War was coming to its end, a young Japanese pilot, Ensign Teruo Yamaguchi, penned a farewell letter to his father. In it he reflected on the Japanese world in words of almost unbearable simplicity:

> The Japanese way of life is indeed beautiful, and I am proud of it, as I am of Japanese history and mythology, which reflect the purity of our ances-tors and their belief in the past – whether or not those beliefs are true. That way of life is the product of all the best things, which our ancestors have handed down to us. And the living embodiment of all wonderful things out of our past is the Imperial Family which, too, is the crystallisation of the splendour and beauty of Japan and its people. It is an honour to be able to give my life in defence of these beautiful and lofty things.[4]

That devotion to an Emperor divinely appointed, that love of past glory, that sense of history and of a spiritual destiny for the nation, went back in a straight line for nearly 700 years, to a time when Japan's survival seemed to be unlikely, until the gods intervened. This all happened because of Kublai's determination to add Japan to his empire. He was about to suffer cataclysmic defeat and in the process breathe spiritual life into the islands of Japan.

The debacle experienced during the first attempt to conquer Japan rankled with Kublai. It was a blot on an impressive record that could only be erased by conquest. So he plotted for revenge, for a chance to put the record right. He would need the help of Korea again to do so, but the country was in trouble. It had been denuded of manpower for the previous attempt on Japan and had also contributed huge amounts of resources to the shipbuilding programme. It was also short of food; harvests had not been good, and Kublai had been forced to send in provisions to top up supplies.

A stickler for protocol, Kublai again sent an embassy to Japan in 1279 demanding the surrender of the islands to his rule. His envoys were told to tread carefully and keep their calm whatever happened. The emperor was to be informed that he would be allowed to keep his kingdom as a client monarch, if he agreed to recognise Kublai as his overlord. However, Japan was nervous. There were rumours of Mongol spies abroad in the country, and nerve ends were frayed. The ambassadors were promptly executed.

So the orders went out from Kublai to the shipbuilders once more, this time not for one fleet but for two. One was to sail to Japan from Korea, the other from the south of China. The two fleets were to combine into one at the island of Iki, about twenty miles off the mainland of Japan. But there was a big risk taken in the timing of the enterprise. It would take place in late summer and the typhoon season normally arrived in August. If the fleet were to be caught by one, then disaster might ensue. It was to be a huge invasion fleet, much bigger than the first expedition that had previously made its way to Japan. But from the outset there were problems. The Korean fleet arrived on time, but the Chinese fleet was late. The latter had been unable to leave when it should, and, with food rotted, key commanders were taken ill and momentum was already being lost. Given the fact that time was of the essence, these delays were worrisome.

In the meantime the commander of the Korean fleet ran out of patience. He landed some of his men on Iki, and took the outpost easily enough. However, the mainland was an altogether different proposition. When, with the Chinese fleet still not in sight, the Koreans pushed on to the mainland near Munakata, they were forced back by a determined defence onto an island in the middle of a bay. The walls that the Japanese had erected to keep the enemy out were too formidable to be bypassed without the assistance of Mongol soldiers. The Chinese fleet eventually set out a month behind schedule and, realising that there was probably no point in making for a rendezvous that was no longer likely to be met, they made their way straight to the mainland, or at least a small island just off it called Takashima. Here they regrouped, replenished and made themselves ready for the main assault. Those unfortunate enough to live on the island, just a few hundred wretched souls, were all slaughtered. There was a local legend that the last few survivors hid away in a cave, but their presence was revealed to the Mongols by a treacherous cockerel. They were all dragged out of their hidey-hole and killed.

However, the Chinese fleet had chosen its position poorly. The landing place opposite was narrow; there was little room to manoeuvre, few spaces to land, and plenty of spots for the Japanese to rush reinforcements in. The Japanese also went onto the offensive, using small craft to sail in amongst the Chinese and create havoc. There were acts of extraordinary individual valour. The small Japanese boats carried about fifteen samurai, who attacked the Mongol ships at night by lowering boarding bridges under cover of darkness. In one attack thirty samurai swam out to a Mongol ship, decapitated the entire crew and then swam back to shore again. Another warrior, Kusano Jiro, set fire to a Mongol ship even though his arm had been cut off. They were more than holding their own. Their cause was helped no end by the fact that the enemy facing them were substantially composed of Chinese and Korean men; their hearts were simply not in the fight.

For two months the fight went on. The fleet were too intimidated by the Japanese defences for the soldiers onboard to land. However, worse was to come for the Mongols. It was now August, the typhoon season, there were ominous clouds billowing in and every sign that the weather was about to break. The storm hit on 15 August. The craft assembled off the coast of Japan were generally not very large. There are increasingly suggestions, based on underwater archaeology, that many of the vessels were little more than river barges, hopelessly inadequate for an expedition across an open sea, especially when the wind blew like this. It has even been suggested that sabotage might have played a part in what was to come, as neither Koreans nor Chinese were particularly enamoured of Mongol rule and wished the expedition to fail.

At any event, the disaster that now befell the Mongol fleet was cataclysmic in scale. Sea captains, realising with terror what was about to befall them, tried to put out to sea to ride out the storm. When they were forced inexorably towards the shore they threw their massive granite anchors over the side in a frantic effort to stay out in the bay. For all too many of them, the attempt was hopeless and their craft were thrown like helpless puppies against the rocks and onto the beaches. Their men died in their thousands, perhaps upwards of 50,000. It was the most complete maritime disaster in history.

This was the end. The remnants of this once proud fleet limped back to mainland Asia, their commanders – those who had lived – trembling in trepidation at the thought of having to explain to Kublai what had gone wrong – again. The gods had not smiled on them, and this must have been the most difficult thing of all to explain away, for had not heaven decreed that the entire world belonged to the Mongols? A debacle of this scale would take some explanation – it did not fit at all comfortably with the perception of Mongol invincibility that was required.

The Japanese of course could not believe their luck. But when they reflected they did not put the outcome down to mere good fortune. Many a prayer had been uttered to the gods by a people terrified at the fate that it seemed imminently awaited them. No, this was nothing less than a divine intervention. The breath of the gods had scattered the greatest fleet in the world. There was a name for this divine wind, one that was going to become an everyday word centuries later – *kamikaze*. Such was the myth and it was true to an extent. The winds had indeed blown and the fleet was indeed scattered. But this had just been the final nail in the coffin. There were in fact two reasons why the expedition was in tatters. The first was that the Mongol expedition had been a shambles. The two fleets had not become one as planned, and there were insufficient troops – and insufficient will to fight.

And in that latter issue the Mongols perhaps had a warning of a weakness that so many other empires have discovered before and since; the problem that arises when that empire has to rely on the troops of a subject nation to fight its battles for it. A determined Mongol commander would have forced his troops ashore and when the typhoon struck most of them would have been off the ships. The second reason for the reverse was the fighting spirit of the Japanese defenders. Faced with a terrifying challenge against the mightiest army in the world, they had fought with spirit and resilience. It was true that the Mongols had been fighting in an environment – that is, at sea – that was alien to them. But they had been prevented from landing by a combination of the bravery of their fighting men and the strategically sited walls that had prevented the Mongols from storming ashore.

Kublai never gave up on the idea of conquering Japan. He would even occasionally send another summons to the emperor of Japan demanding that he hand over his country as decreed by the gods. But the emperor was now more confident than ever. Heaven had spoken, and it had spoken against Kublai and his Mongols. Kublai was now faced with a predicament. It was required of a Mongol emperor that he should go forth and conquer, and – in the case of Japan at least – he had failed in his divinely appointed mission. It must have come as a shock after all those decades of conquest to find that the Mongols had been defeated. It was not the first setback ever, of course. Ail Jalut had been a bad reverse and there had been others. But the sheer scale of the Japanese defeat was breathtaking.

What was worrying for Kublai was that this was not the only setback during this period. Burma was also a desirable target for the Mongols. Given its proximity to China it was the logical next step. Kublai initiated the traditional first step by sending three envoys to the king of Burma, Narathihipate, demanding his submission. However, the king was not popular, he was a usurper and he had not won the people over to his side. He was vainglorious, delighting in building extravagant new temples that he could ill afford, and spending much of his time cosseted with one or another of his 3,000 concubines. When Mongol envoys were sent demanding surrender, Narathihipate took the imprudent step of having them executed, inevitably calling down the wrath of the Mongols on his head. The king was a man who did things to excess: inscriptions on Burmese temples describe him as having an army of 36 million and of enjoying curries so much that he ate 300 of them a day! Kublai could not respond straightaway because of distractions elsewhere, but in 1277 he at last sent in an army to subdue Burma and punish the king for his intransigence. It was led by Nasir al-Din, whose father Saiyid Ajall, a Central Asian subject from Bokhara, was one of Kublai's favourites.

The Burmese moved confidently up to the border to face off the invaders. They were accompanied by several hundred war-elephants. The Mongol horses were terrified at this sight, new to their eyes as it was, and would not move forward. However, Mongol archers were not so timid, and they dismounted and moved forward to loose hundreds of arrows towards this unmissable target. When wounded, an elephant was uncontrollable and was most likely to run away from the source of its pain, the Mongol army. This meant that they turned about and stampeded back through their own lines, trampling anyone unlucky enough to be in their way beneath their enormous feet. Utter carnage ensued.

Now that the Burmese were in flight, and the terrifying elephants were heading into the far distance, the horses recovered their nerve and the Mongol cavalry raced after a broken enemy, adding to the slaughter. Among the prizes captured were a number of elephants, which formed a menagerie later presented to Kublai for his entertainment. However, although the battle was won, the war was not. The king ran away but the Mongols were overwhelmed by the disease so prevalent in the jungles of Burma and against which they had no sort of immunity. The move into Burma was taking the Mongols into strange new environments, characterised by jungle, humidity and debilitating heat and disease. So, their mission unaccomplished, they returned to Kublai with a victory to boast of but no conquest.

Kublai also had his eyes firmly fixed on Vietnam, which was in those days divided into two countries, one in the north known as Annam, and the other as Champa. Of course, these two were believed to be part of Kublai's empire by virtue of his divine birthright. The usual formalities were followed, envoys were sent demanding submission. The two countries showed more temperance than the Burmese and sent back some gifts but no more (these included another elephant and a rhinoceros to add to the menagerie). Kublai wanted more and in 1280 insisted on formal recognition from Champa, a country famed for its elephants, its aloe wood and its ebony.

The campaign to enforce this demand was entrusted to the governor of Canton, Sodu. He took a fleet with 5,000 men to what was, until recently South Vietnam, and on landing there demanded the submission of the people. But the king of Champa, Indravarman V, was having none of it. He took to the jungle and prepared to embark on a determined guerrilla campaign. The Mongols were about to find out, as later superpowers would, just how difficult Vietnamese territory could be to subdue. Parallels with later Vietnamese campaigns are hard to avoid. Fighting went on for several years, much longer than anticipated. The Chams were fierce fighters: their strongest weapons were perhaps their great war-elephants, some of which were used as platforms for crossbowmen. When Sodu found that the guerrilla campaign was proving impossible to subdue, he sent for reinforcements. They achieved nothing. Indravarman fought on resolutely and in his mountainous jungle hideouts were impervious to the Mongols. Sodu believed that a change of strategy was needed, and embarked on one that was to make the situation worse rather than better.

Sodu did not like the idea that reinforcements had to be sent by sea, and so he ran a suggestion past Kublai. There was a land route available to the Mongols through Annam. In the *khan's* view, Annam was Mongol territory anyway so why not send a message to the king of Annam, Tran Nhan Tong, demanding that he let a Mongol army cross his lands to get to the south? Kublai loved the idea: it would be militarily expedient but it would also draw the king of Annam out. He would either have to accept Mongol supremacy or deny it. The ultimatum was duly sent placing the king in something of a quandary. By failing to agree to the demand he would inevitably invite retribution, yet if he let the Mongols in, he felt that they would never leave again. Tran prevaricated, genuinely not knowing what to do. He eventually found courage and decided that he would rebuff Kublai, knowing full well what was likely to follow.

His decision was taken in council in January 1285. There was a strong will to fight. This was a fighter's country, with every male required to provide military service. Everywhere people came to join the army, fired up by nationalistic fervour, and a deep-set hatred of the Mongol scourge. They would not have long to wait to prove their devotion to the king's cause, for a Mongol army under Kublai's son Toghan was already on its way.

Toghan was confident when he should have been cautious. Back in 1257 a Mongol army under a famous general Uriyang-kadai had attempted to subdue Annam. It had been forced to retreat by a combination of stubborn resistance and disease, though the year after the king of Annam had nominally recognised Mongol supremacy, and sent his son to the Mongols as a hostage. But now Toghan had a huge army with him, hundreds of thousands strong, recruited in the south of China. This gave him a huge numerical advantage, and he rapidly pushed into Annam, reaching Hanoi in June 1285. All had gone very well, or so Toghan thought to himself. But it was all a ruse. The people of Annam had adopted a scorched earth policy, stripping the country of provisions as the Mongols moved further into it. Hanoi was a ghost town by the time that they arrived there. They could re-supply by sea, but it would take time. The warriors of Annam were fighting a determined guerrilla war from the hinterland of their country, and disease was starting to take its toll on the Mongols again.

The supreme commander of the army of Annam was Tran Hung Dao. He was waiting for the right moment to launch a counter-attack against the invaders. When it was instigated, a fierce battle followed at Chuong Duong. It ended in a stunning victory for Annam over the Mongols. The victors moved back into Hanoi, whilst the losers retreated over the Red River. This was not the end. The Mongols were chased across the river and another battle followed, with Annam once again triumphant. Sodu was captured and beheaded, paying the ultimate price for the folly of the policy that he had advocated. Thousands of Mongols were taken prisoner. The rest fled out of the country. It was another stunning reverse for the Mongols, coming just a few years after the disaster that was the Japanese invasion. Kublai could not let such a rebuff go unanswered. In 1288 an army returned to Annam. It would be led by some of Kublai's most senior commanders, although Toghan would also be given a chance to redeem himself. It was to be an overwhelming assault. A huge land base would be set up, and an attack from the sea launched to coincide with that from onshore.

However, the Mongols had met their match in Tran Hung Dao, who came up with an amazingly successful strategy to fight off the Mongols. On land, it would be a scorched earth policy again. By contrast it was the response to the attack from the water that showed real brilliance. The Mongols sailed upriver into the hinterland of Annam. As they did so they were being watched. When they had passed, hundreds of warriors waded into the water and planted long pointed stakes in the river-bed. Their tops were hidden just below the waterline. Packed closely together, they represented a death trap for large ships that were unaware of their presence. Like a giant submarine porcupine, the stakes lurked out of sight, a devastating threat to the Mongol fleet.

The attacks that the Mongol vessels launched upriver were beaten off, and they sailed in disorder back the way they had come. Before them, much smaller enemy craft fled. Because of their shallow draft they sailed safely over the stakes. The Mongol ships, however, being bigger vessels, did not. They impaled themselves on the sharp underwater points. To complete the carnage, fire-ships were then sent into the midst of the Mongol fleet, turning what was already a decisive defeat into a rout. Toghan escaped and made his way back to Kublai, who was far from pleased at a second major defeat in Annam. Toghan was sent into exile to ponder on the vicissitudes of fate. Annam remained tantalisingly beyond the reach of Kublai, another black mark in his far from unblemished record of conquest. Both Annam and Champa later sent nominal tributes to Kublai, in theory recognising his supremacy, as a way of ensuring that he did not return; in practice, his writ did not run in either country.

Burma was another blot to be erased from the record. Kublai continued to send delegations to the country demanding submission, but the response from Burma was to ask for mercy; Kublai had great domains already, they said, and they appealed to his Buddhist beliefs (Burma was a Buddhist country) in an effort to induce him to stay away. This tactic did not work for long. In 1286 an opportunity for Kublai arose when Narathihipate was murdered by his son, who held a knife to his throat and forced him to drink poison. Understandably this led to a great deal of internal disturbance in Burma. Sensing the weakness, Kublai sent a small army commanded by Esun Timür, grandson of Genghis, to take advantage of the situation. However, this turned out to be little more than a grubby raid. The temples of the capital, Pagan, were stripped of their gold, a sacrilege that did Kublai little credit. Burma agreed to pay tribute in token recognition of Mongol supremacy, but Kublai played little part in Burmese affairs.

Burma itself returned to being a nation at war with itself, another disturbing resonance of modern times.

There was one last major enterprise undertaken in Kublai's reign, perhaps the most ambitious Mongol adventure yet. Hundreds of miles away from the heartlands of the Mongol empire, across storm-tossed oceans and wind-swept seas, a powerful and rich empire had been established in Java. In 1289, its emperor was a man named Kertenagara. He had intervened to an extent in mainland Asian affairs by arranging a marriage to a Champa princess. He also sought to extend his dominions to the detriment of the neighbouring princes who ruled in Sumatra and Bali.

In that year a delegation arrived out of the blue. It had been despatched by Kublai and it brought with it a familiar message. Submit, demanded the great *khan*, or suffer the consequences. Kertenagara's response had the virtue of being innovative. He had a scornful message tattooed on the face of Kublai's foremost envoy, so that all might be able to read exactly what the emperor of Java thought of his demands. It was a proud riposte, though it is fair to venture that the pride emanated from a sense of security felt by Kertenagara in the light of the distance from Kublai's empire. The sea, he felt, might be a greater barrier than the highest and thickest of walls. He had also no doubt heard of the debacle suffered by the Mongols in Japan. The Mongols' defeats there seemed to prove that they had no aptitude for naval warfare. The insult meted out to the envoy could not be ignored by Kublai. A war-fleet was assembled to teach the imprudent emperor a lesson he would never forget. It took three years to build the fleet; shipbuilders by this time must have been a little tired of constructing hundreds of ships with no guarantee of success in the campaign that they were to be used in. It gave Kertenagara plenty of time to prepare, and he took advantage of this to launch what he thought would be a decisive counter-stroke.

His plan was to ambush the Mongols as they made their way slowly down the coasts of Champa and Malaya, to hit them hard before they were within a thousand miles of his kingdom. The plan was not without its merits save for one ultimately fatal flaw; the Mongols had no intention of taking the circuitous route that Kertenagara thought they would employ. Instead they sailed direct to Java, a distance of 2,500 miles. This was an immense undertaking, a high-risk strategy that could have ended in disaster if the weather had turned (and memories of what had happened in Japan no doubt weighed heavily on some minds). But this time the gods were with the Mongols. When they made land, Kertenagara was more than unprepared – he was actually dead.

He had become embroiled in a war with his neighbours and had died on campaign. His forces were spread all over the place, and his kingdom was incapable of fighting off the Mongol invaders. Shi-pi, the commander of the Mongol forces, could not believe his luck. He appeared to be on the verge of a momentous victory when he allowed himself to be distracted. Kertenagara's son-in-law, Vijaya, offered submission to the Mongols, along with sumptuous gifts, if they would in return help him fight the neighbouring state of Kediri. Delighted at the offer, Shi-pi went to war with Kediri on behalf of Vijaya, and won a bloody victory against an outmatched enemy.

Shi-pi, no doubt ecstatic at his success, returned to Vijaya for his reward. It was not quite as welcome a prize as he might have hoped. Now that the Mongols had done his work for him, Vijaya turned on them. Caught far away from his ships, Shi-pi had to fight his way back to the coast 100 miles away. He made it and sailed back to Kublai who was furious at his failure. He was whipped for his poor judgement and deprived of a third of his property. There had then been a collection of failures; Japan was the worst but Champa, Annam and Java also represented unsuccessful ventures, whilst the intervention in Burma had achieved next to nothing. Collectively, these reverses suggested that the Mongol empire had reached its natural limits. Some of those limits were due to natural barriers, not least the Mongols' inability to conquer the sea. But there was also an unwritten natural equation at work; in the final analysis, no empire has been strong enough to conquer the whole world, much less to hold it. Fuelled by success, ambitions grow until the empire becomes bloated, lethargic, and incapable of reacting to changing circumstances quickly enough.

During the Second World War, when another great Asiatic power won a victory at Pearl Harbour, a later would-be empire went on to conquer every target it set itself for a time. When this happened, some observers noticed the emergence of a trait of arrogant over-confidence by which Japanese generals believed they held the moral ascendancy over every enemy that might stand up to them. This led them to overstretch themselves. The observers called the cause of this problem 'victory disease' and it provides a good explanation for what happened to the Mongols. 'Victory disease', had infected them too, and they were slowly succumbing to its debilitating effects. In the 1280s Kublai slowly declined physically. It is easy to forget that, unlike Genghis, he was not a young man when he came to the throne. When he was fighting for the *khanate* in the early years of the 1260s, he was not far off fifty years old. As time went on, his fondness for the good life increasingly showed itself. He became overweight, then corpulent, then obese. As his weight increased, so his dynamism reduced proportionately. He suffered a bitter personal blow in 1281 when his beloved Chabi died. She had been a wise, moderating influence on him, making sure whilst she was alive that success never went to his head. She left behind her a number of children including Jingim, Kublai's nominated heir. Kublai, when he was nearly seventy, took a new wife to help him cope with the loss of Chabi. Clearly there was still some life and vitality in him yet, for soon after he fathered a child by her.

In 1285 an adviser to Jingim, perhaps seeing his father declining, suggested privately to confidantes that Kublai should abdicate. Word of this imprudent suggestion filtered through to the *khan* who was outraged at the suggestion. Soon after, Jingim fell ill and died; from what no one is sure. Once again a potential problem child had died in strange circumstances soon after having been involved in strained circumstances with his father, in just the same way as it had happened to Jochi with Genghis. There is absolutely no evidence of foul play in connection to Jingim's death, but the timing of it seems very suspicious. One should never doubt the ruthlessness of a Mongol ruler who felt threatened from whatever source. As if to prove the point, at this late stage of Kublai's reign an old adversary, close to home, reappeared. It is significant that most of the key events that marked his *khanate* occurred in the east. With Kublai's gaze seemingly fixed on the Orient, Kaidu took advantage of any problem further west to advance his own interests. In Tibet, Phags-Pa had died in 1280 and left behind a vacuum. An ally of Kaidu, Duwa, involved himself in the rebellion that followed. The fighting was both lengthy and inconclusive, but the mere fact that Kaidu's ally was at war with the established order in Tibet, which was explicitly supported by Kublai, spoke volumes.

In 1288, Kaidu moved into Uighur territory, which was towards the heart of the Mongol empire. Kublai was forced to temporarily abandon it. However, he was not prepared to do so on a permanent basis, and the year after its abandonment he sent an army to sort Kaidu out. A fierce battle followed in which, allegedly, thousands of Mongols died. But Kaidu was spreading his wings. He also involved himself with a challenger to Kublai in Manchuria, Nayan. It was, according to Marco Polo, Nayan who approached Kaidu and suggested that they cooperated together against Kublai. This was a grave threat. The long arms of Kaidu were wrapped wide around Kublai's heartlands in China, as if moving in to strangle the life out of him and his empire. Although old and obese, Kublai still had fight in him. He called on Bayan, the conqueror of the

Song all those years before, once more. He was sent to Karakorum, still symbolically crucial, to reassert Kublai's authority there. Kublai himself set off to face up to Nayan. He gathered together a large army to face up to the threat. We can take Marco Polo's assertion that he collected an army of 360,000 men with a generous pinch of salt. However, his statement that he was forced to rely on locally available levies for his army, because many of his men were dispersed elsewhere, has more of a ring of truth about it.

Kublai sought advice from his astrologers and they advised him that he would be successful in the campaign ahead. He caught up with Nayan, catching him off guard asleep in bed with his wife, if Marco is to be believed. Off balance, Nayan's troops assembled themselves hurriedly for battle. The sky was filled with the voices of the warriors chanting their war psalms on the eve of the fight. Then the great war drums beat out their insistent rhythm, and the two great armies moved in on each other. A fierce battle ensued, lasting for hours. It was said that Kublai watched over events in the battle from a great tower carried on the back of four war-elephants. At the end of it all, Nayan was captured. He then suffered the 'bloodless' death reserved for princes of the Mongol royal family (he was distantly related to Genghis) by being wrapped in a carpet and trampled. In fact, this was probably far from bloodless, given the violence with which he was thrown around, but the important symbolic point was to prevent his blood from being spilt on the earth. He was an irritating itch, little more, though Kublai was glad to put an end to his challenge. Kaidu in the meantime retreated west, abandoning some of his conquests in the process.

Bayan did not come out of these events too well. Some felt that his position in Karakorum meant that he was well placed to stop Kaidu escaping, but he had failed to do so. It was even suggested that he was secretly collaborating with him. Kublai was forced to banish Bayan until the rumours died down. In the meantime Kaidu was rash and moved too close to Kublai's men. There was another clash and several thousand of Kaidu's men were captured, though once again he managed to escape. But Kublai was forced to let him be. His energy was slipping away as age and overindulgence took its toll. The closing years of his reign were a metaphor for the Mongol empire; debilitation and decline in old age, a pale reflection of the glory and virility of earlier life. Time was catching up with Kublai. He must have known it himself but he made no effort to embark on a healthier way of life in order to buy himself a few more years. He struggled to cope without his treasured Chabi. She seems genuinely to have been his pride and joy, and certainly a trusted confidante in the mould of other great Mongol women. Deprived of his trusted wife and worn out by many battles as well as affairs of state, his love of life died long before he did.

Marco Polo had gone too, leaving in 1292, supposedly after undertaking one last mission for Kublai to India; he claimed to have been on many such for him, though not all critics are convinced of the veracity of the claim. He took with him a bride for Arghun, the *ilkhan* of Persia. They went by sea, landing at Sumatra and then sailing across the Indian Ocean, a remarkable journey to end an amazing sojourn. Unfortunately, their good deed in accompanying the bride-to-be seemed to be wasted, as Arghun was already dead by the time that they arrived in Persia. However, all ended happily enough when she was married to Arghun's ultimate successor Ghazan instead: the Mongols did not like wasted effort. The Polos continued their long journey, eventually arriving back in Venice in 1295.

For Kublai, there were still some small triumphs left to celebrate in his life. The kingdom of Siam (modern Thailand) was ruled by Ramkhamhaeng and he decided that he would stay on good terms with the Mongols at all costs. He had signed a treaty with the Mongols in 1282 and now, late on in Kublai's reign, he presented himself in person to Kublai. He was well received by the *khan*, and his obeisance undoubtedly saved his kingdom from being invaded as some of his neighbours had. The quasi-annexation of his country marked the widest reach of the Mongol empire.

On New Year's Day it was traditional that Kublai would attend festivities to mark the event in Beijing. When the festivities were held in 1294, he was not there, too ill to attend. He had suffered from gout for many years, and as far back as 1267 he had sent to Korea to ask for some fish-skins to be sent to him from which shoes could be made to ease the pain in his swollen feet. Now he was lonely and had lost the will to live. He was obese and, like other *khans* before him, he was drinking far too much. It seemed that the end was approaching and messengers were sent to Bayan in exile, urgently summoning him to Kublai's side. By the time he arrived it was obvious that the *khan* was dying. Nothing remained to be done but to ease his passing to the next world.

It had been a reign of contradictory progress, with great gains but also unprecedented defeats. The destruction of the Mongol invasion fleet sent to Japan, contrasted starkly with the final conquest of Song China. Unsatisfactory outcomes too had been the result of many of his endeavours in south-east Asia. However, these were not the greatest or most significant reverses of his time on the throne. The major failure of his reign was his inability to bring Kaidu to book. Another Mongol had defied his authority and lived to tell the tale with his power largely unbroken. Such a pass would have been unthinkable if Genghis has been *khan*.

Marco Polo described Kublai, whom he called incorrectly the sixth khan of the Mongols, as 'greater and more powerful than any of the others. For all the other five put together would not have such power as belongs to Kublai.'[5] But he was wrong – he was confusing territory nominally held with power. The latter is all about authority, the ability to impose one's will on his subjects, and in that respect Genghis was greater than Kublai by far. And yet perhaps it is not as simple as that. Kublai and Genghis were two great men who were in many ways vastly different. Kublai was trying to be something that his grandfather had never been, both the Emperor of China and the Great Khan. If he failed substantially in the latter respect – and that must be the conclusion given the disunity of the empire on his death – he made a much better fist of the former.

Throughout his life he walked a fine line, wanting to integrate with his Chinese subjects whilst being as careful as he could be to avoid upsetting Mongol traditionalists in the process. He paid attention to the needs of the peasants of China in stark contrast to earlier Mongol incursions into the north. Artisans had been supported by him, as had merchants. Economic reforms were made: when foreign merchants entered China they were forced to exchange any precious metals they had for paper money.

His economic approach was radical in some ways but reassuringly prudent in others. When the south was conquered, he was faced with the problem of how to integrate the currency with that of the former Chin north. His solution was to adopt the northern currency but only gradually, over time, so as to avoid a meltdown in the south. He developed what was effectively a simple form of central bank, the *ortogh*, whose role was to make loans to merchants. During his long reign there is no evidence of any significant degree of inflation in the economy.

Kublai was accepted as emperor by many of the Chinese, but in the end it was because they had no choice. Kublai tried to be a benevolent ruler, and in many ways he succeeded, yet he was, when all was said and done, a foreigner who would never be loved by his people. There were frequent uprisings in China during his reign, but they were all kept under control. Despite Kublai's attempts to integrate he was always aware that he was tolerated by many of his Chinese subjects only because they were not strong enough to dethrone him. And so, on the one hand, during his reign Kublai encouraged the porcelain trade in China and it proved to be a good time for some of the arts, such as the theatre, although poetry suffered partly because of language difficulties; much was lost in translation when verses were transcribed from Chinese into Mongolian. Painting also continued to do well, although trends changed with the Mongols at the helm, when equine subjects became popular for obvious reasons.

But on the other hand, the Chinese could not be completely trusted. Large numbers of them might be included in Kublai's armies, but his bodyguard would stay Mongol. As one example of the fear that Kublai felt, bamboo could not be traded freely because it might be used to make bows. Chinese were debarred from senior civil service positions, in the past the bedrock of many a lucrative career. There were even frequent restrictions imposed on the Chinese being allowed to learn the Mongolian language. Even in the bedchamber discrimination was practised: not only all his wives but all Kublai's harem were non-Chinese. Kublai tried to maintain a delicate equilibrium, to be both Mongol and Chinese, but in this he ultimately failed and perhaps was truly neither, but it was a fantastically brave effort on his part to try and achieve the impossible. Now the sands of time were running out.

The end came on 18 February. Kublai died in China, where he had spent his life, expiring at the last in the capital city that he had built at Beijing. Yet it is significant that this was not to be his burial place. In life, Kublai was never in Mongolia: in death, he would never leave it. His body was packed in spices and put in a coffin which was carried reverentially back towards the homeland. Marco Polo described how former *khans* had been joined in death by any of their subjects unfortunate enough to cross the path of the cortege on its way to its final destination. He said that Möngke was accompanied by 20,000 such wretched souls. No doubt it was the same for Kublai; or had his appreciation of the Chinese way of life interfered with such savage customs?

At last, after a journey of many days, the procession arrived back in the rolling steppes of Mongolia. Here, Kublai was buried in secret on the sacred hill of Bhurkan Khaldun, somewhere close to his grandfather Genghis. Although he had not quite achieved the eminence of him, he had taken his conquests on to another level. Now he was dead, and with him died the greatness of the Mongol empire.

CHAPTER 11
Decline and Fall:
The Successors of Kublai
1295-1359

The death of Kublai marked a critical change in Mongol fortunes. The glories of his reign can blind the observer to the reality, which is that during his years as Great Khan his power became increasingly restricted in its universality. The *ilkhans* of Persia, the successors of Hülegü, were nominally his subjects, but they operated almost completely autonomously of his command. The name *ilkhan* means 'lesser *khan*' a tacit recognition of Kublai's authority but in practice, the vast distance from China gave them a great deal of independence. Kaidu of course had staked a claim for freedom in large parts of Central Asia, and to a great extent succeeded in getting it. The *khans* of the Golden Horde were against Kublai too. Mongol unity was now nothing save a rapidly fading chimera.

The story of the Mongol empire in the fourteenth century is inevitably bitty, for it is no longer the story of one united Greater Mongolia (it never was in truth) but rather a tale of the fate of several different states, all of them large and significant, but none of them truly part of a greater whole. As the century progressed, the fabric of the empire in most of its constituent parts came crashing down until at the end just a rump was left. But things went at a different pace in different parts of this rapidly fragmenting superstructure, and the rest of the story of the Mongol empire must be told with an increasing emphasis on the divided and increasingly unconnected states that remained now that the empire was on the road to disintegration.

Approaching the subject is one that causes some problems. One early twentieth-century writer, Jeremiah Curtin, got round the problem by simply pretending that the Mongols didn't exist anywhere other then China after the death of Kublai. The last chapter of his work starts with the death of Kublai, and ends with the final loss of China. Of Persia and the lands of the Golden Horde, or the Chagataids in Central Asia, there is never a mention. Rather than repeat the error, I propose to face up to the problem by briefly looking at what happened in each part of the old Mongol empire: an implicit recognition that the Mongol empire had already ceased to exist in its old form when Kublai died.

One of the great problems of the Mongols was their inability to resist the cultures with which they came into contact rather than impose their own poorly defined way of life on their subjects. This meant that they were overwhelmed by those they meant to conquer, not invariably by acts of war, but more insidiously by assimilation. This meant that in several parts of the old empire the Mongols, massively outnumbered invaders, were overwhelmed by those they sought to govern. Marco Polo for one, noticed it. He talked about the 'genuine Tartars', that is the Mongol traditionalists. He then remarks that:

> Nowadays their stock had degenerated. Those who live in Cathay [China] have adopted the manners and customs of the idolaters [the name given to Buddhists] and abandoned their own faith, while those who live in the Levant have adopted the manners of the Saracens [that is they had become Muslims].[1]

The Mongols themselves were being conquered and yet they barely seemed to notice.

After Marco Polo left on his homeward journey, the Mongols were then lost to the West for a while. They had never been understood by Western princes, and with Marco Polo gone events amongst the Mongols became obscure once more. News travelled slowly: Marco wrote his book in 1298 but was not yet aware that Kublai was dead. The attention of the Mongol world was to turn more towards the Middle East, in particular to the lands around Persia. This part of the Mongol empire was frankly a mess, and had been for some time. It recognised Kublai as the Great Khan but lived largely unconnected from the centre of his world in China. On the death of Abaka in 1284, it was expected that his son Arghun would become the *ilkhan* of Persia. However, Arghun was six weeks away from court when Abaka died, and almost at once another succession dispute loomed, this time in Persia.

Arghun's uncle Ahmad (the name gives a clue that he had become a Muslim) saw a chance to seize the inheritance for himself. Born with the traditional Mongol name of Tegüder, Ahmad perhaps felt that the adoption of the Islamic faith would strengthen his hand over those he wished to be his subjects. Declaring himself as the new ruler, he generously distributed large parts of the huge fortune that he took in the process to the great men of Persia, in an effort to buy their loyalty.

His coup appeared to have succeeded, though some men muttered under their breath when he took all of Arghun's wives for his harem. Arghun, as might be expected, was not prepared to accept this disinheritance without a fight. He gathered together a large army and moved on Ahmad. They came face to face on a great plain. Arghun sent emissaries across to his uncle demanding his submission. Ahmad, in the stronger position, responded confidently that he was in charge and he would reward Arghun well if he would submit but on no account would he give up the predominant position he had won. If he refused to accept Ahmad's takeover as a *fait accompli*, then this would be a fight to the death. The scene was set for another intrafamilial battle.

When the messengers returned to Arghun with this strident rebuff, he was furious, and vowed that he too would fight to the death. A fierce fight followed on the morrow. It ended when Arghun's men broke and fled. Euphoric, Ahmad's men chased after them and a bloody rout ensued. During it Arghun was captured. His seizure ended the chase and he was taken back to Ahmad's camp where he was put in chains to await his fate. That was that, it appeared; but it was not. Arghun had sympathisers in the camp, men who believed him to be the legitimate successor to Abaka. A group of them crept to his tent and announced that they planned to rescue him. Arghun at first did not believe them, and told them not to mock him. It may be that he believed they were trying to lure him into an escape, and that they would then kill him when he fled – it would save Ahmad from an embarrassing execution. But it slowly dawned on Arghun that this was no ruse. His rescuers broke his fetters and left with him. Before they did so, he ordered them to unleash a volley of arrows into the tent of the guard's commander which they did, killing him. Men flocked to him as the rightful *ilkhan*. Word soon reached Ahmad that Arghun was free, and heading for court with a large number of supporters. The game was up.

Ahmad headed for Egypt, but his luck was out. As he made his way through one of the passes through which he must journey, a sentry intercepted him. Ahmad tried to bribe his way through, but the sentry would have none of it. He summoned the rest of the guard and easily overpowered the small escort with the fleeing would-be *ilkhan*. Ahmad was taken back to Arghun to receive what justice he might at his hands. It would be rough justice, but he was done to death out of the public gaze. He was taken to a secret place of execution and his body buried in an unknown spot.

Arghun reigned until March 1291, when he died (there were rumours that he was poisoned). There was then another succession dispute; the regularity of such events providing strong evidence of the state of decline that the Mongol empire was then in. History repeated itself with uncanny exactitude. The expected successor was Arghun's son Ghazan, but the *ilkhanate* was usurped by the late ruler's brother Geikhatu. Ghazan was, for the time being, powerless to intervene. However, just a few years after seizing the throne Geikhatu died, allegedly from poisoning. But Ghazan still had to bide his time. When Geikhatu conveniently vacated the throne, it was then taken by another prominent Mongol, Baidu. But Ghazan sensed that the time was now ripe to make his move. He got together an army and moved against Baidu. His intuition was right; a number of Baidu's men deserted him in the battle that followed. His army was crushed and he himself killed. Ghazan at last became ruler of Persia, along with the wife that Marco Polo had helpfully delivered from Kublai Khan.

In 1295, Ghazan took a momentous step. He had been made the *ilkhan* of Persia partly through the help of Nawruz, a Muslim general. The general now prevailed on the *ilkhan* to become a Muslim. Ghazan decided to do so and, in the process, instituted a massive change to former Mongol policy. He would from now on be a Muslim, adopt Muslim customs, and govern as a Muslim ruler. Although he would not generally be intolerant of other religions, he was firmly wedded to the Muslim cause, a sea-change in Mongol policy.

Many of his Mongol adherents followed suit, though for a number it appears that the change was largely cosmetic. The example of Ghazan's ultimate successor, Öljeitü, might not be typical, but it is interesting nonetheless. At various stages of his life he was a Christian, a Buddhist and a Muslim (changing allegiance at various times from Sunni to Shi'a forms of the faith). As he would also have been subject to traditional Mongol shamanist beliefs, this must have been a man with a very confused theology. Or, more likely, Öljeitü was a man who put on differing religious clothes as a matter of expediency, according to the needs of each given moment in time.

Ghazan, however, proved to be a largely successful ruler. He attempted to institute fundamental reforms in his Persian lands, reforms which were much needed. During the reign of Abaka (1265-1282) Persia had been governed from Tabriz. It had the virtue of being located in the grasslands of the northern part of the country, which were of course crucial for the Mongol horse herds. However, 'governed' might be a slightly generous description to apply, for it appears that Persia had for years been an economic mess. Taxes were raised erratically and often- sometimes up to thirty times a year. The situation continued on into the reign of Arghun.

His finance minister was a rapacious, ruthless man, Sa'd al-Dawla. During one mission to Baghdad, he extorted money from the populace by the widespread use of torture, including *bastinado*, repeated beating of the soles of the feet with a cane. It was successful in forcing people to reveal where they had secreted their wealth, but so extreme were his measures that the peasants who were integral to working the land fled and parts of Persia fell out of cultivated use as a result.

There was at least a degree of efficiency about Sa'd al-Dawla, in that he did succeed in balancing the budget, albeit through some pretty extreme policies. However, it is the fate of finance ministers, in most ages it seems to be unpopular, and he was no exception. When Arghun fell ill in 1291, the resultant loss of control allowed his enemies to seize Sa'd al-Dawla and put him to the sword. During the subsequent reign of Geikhatu, even more radical policies had been adopted. With the economy hit hard by a plague that had decimated the cattle herds, he decided to adopt paper money in the style of the Chinese. It was an idea before its time. Merchants did not trust this new-fangled concept and the economy soon ground to a halt. The move proved to be a disaster and the money had to be withdrawn. Ghazan, by now governor of Khorasan, refused to have anything to do with the scheme – possibly hoping to win the support of dissidents as a result – and positioned himself to take advantage of the chaos that had ensued.

When Ghazan's moment finally came, he attempted to secure the support of the Persian people by introducing a more egalitarian and less exploitative style of government, something of a novelty for the Mongols. He introduced a wide-ranging reform programme, regulating the taxes imposed for example. The powers of judges were better controlled too, and grants were offered to encourage farmers to start working uncultivated land again. Ghazan's reign was something of a watershed for Mongol rule in Persia. Widespread conversion to Islam broke down social barriers too, and there is evidence of increased inter-marriage between Mongol and Persian. However, Ghazan did not live for long. His radical ideas did not get a chance to develop, and Mongol rule in Persia went out not with a bang, but with a whimper too.

On Ghazan's death, his brother Öljeitü, the indecisive theologian, took the helm. The major feature of his reign was to move the capital of the Persian *ilkhanate* from Tabriz to Sultaniya, where his magnificent mausoleum still stands as perhaps the greatest architectural memorial to the Mongols. When he died, his place was taken by his son Abu Sa'id. He was still very young when he became the *ilkhan*, and the early part of his rule was characterised by bitter infighting, as men struggled to gain supremacy in a divisive battle to usurp authority. However, when he emerged with his power cemented from these trying years, he proved to be an *ilkhan* who was not without merit. There were some notable achievements in his reign, in particular a peace agreement with the Mamelukes which in theory bought Mongol Persia much needed protection. But when he died in 1335 the *ilkhanate* died with him. Within years, Mongol rule in Persia was a thing of the past.

The complete collapse of Mongol Persia leaves historians with something of a predicament: how can such a sudden event be explained? As one leading analyst of the Mongols noted 'we appear to have here the perplexing phenomenon of an empire which fell without having previously declined'.[2] Biological bad luck played a part: Abu Sa'id failed to leave a son as an heir, and in the crucial absence of one, there was no other representative of the house of Hülegü to stake a convincing claim.

But the reality was that in Persia, the local populace overwhelmingly outnumbered the Mongols, and in attempting to assimilate with them they had in fact achieved precisely the reverse effect. With no powerful leader left to act as a figurehead, the Mongols were absorbed into Persian society, and the conquerors were themselves conquered, not on the field of battle, but in far more subtle non-violent ways. Their arrival in Persia was dramatic and apocalyptic: their departure could not have been more different. It is impossible to give a date when Mongol rule ended, as it simply sank without trace, leaving barely a ripple on the surface. The Mongols were absorbed into Persian society, and there was no wholesale dismissal of them from the country. This contrasted markedly with what was to happen in China.

The assimilation of China into the Mongol empire helped to create the illusion of what was known as the 'Pax Mongolica', a visage of stability and cohesion, sometimes referred to by historians, but hard to identify in reality. The 'Pax' was supposedly something equivalent to the stability that Rome introduced to the world when its empire was at its zenith. It was said that travellers could cross the length and breadth of the Mongol empire without being molested: a classic folktale found all over the world to justify the reign of many a dictator – similar tales have been told of Vlad the Impaler, the medieval Romanian prince, for example.

The briefest review of the evidence will show that no such thing ever existed. The Mongols were always at war, sometimes against rebellious subjects, increasingly against other Mongols. If this were so, how could there be peace and stability? The reality was that at times there may have been security, at other times – with the Mongols increasingly divided and fighting each other – there was not.

Maybe in parts of the empire, travellers could travel safely in contrast to what had gone before, but not everywhere. And with the empire increasingly divided, the problems must have got worse. After all, the Polos had ended up in the court of Kublai precisely because they could not travel in the opposite direction because the Mongols were involved in a bitter civil war. Now, four decades later, just as the loss of Persia shattered illusions, so too did increasing tension in the east, in the land that Kublai had made his heartland but which, after his death, became increasingly unstable.

Not that men did not try and make their way across vast distances to China. One such was an Italian, Francesco Pegolotti. He journeyed across Asia in about 1340, and even committed a number of helpful hints to writing in an attempt to help would-be travellers. His account gives some insight into why the goods that could be purchased from the east were so highly regarded in the West, where the list of locally produced goods was so limited. This list included exotic spices such as pepper, ginger, saffron, cloves, nutmegs, and other luxury goods: silk, salted sturgeons' tails, and gold wire for example. China, at the end of the fabled Silk Road, was critical to the safe delivery of all this to the rest of the world, and whoever controlled that region was in a position of immense power. It is easy to see why, for Kublai, this was indeed the jewel in the crown. The Mongol empire opened up new opportunities to Europe, an increasingly confident though still backward part of the world where traders were always on the lookout for new ways to make money. Exotic goods from the east had a ready made market in the courts of kings and rich nobles back in the West.

Despite these opportunities, there were some obvious weaknesses with the Mongol empire, especially as far as China was concerned, as well as some that were not so readily apparent. The use of paper money, widely employed by Kublai, was not new – the Song had done the same long before – but the science of economics was not well understood. The eventual successors to the Mongol emperors in China eventually abandoned paper money – a sure sign that it was not proving effective, and that economic problems had resulted from its use.

Economic issues played a major part in the decline of Mongol China, but this was not all. The simple fact was that the Mongols were invaders, and aliens therefore, and were not welcome. The fact that they were also regarded as barbarian interlopers can not have helped their cause one iota. At any event, even during Kublai's time, the apogee of Mongol power in China, a foreigner like Marco Polo noticed that the locals bristled at the approach of the *khan's* soldiers. Yet there was an interesting corollary to Mongol rule in China. Some have observed that the Mongols did nothing to develop culture in China, and that may be true. Yet they did nothing to stop it either. Artists continued to produce works of art. Some have even suggested that there are hidden messages in the Chinese art of the time, bamboos swaying in the wind, blossom trees blooming. These are allegedly symbols of resistance; such signs may be, according to some, hidden messages, suggesting stubborn resistance to the rule of the barbarian: a difficult argument to sustain, as there is little empirical evidence to support it, but an interesting one nonetheless.[3]

When Kublai died, his grandson Timür succeeded him in China. Kublai was old at the time of his death, and therefore the dynasty skipped a generation. Timür managed to hold the Chinese portion of the empire together until 1307, but on his death matters went downhill alarmingly. The forces of nature, far more powerful than any human foe, were partly responsible for the demise. A series of natural calamities hit China, in particular when the Yellow River burst its banks and flooded a vast area. When such an event occurred, the results were often, in a terrifying way, spectacular. Sometimes the mouth of the river shifted by as much as 300 miles.[4] The only answer to this seemingly insoluble problem, was to construct flood defences on a massive scale, and the only way that such ambitious schemes could even be considered, was if the local peasantry were recruited *en masse*. Although such measures might be necessary if the waters were to be controlled and contained, they were understandably not popular, so much so that rebellions became an increasingly regular irritant for the Mongols to worry about.

There were other side effects which only made the problem worse. In the areas where the flooding took place, there was inevitably major economic damage too. This meant that the taxes that had previously been levied there could no longer be collected. To make up for the shortfall, other areas, especially in the south of China, had to pay more. This was also, predictably enough, unpopular and here too revolts broke out.

Revolts were a common feature of most periods of Mongol rule; even Genghis had had to contend with them. However, what differed now was the Mongols' inability to cope with them and keep them under control. There were rumours of secret societies determined to remove the Chinese version of the 'Tartar Yoke'. Leaders emerged to challenge the heavy-handed imposition of Mongol rule.

An earthquake was about to bring the façade on Mongol rule crashing down, and its epicentre was found in an unexpected location. A humble Buddhist monk proved surprisingly adept at building up resistance against the Mongols. His name was Zhu Yuanzhang and he came from peasant stock, socially the lowest of the low. It was said his parents had donated him to the local Buddhist temple when he was a child so that he might benefit from the two bowls of rice a day he would be fed there. This was an inauspicious start, but from such insignificant beginnings, Zhu developed incredible leadership skills, though at first things went from bad to worse. The temple where he had taken up residence was unable to support even this basic level of subsistence, and Zhu found himself out on the streets with a begging bowl, and then entered the shady world of Chinese secret societies. It was said that he was a member of a shadowy organisation known as 'The White Lotus Society'. Later, when he reached the stars, he would deny that he had ever been involved with any such organisation, but the rumours proved stubbornly resilient.

By 1355 Zhu was the leader of a band of rebels actively campaigning against Mongol rule. The next year he succeeded in conquering the city of Nanjing and this became the focal point of ongoing activity directed against the barbarian invader. His strength grew even as that of the Mongols waned, and in 1368 he marched north against the enemy. He led a stunning campaign which ended with Beijing, the Mongols' great capital, in his hands.

The Chinese were fatalistic about changes in dynasty. Their civilisation was so old that they knew that such things happened from time to time. They believed that it was the will of the gods that decided such things. Quite simply, the gods gave their blessing to those who wished to be emperor when it suited their plan to do so, but they could just as easily withdraw their favour. They even had a phrase to describe such happenings: The Mandate of Heaven. Now, the Mandate of Heaven had decreed it was time for a change. The Mongol Dynasty, the 'Yuan' would soon be no more. A new power would take its place: the Ming, 'The Brilliant'. Mongol rule disintegrated as quickly as it had arrived. For a few more years the Mongols hung on in far-flung corners of China, before they were ejected even from there, and returned to the distant and uninviting steppes from whence they had come. It has frequently been claimed that the Mongols made no lasting cultural impact on China; that art developed without interference (allegedly in spite of them) and that little changed in terms of the Chinese way of life. Yet this is a gross simplification. They succeeded in uniting two great dynasties into one; the Song and the Chin. They therefore built the foundations of a Chinese super-state, one that lives on to this day.

They also had another profound effect on the psyche of China. When the Mongols were ejected, most traces of their rule were eliminated in peremptory fashion. Beijing, their capital, was largely obliterated. Over its ruins the edifices of a new and confident nation were erected, the Forbidden City in particular. But the bitter taste of Mongol rule would not go away. So sharp was it that it left the Chinese with an aversion to most things foreign and so, for centuries, China became a closed nation, a state that was distrusting of aliens, and lived by its own set of rules. Only recently has this state of mind started to change, and even now it forms a major part of the Chinese mindset.

Whilst Mongol rule in China and Persia collapsed, in the regions occupied by the Golden Horde it continued. Permanent Mongol rule in what we now term Russia was in fact limited. The Mongol settlers based themselves in the steppes, by the Caspian Sea for example. The area was rich in pasture for their horses and it offered them a way of life that they were well used to, and which in fact had given them the initial basis of their success in terms of military conquest.

Large parts of Russia were never conquered by the Mongols for several reasons; the first issue being that the country in the north would not support the horses that they needed to give them their victories. The other point was this: the Mongol plan, increasingly, was to rule the world, not to conquer it, and the two are vastly different things. It was equally acceptable for pliant, client kings to run a country responding appropriately to Mongol dictate as it was to militarily subdue it. The Mongols were prepared to be pragmatic. Voluntary acceptance of Mongol demands, for example the payment of tribute, favourable treatment of Mongol traders or military assistance, were often as acceptable as an alternative to military conquest. This meant that Mongol policy could be implemented without the need for a fight.

Some major Russian cities never fell to Mongol arms. One major example of this is found in Novgorod, then the leading city of Russia. But it has been pointed out that 'the Mongols never reduced Novgorod militarily because they did not need to'.[5] The people of the city became very adept at playing by the rules imposed by the regional Mongol superpower, and using them to their own benefit. When the Mongols, for example, insisted that the authorities there take a census of the population (a favourite approach of the Mongols in working out how large a tribute was reasonable) they meekly complied. This might seem little better than cowardice. It has been persuasively argued that Russian historians have sought to gloss over the Mongol incursions, because of a sense of national embarrassment, a process called by Charles Halperin 'the ideology of silence'.[6] Such revisionism is of course far from unique. The problem of the approach though, is that if Russian historians do not

26. Louis IX, King of France, sets out on Crusade. The saintly Crusader 'enjoyed' a problematic relationship with the Mongols.

27. Western knights attack a Muslim city, exemplifying the state of Western arms at the time in a medieval manuscript.

28. A romanticised view of a Mongol shaman from an old French manuscript.

29. A Persian manuscript illustrating lamellar armour as used by the Mongols.

30. A hunting scene from Khwarezm illustrating the tactics of the 'Great Hunt' employed by the Mongols so effectively, both in peacetime training and in the heat of battle.

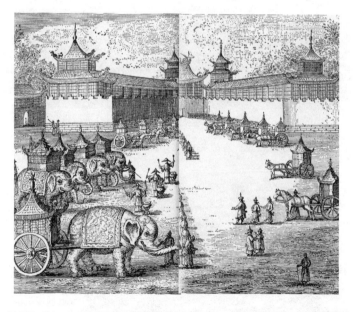

31. This Chinese manuscript, showing the court in China, shows some rather fanciful illustrations of the Mongol *yurts* transported on the backs of wagons. The wagons tended to be much bigger and the *yurts* less Oriental in appearance.

32. Genghis Khan, the founder of the greatest empire the world has ever seen.

33. An early twentieth-century photograph of Mongols wrestling. The Mongols loved their wrestling (and still do). Breaking a troublemaker's back in a wrestling match was one of the more bizarre and painful ways of execution employed by the Great Khans.

34. A Mongolian horseman with a lasso to capture a horse from the herds that roamed the steppes.

35. An early twentieth-century Mongolian princess: a picture that captures both the beauty and elegance for which some medieval Mongol princesses were renowned.

36. An early twentieth-century Mongol prince, a successor to the great Khans such as Genghis, though by the time that this picture was taken, Mongolia was a pale reflection of the great empire it had once been.

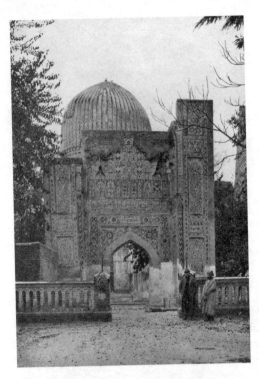

37. An old photograph of
the great mausoleum of
Tamerlane in Samarkand,
his opulent capital.

38. The coronation of Henry IV of England – he was nervous enough to correspond
enthusiastically with Tamerlane.

mention much about the Mongol incursions, then no one else is likely to (the Mongols never becoming great historians themselves, even when they became literate; their traditions and histories remained largely oral in line with their steppe roots).

However, to view the people of Novgorod, for example, as being meekly submissive, is to do them a disservice. Realising that military defeat of the Mongols was not an option, they instead sought to proactively benefit from co-operating with them. By collaborating with them and doing largely as they were told, they earned themselves the option of gaining Mongol military assistance when they needed it. By taking advantage of this, they were able to strengthen their position inside a very divided and inherently weak Russian hinterland. Others took advantage of the situation too; the city of Moscow grew in power partly as a result of being the 'Mongols' chief tribute-gatherers'.[7]

Not everywhere was submissive though. Areas under more direct Mongol rule did revolt against their overlords. There were uprisings at Rostov (1289), Nizhnii Novgorod (1305) and Tver (1327) for example. But they were put down with ruthless efficiency. Elsewhere, in more peripheral areas, Mongol rule did weaken. The Ukraine had been decimated by the Mongols, and the position of Kiev suffered significantly as a result. The city declined but Mongol rule started to slacken in the fourteenth century and other regional powers, for example the Lithuanians, began to conquer Ukrainian territory for themselves.

The Mongols of the Golden Horde established their base in the city of Sarai, on the mighty Volga. Here they established a bureaucracy to govern their part of the empire. Religious toleration proved beneficial to a number of subjects, not least the Orthodox Church, whose position actually improved under Mongol rule. A bishopric was established there. Later though, as the rulers of the Golden Horde increasingly demonstrated their Islamic credentials, the city became a great centre of the Muslim faith, whose architecture could match that of some of the finest cities of the Middle East.

Trade was forcibly routed through Sarai so that the Mongols could take advantage of their dominance of the trade routes to increase their wealth. As a crossroads of major trading networks from east to west and being close to the Caspian Sea, it was perfectly positioned to become a wealthy Mongol capital and it did so. Here, close by the steppes, the Mongol influence in the region of Russia became strongest. Further north, large parts of Russia became effectively a buffer zone between two vastly different worlds of east and west, with the people of that territory culturally influenced by both to an extent, though dominated by neither.

But on the steppes Mongol influence became more permanent; old tribes took new Mongolised names, hence the emergence of Tatars, Uzbeks and Nogais. The latter were named after a leader called Nogai, who claimed for himself the rule of the Golden Horde though not everyone believed that he was a member of the 'Golden Kin', that is the family of Genghis Khan. For a while, Nogai led his nomads across the steppes of Russia in a mirror image of the traditional way of life that the Mongols of Genghis Khan had enjoyed. In the process, he became a very powerful force in Russia.

He built up his power around the Crimea and the Balkans and his followers followed the archetypal pattern of traditionalist Mongols, a nomadic life wandering from base to base. Many of the other Mongols of the Golden Horde had lost touch with their roots; now that China and Persia had gone there was little to make them look east, so they looked west instead. The Mongols in Russia had long been fragmenting. By 1297, Nogai was at war with another claimant for the *khanate* in Russia, Tokhta, the son of Mongkë Timür who had replaced Berke in 1266. In the war that followed, Tokhta won and Nogai was killed. The new emperor confirmed his newly-won prestige by marrying the illegitimate daughter of the Emperor of Byzantium. He lived long, dying at Sarai in 1341. During the reign of his successor, Janibeg, the fortunes of the Golden Horde went into terminal decline. When he was murdered in 1359, chaos ensued.

In the end the Mongols of the Golden Horde would fade away from the pages of history too, though much more slowly than their brethren in China and Persia; but there would be one last flaring up of the Mongol flame, and they would be right at the heart of events when this took place. A great power was stirring to the south of the lands of the Golden Horde. From the Mongol-occupied lands of Central Asia a mighty leader of Mongol stock was to emerge. He would not be of the family of Genghis, and so he would resist any claim to be the Great Khan, though he would wisely support puppets that were. He would wreak terror onto the world, at a level that Genghis had rarely reached. A trail of destruction was about to tear its way across Asia, destroying great cities, some of which had as yet proved impervious to Mongol attack. Mighty empires were about to be brought to the brink of oblivion. The age of Tamerlane had arrived.

CHAPTER 12
The End of Empire:
Tamerlane & the Brief Revival of the Empire
1360-1510

Whilst great upheavals had been taking place in Persia, China and the lands of the Golden Horde, the territories which made up the Chagataid part of the Mongol empire had also been going through some major changes. These lands, covering parts of Central Asia and much of modern Afghanistan, had been peopled by Mongol settlers who remained in the main steppe-dwellers and nomads. More traditionalist than other parts of the Mongol world, they were about to ignite a final flare-up of Mongol fortunes, sending shockwaves across the known world as a result. In common with those other Mongol regions that had eventually imploded, these lands too had seen contention and conflict. The effects, though, had been relatively localised and this part of the Mongol empire was one of the less influential, so their effects were not felt far and wide. The Chagataid lands remained in essence a backwater as far as geopolitics was concerned. All this was about to change with spectacular effect.

Again there were disputes between traditionalists and those who wished to change, the modernisers. These dated back some time. Chagatai, the man who had initially shaped this part of the empire, and an arch-traditionalist if ever there was one, had decided that the *kuriltais* should elect new leaders, for his lands should be held at a camp on the River Ili in what is now Kazakhstan. As early as 1266, the new *khan* of these territories, Mubarak, decided to be enthroned at Mawarannahr, hundreds of miles away.

This was bad enough. When Mubarak, in common with the lords of the Golden Horde, decided to adopt the doctrines of Islam for his guiding principles, there were ructions. The traditionalists, the steppe dwellers, rose up in arms, and the region was soon divided in a bitter civil war. Mubarak was the loser, and lost his *khanate* as a result. However, this attempt to turn back the tide of change eventually faltered, and Islam in the end emerged victorious, overwhelming the resistance of shamanists in the process. By the end of the thirteenth century, the Muslim faith had taken root across the region.

But the traditionalists hung on determinedly. They refused to accept the triumph of Islam or the advance of what they saw as modernism. In the end, the region split in two. Islamic Mawarannahr made up the western part of this land; the east, mountainous and harsh, the powerbase of the traditionalists, became Moghulistan. It was a shattered, contentious world, unsure of where it was going. It was no longer truly Mongol either, with Turkish influence increasingly significant. Once more, the Mongol way of life was being overwhelmed by cultural influences that were far more powerful.

Into this fractured and fractious land, a boy was born who would later rewrite the pages of history. The date, according to the chroniclers, was 9 April, 1336. It was said that he was born clutching blood in his tiny hands. This might ring a few bells, for the same was said of Genghis, suggesting that this was not a statement of fact, but a necessary prerequisite for writers to mark down when any great conqueror was born at the time. The similarities do not end there; Timür, like Genghis, was the son of a leader, but not a prominent one, his father being Taraghay, chief of the Barlas tribe. The child was given the name of Timür, though he is better known to most as Tamerlane. His early life left little impression with the chroniclers of the time, as he was not marked out for greatness by his birth.

His chance to make his mark came in around 1360, when the Moghuls invaded the western part of the region where Timür resided. He fled with Haji Beg, then chief of the Barlas, but had not gone far when he persuaded his overlord that he should be allowed to go back and face up to the threat. It appeared to be an act of youthful bravado but it was a ruse; when Timür had moved his men close to the forces of the Moghul *khan*, he sent him a message offering to serve him. The approach was duly accepted. Timür was rewarded for his betrayal with the overlordship of the Barlas. Although this made him locally significant, he was still a minor player on the big stage. He returned to a life that was characterised by petty banditry and violence. His act of duplicity had merely achieved localised status for him.

It was whilst engaged in low-level raiding that the event that was to change his name, as well as his life, occurred. Whilst involved in offensive actions against a flock of sheep (of all things) he badly injured his leg. Some accounts state that he was set upon by a much larger body of soldiers whilst trying to seize the sheep, and was injured in the affray that followed. Others blamed his injury on the arrows unleashed by a belligerent shepherd. Whatever the cause, Timür was left with a bad wound which severely limited his ability to walk. From that day on he would be known as Timür the Lame – 'Tamerlane'. At least, to his enemies he would be known that way. The name was regarded as an insult by his adherents, and indeed, it is still perceived this way by the people of Uzbekistan, the country that eventually established itself in the place of his birth, where he is a major national hero *à la* Genghis in Mongolia. At some time, Timür would also lose two fingers. These were not the sort of setbacks likely to make a young and ambitious chieftain particularly sensitive towards his fellow man.

Timür developed a strong bond of friendship with another ambitious youth who was named Husayn. This alliance ended in tears for the same reasons which led to the demise of the friendship between Genghis and Jamuka, all those years before. Both men were so ambitious that they inevitably came to blows. Like Jamuka, Husayn alienated men through his harsh rule and extortionate levels of taxation. When the two men came to open conflict in 1365, it was Timür who emerged triumphant. Husayn was captured. Timür had promised that he would not kill him. This promise proved to be mere semantics; Timür did nothing to intervene when another noble who had been wronged by Husayn put him to death.

This was the start of an impressive rise to power. Despite the influences that Turkic culture had had on him, Timür was very conscious of his Mongol heritage, an awareness that helped to shape his marital alliances. A Muslim himself, he was not limited to the number of wives that he took. However, his chief wife was Saray Mulk-Khanam, the widow of Husayn. She was a princess of Genghis Khan's own bloodline. This gave Timür a direct connection to the Genghisid line of succession. However, he was scrupulous in not declaring himself to be the successor to Genghis. He was now one of the 'Golden Kin' and therefore he could not declare himself a *khan* without alienating Mongol traditionalists. Instead, he would support the legitimate Chagataid line in Central Asia, even though members of that august group would be mere puppets in the hands of Timür, the real master pulling the strings.

As an up and coming young chieftain, Timür's first aims in terms of wider conquest were to reunite the lands that had previously formed the Chagataid part of the Mongol empire. This meant the reunification of Timür's lands with those of Khwarezm to the north, and the Moghul lands to the east of him. It would take several decades for the east to come to heel, a long, extended series of raids and campaigns, which finally resulted in the reunification of east and west through the age-old policy of marrying a prominent princess from the bloodline of the former to Timür.

Khwarezm was a more attractive proposition. It straddled the great trade routes from eastern Asia to the borders of Europe and the Mediterranean, and as such was a land of great wealth. The benefits of bringing this under Timür's control were obvious. For someone who would have been well aware of Mongol history, Genghis' conquests there might have been an attraction too; if he were to recover the land once won by his illustrious predecessor, then great kudos would accrue to him.

The campaign against Khwarezm began in typical Mongol fashion with a peremptory letter to the ruler of the region, Husayn Sufi, to surrender the lands he held back to the legitimate Mongol successors of Chagatai. The response was predictable: a blunt message telling Timür that if he wanted to have Khwarezm he would have to conquer it. Timür (who had adopted another old Mongol tactic, by incorporating many of the men of his old ally and rival, Husayn, into his own forces once he had defeated him) was ready for the fight. He invaded in 1372 and took the important city of Kat. As the city had dared to defy him, Timür took the course so often adopted by Genghis in moments of victory; the men who had defended the city were butchered, and the women and children were taken away to lives of slavery.

Husayn Sufi died soon after and his brother Yusef quickly recognised the superiority of Timür's armies. He sought peace and offered to seal the deal by offering a princess to Timür as a wife. Satisfied at this offer, Timür returned to his capital at Samarkand and waited. Nothing happened. Time went by, and the only news to arrive was that Yusuf had regathered his strength and retaken Kat. Timür returned to Khwarezm, once again besting the armies of Yusuf, who sought new terms. These were granted, but Timür took the precaution of more firmly integrating the lands of southern Khwarezm into his own territories.

Soon after, two events happened which were to shape the future direction of Timür's life. The first concerned his son Jahingir. He was the apple of Timür's eye, his great hope of the future. In 1376, he was just twenty years old, but he had already proved himself a great warrior. He was clearly earmarked to be Timür's successor. In that year came the shattering news that he had not fallen victim to an arrow or a sword-stroke, but to disease. Timür was distraught. The chronicler Saharaf ad-Din Ali Yazdi wrote that:

> Everything then became melancholy and disagreeable to him, and his cheeks were almost always bathed in tears; he clothed himself with mourning and his life became uneasy to him. The whole kingdom, which used to be overjoyed at the arrival of this great emperor, was turned into a place of sorrow and weeping.[1]

The joy of life had gone from him (amateur psychologists cannot fail to trace a connection between this event and the brutality of his future career). At about this time, too, another seminal event occurred. A young Mongol prince from the north arrived at Timür's court. His name was Tokhtamish, and he was a prince of Genghis' own bloodline. He was a prominent member of the White Horde to the north. His father had been murdered and he sought revenge, but his ambitions did not stop there. Tokhtamish sought nothing less than to reunite the Golden Horde itself under his leadership.

For several decades the lands of the Golden Horde had been in decline. Riven by internal dispute, the Mongol territories populated by the Horde had started to fragment. Tokhtamish saw great potential in this much weakened empire. He threw himself of Timür's mercy and sought an alliance with him. Timür responded positively. He saw a sparkle of greatness in the disinherited prince's eyes. He adopted Tokhtamish as his son and dedicated himself to assisting him in his attempt to avenge himself against Urus, the man who had killed his father.

Two expeditions led by Tokhtamish failed. The third was led by Timür in person, and ended in triumph. Urus died in the aftermath. Tokhtamish became *khan* of the White Horde. For him, it was not enough. However, Timür's attention was about to be drawn elsewhere in this moment of triumph when news reached him that Yusuf had rebelled against him in Khwarezm. Rebellion by a man who had sworn loyalty to him was an unforgivable sin as far as Timür was concerned. He bore down on the city of Urganch, set on revenge. Yusuf sought to buy time. He sent out a message to Timür: it was wrong for the lives of so many to be put on the line because of a dispute between two men, let them fight it out in a duel he suggested. Timür, lamed as he was, took up the challenge, and duly appeared on the field appointed, dressed in his battle armour. Yusuf was nowhere to be seen.

Timür returned to the ranks of his men to be greeted with a hero's welcome. Yusuf was a broken man with a shattered reputation. Shortly after, he sickened and died, probably saving himself a far more painful fate in the process. The city fell to Timür in 1379, and was brutally ravaged. Nine years later it rebelled against him. Its fate on this occasion was even harsher. Ten days of pillaging and rapine followed. At the end of this time, all that remained of a once great city was a single mosque. It was a dangerous policy to rebel against Timür. His armies would inevitably best any that could be put in the field against him, and the punishment that inevitably followed was draconian.

The savagery that accompanied the recapture of the city helped to evolve the reputation for ruthlessness which Timür was rapidly acquiring. But he had some ambivalent traits. He was a Muslim who would refer to the teachings of the Koran when it suited his purposes to do so. Yet he would also refer to astrologers when he wished for advice. He would sometimes pick and choose which advice suited him better; in other words, he was a pragmatist rather than a zealot. He was a Sufi adherent, a follower of one of the more mystical elements of Islam, but he also had pronounced sympathy for the Shi'a strand of the faith. The geneology on his tomb traces his line back to that of Ali, the son-in-law of the Prophet and the founder of the Shi'a movement. Sunni Muslims were as likely to feel the bitter edge of his sword as Christians or pagans. Although he played on the fact that he sought to advance the cause of Islam, his attachment to it seems to be rather more cynical than fanatical.

This adherence to Islam when it suited him was reflected in his private as well as political life. The Prophet had decreed that a man might have four wives, for example, but Timür had considerably more (the exact number is unknown). Similarly, the Islamic faith frowned on the use of alcohol, but on many occasions this inconvenient injunction was overlooked, and riotous orgies of drunken excess were far from unknown. Timür believed himself to be above the law; he was instead the maker of the law.

Comparisons with Genghis are inevitable. Indeed, Timür owed much to Genghis. The organisation of their armies had much in common, as did the reliance on the composite bow. Tactics in battle too were similar, with the use of the feigned retreat as frequent a tactic of Timür's men as of Genghis'. In some ways, though, there were marked differences between them. Timür was a lover of great cities for example, and whilst Genghis could enjoy himself in such places too, he seems to have loved his rural roots even more – no prominent tomb in a great city for him, but a hidden mausoleum of earth in the steppes. Significantly, Genghis never sought to build his people a capital city as his successors did. Sometimes, commentators on Timür try to hard to accentuate the differences. One recent writer on Timür opines that he formed 'a new military class directly loyal to his person, free from the political constraints of the tribe'.[2] Yet there was nothing new about this, Genghis had adopted an identical strategy nearly two centuries before.

In promotion policy too, with its emphasis on merit, Timür replicated what Genghis had done. His debt to the great *khan* of old was acknowledged by Timür in person, yet the connections should not be over-stated either. Timür was a brilliant, albeit terrifying, strategist. The fact that he was quick to recognise the genius of Genghis should not blind us from the fact that he too was a genius in his own right.

Detailed planning above all was the key to success in Timür's philosophy. He was credited by a contemporary with a phrase that should become a maxim for modern civil servants as much as military strategists: 'one skilful plan can perform the services of a hundred thousand warriors'.[3] In line with this maxim, campaigns were planned with passionate attention to detail with stunning results.

Timür had launched his career with significant success. Now it was time to turn his attention to a wider international stage. In 1379, he sent a message to the ruler of the city of Herat, in modern Afghanistan, instructing him to attend a *kuriltai* at his court. It was a demand that could not be complied with without that ruler recognising the supremacy of Timür. This he opted not to do. In order to assert his authority over the city, Timür set out on the start of what was to become known as his Three-Year Campaign, a period of almost uninterrupted triumph. Herat saw that its position was hopeless when faced with the huge and seemingly invincible army arrayed before it. It opted for surrender rather than defiance, a good move, as its citizens were allowed to live. They paid for their freedom with a huge ransom. This was another legacy owed to Genghis; cities that surrendered might survive, though they would pay extravagantly for the privilege.

The wisdom of the people of Herat later evaporated. Two years later they rebelled against the rule of Timür. He sent his son Miranshah to deal with the rebels, which he did with chilling efficiency. In a symbolic statement that would become irrevocably associated with Timür and his savagery, a huge pile of skulls was made of the citizens who were slain in their thousands as a result of their temerity.

In the meantime, Timür had moved west into Persia to the region of Mazandaran. In 1382 his vast army stormed into this mountainous region whose peaks seemed to touch the sky. Amir Wali, the local ruler, resisted, but was defeated and surrendered. He was allowed to live and carry on ruling, a rather misguided display of mercy on Timür's part as a few years later Mazandaran too revolted. Wali was defeated and killed, and his head presented to Timür as an unusual gift. Timür was by now in a bad mood: when he took the city of Isfizar soon after, a tower was constructed from the still living inhabitants of the city who had been captured. They were piled on top of each other along with bricks and mortar, a terrifying end indeed.

The list of conquests continued, places far apart and wealthy like Kandahar in Afghanistan, Sultaniya in Persia and Tabriz in Azerbaijan. From this distance in time, it is difficult to distinguish one from another; a long catalogue of names now largely lost to the cognisance of those outside the countries where these places are located. The trend was largely predictable: surrender, pay a ransom and survive; resist and be slaughtered – a stark choice indeed.

But a new threat to Timür was emerging in the north. The source of it angered Timür greatly, for it emanated from Tokhtamish, increasingly prominent in the Golden Horde. His position had been improved greatly when his Mongol rival in the lands bordering Russia, Mamai, was involved in a battle at Kulikovo. This took place on 8 September 1380 close to the River Don. An army of over 100,000 Mongols took on a slightly smaller force composed mainly of Russians with some Lithuanian allies. That morning broke with a heavy fog blanketing the field. At about eleven o'clock the two armies advanced towards each other as the mists started to lift. Legend has it that the battle commenced with two champions facing each other in single combat. Both were killed in the charge against each other, though by some miracle the Russian champion stayed on his horse whilst his Mongol counterpart was unseated.

The battle was hard fought for three hours. Despite heavy losses, the Russians stood firm. They then edged their way forward against the Mongol army. The battle was won and lost by a sudden attack on the Mongol flank. They broke and fled and the field was won for the Russians. Later nationalist historians claimed that this was a critical victory for a reunited Russia, an argument that is somewhat undermined by the fact that there were a large number of Mongols fighting alongside the Russians as allies. Mamai died soon after. This left the way clear for Tokhtamish to claim the *khanate* of the Golden Horde. In 1382, he led his army against the Russians and won a victory against them, in the process securing his hold on the Horde. He later turned his attention to Lithuania and Poland, invading their lands and creating havoc in the process. Now he had turned south to lands that were within Timür's sphere of influence. It was a direct challenge to his authority.

The fact that it was Timür who had first supported Tokhtamish must have been hard for him to bear. Nevertheless, he was not going to run away from the looming confrontation. He tackled the problem, as was his wont, head on. The kingdom of Georgia was no friend of the Golden Horde, but it was an important buffer zone against a threat to Timür from that direction. Because of this, it was a natural target for him. Unusually, he launched his attack in winter. This intimates how seriously Timür took the threat. In contrast to Genghis and many other Mongol *khans* in the past, for Timür this was normally a season for rest and relaxation. Spring was invariably the time of year at which the army marched. Not now though. In 1387 Timür descended on Tiflis, the capital of Georgia. Once more suffering because it was in the wrong place at the wrong time, the city fell after a tough scrap.

Bagrat, the king of Georgia, was brought before Timür in chains, but he was allowed to live. His country was decimated by Timür. Eventually, he would be 'persuaded' to convert to Islam. But his conversion was only skin deep. When the pressure was off, and Timür was far away, he threw off the pretence and reverted to Christianity. His country rebelled against Timür who had to return six years later and decimate it once more. It was a recurring theme: conquest, rebellion, reconquest.

Progress towards wider domination continued apace. Timür moved into the eastern extremes of Asia Minor. This brought him right up against a powerful potential adversary, the Ottoman Empire. The time was not yet ripe for open conflict, but it could not be too far away. Tensions with Tokhtamish continued too, though for now the two men were not openly battling each other. Like all great conquerors, Timür divided opinion, depending on whether one was a victim or a beneficiary of him. His army gloried in his triumphs, revelled in the plunder, the gold that came to them (though in a strictly controlled fashion: uncontrolled pillaging cost Timür money and would not be countenanced), the riches that they grabbed, the women that they ravished.

Enemies not unsurprisingly thought rather differently about him. A chronicle from Asia Minor described how:

A man named Tamerlane, holding the faith and precepts of the obscene Mahomet, precursor of the Antichrist, appeared in the East, in the city of Samarkand, merciless, cruel, treacherous, filled with all the evil, impurity and stratagems of the tempter Satan.[4]

The hatred that Timür inspired leaps off the page across the centuries.

Nowhere was the reason for such antipathy better illustrated than at Isfahan. A great city, situated in what was effectively a lush oasis in the middle of an arid part of Persia, it inevitably attracted Timür's attention. His army moved on the city, which trembled in fear before him. Rather than fight, the city surrendered. An atmosphere of fear gripped Isfahan. There was no sack though. A small garrison of Timür's soldiers took up residence. That very night, panic took over. Quite why the people decided to rise up against the garrison is unclear. The small group of men was soon overwhelmed and slaughtered. It was a catastrophic move. When dawn broke, everyone realised what must happen next. Timür unleashed his infuriated men against the city. They smashed their way in through the city walls.

Timür commanded that every person in the city must be killed. Regardless of sex or age, the order was meticulously carried out. One observer wrote how a group of 7,000 women and children were placed in a field and then crushed below the hooves of Timür's cavalry. Men were paid for the butchery by Timür, a fixed fee being given for each head they brought back to be counted. An observer later walked past the site of the city, counting twenty-eight pyramids of skulls with 1,500 heads in each of them.

Happy with his conquests, Timür resolved to return to Samarkand to recuperate for the next season's campaigning. As he made his plans to do so, stunning news arrived. The very heartland of his kingdom was under attack. In an act of both impressive boldness and proud defiance, it was Tokhtamish who had led an army towards Samarkand. The warning signs had been there shortly before when he had led his hordes into Azerbaijan, an uncertain frontier territory between the lands of the Golden Horde and those ruled by Timür. It is worth remembering that Tokhtamish could claim something that Timür could not, direct and traceable descent from the royal family of Genghis Khan through Jochi, the son of doubtful paternity. It would have been quite natural for him to see himself as Timür's superior. However, although Tokhtamish might claim royal blood, that did not necessarily mean that he was the better strategist. A terrifying yet intriguing battle for dominance was about to begin.

By the time that Timür returned to Samarkand in the autumn of 1388, the immediate danger had passed. Although Bokhara had almost fallen to Tokhtamish's lightning assault, the raid had in the end run out of steam, and he had retreated. However, everyone knew that Timür would not let the insult go unavenged. A rebellion in Khwarezm had to be attended to, which was done with typical ruthless efficiency. For the moment, Timür bided his time, deciding on how best to raise an army to deal with the upstart. Unfortunately for him, Tokhtamish was not prepared to meekly wait for an avenging army to descend on him. As Timür settled in to enjoy winter in Samarkand, more stunning news arrived. Tokhtamish had led an invading army into his lands once more. It was an amazing return to old Mongol tactics, hit and run tactics in the winter when everyone else was expecting a period of relaxation. Timür's advisers were shocked by the tidings, and advised Timür to stay behind solid stone walls and let the attack peter out. They clearly did not understand their master very well.

Even would-be world conquerors have finest hours and Timür was about to experience his. Scorning his timid advisers, he led his army by forced marches through the bitter nights with the biting wind and the driving snow. The horses struggled as best they could through drifts that came up to their stomachs. It was an incredible performance for a man who, apart from anything else, had to cope with a serious disability. Seeing the temper of the man before him, Tokhtamish and his horde began to withdraw. The awfulness of that winter prevented a pursuit or any further fighting. In the spring that followed, Timür crushed an uprising in Moghulistan, which had tried to take advantage of the unrest by siding with Tokhtamish. With Khwarezm now subdued too, Timür was ready to go onto the offensive against his enemy, the *khan* of the Golden Horde. As 1390 drew to a close, the army was ready to move off. It headed north, wintering at Tashkent.

However, the troops stopped for a shorter time than most parties anticipated. By January 1391 they were on their way again. It was a momentous move. In the depths of a harsh winter, perhaps 200,000 men were about to march into lands that were shorn of life, into a frigid and barren desert. It would have to live off what it could carry or herd, and that was a highly risky strategy indeed in conditions such as this.

The daring nature of the strategy was a backhanded compliment to Tokhtamish. He had attacked Timür in his own backyard when he had least expected it. He had to be tackled head on, and by attacking now Timür hoped to catch his fearsome enemy when he was off his guard. The surprise tactics were a mark of respect. However, the *khan's* spies gave him ample warning that a large army was on its way to face him. From his capital in Sarai, Tokhtamish sent some of his prize horses to Timür as an act of submission. He apologised for attacking Timür's lands, claiming that evil advisers had misled him and promising to be an obedient subject in the future. Timür sent his messengers back with a stinging rebuke. He reminded Tokhtamish through them that he had raised him up but, once he had taken the throne of Jochi, he had forgotten the debt owed to Timür. If he really meant to submit, then let him send his chief minister Ali-Beg to arrange the terms of surrender. Until he did so, Timür would carry on marching towards him with his army.

Into March the advance went on. The army entered what is now Kazakhstan. Tokhtamish had no intention of facing Timür in an open battle. Instead his army hid itself beyond the seemingly endless horizons whilst Timür moved deeper into hostile territory and towards what seemed to be a looming crisis. First the meat began to run out. Strict orders were given that no bread was to be baked. The men were barely surviving on what were effectively subsistence rations. Men lived on herbs ripped from the ground, on rats or any other animal they could catch, on the flesh of the horses that died beneath them.

It was a moment of truth for Timür who faced a crossroads between a place in history and one in oblivion. He did not panic. He ordered his men to form themselves up as if for a great hunt, just like the Mongols of old had done. Short of food, his army would have to catch it just like their distant forefathers had done. A host of animals was forced to break cover as a gigantic circle of humanity closed in on them, crushing them like a vice. Once the time for the hunt proper had arrived, Timür was the first to shoot down the trapped prey, bringing down several deer. His men, exhilarated, charged in after him after the order to do so was given. That night the heavenly aroma of roasting meat filled the air above a camp now full of happy, relieved men.

Brutal though Timür might be, it is easy to understand the *esprit* that was forged between him and his army in situations such as this. Spirits restored and hunger subdued, the army moved on, now reaching the borders of Siberia. Trackers set out in advance of the main force. Before long, they spotted signs of life, a few recently dead fires scattered here and there at first, then signs of greater concentrations of people as they moved deeper into the country. It was not long before it was clear that at last Tokhtamish and his army was in striking distance, and that a great battle loomed between the forces of a man descended directly from Genghis Khan, and the leader of the newest Mongol power in the world.

The men were so far north now that the long days were a cause of confusion to men unused to the phenomenon. Then one morning, almost anti-climactically, the army topped a hill to find the battle flags of Tokhtamish proudly flying in the breeze less than a mile away. A decisive confrontation loomed. It was 18 June 1391, a seminal day in Mongol history. A hush descended over the field of battle at first, as if everyone present was aware that they were about to take part in an act that would shape the future history of their world. Timür dismounted from his horse, knelt and kissed the ground and begged for the help of Allah. One writer, Arabshah, in a bewildering list of superlatives described how:

> The wolves of war set their teeth and fierce leopards mingled and charged and the lions of the armies rushed upon each other and men's skins bristled, clad with the feathers of arrows ... and the dust was thickened and stood black and the leaders and common soldiers alike plunged into seas of blood ...[5]

Timür's right hurled themselves at the left flank of Tokhtamish's army. A bitter but inconclusive fight followed. These were the two greatest armies in Asia, and the victory would not be won by either side easily. The two leaders moved their men around like pieces on a giant chessboard. It became in the end a battle of wills, and it was that of Tokhtamish that broke first. A cry went up when it was noticed that the standard of Tokhtamish could no longer be seen. His nerve had broken and he had fled. Now his men sought to do the same. Exulted and exhilarated by the whiff of triumph, Timür's men charged after them. There were many non-combatants with the Mongols of the Golden Horde. In the aftermath of the battle at Kanduzcha it was said that 100,000 died.

Perhaps Tokhtamish had shown himself a coward in this monumental confrontation, but he then demonstrated that he had amazing powers of resilience. Deprived of his army, he went away and built another one. He approached the Sultan of Egypt for an alliance against Timür and by 1394 he had descended on Georgia. An imperious demand was sent to Tokhtamish by Timür, demanding his surrender – it was of course ignored. The next year, Timür once more stood at the head of a mighty army resolved to punish the *khan* and show him his place.

This time the chase would be much shorter. Leading his men north up the west coast of the Caspian Sea, Timür's army had soon moved into Chechnya. Tokhtamish had positioned himself to the north of a river. For three days an extraordinary spectacle was played out, with each army shadowing the other as they moved up and down the riverbank. And then a trick won the day. Timür left the women in his camp, dressed in the armour of some of their menfolk. Whilst these surrogate soldiers 'guarded' the camp, he took a large cavalry force to a ford across the river and charged across, taking advantage of the way that he had outmanoeuvred the enemy. They forced the regiments opposing them back. The right wing of the Golden Horde started to break. Shortly after, the left started to crack too. A bitter slogging match ensued in the centre, but Timür's men again sensed victory and pushed on. The armies of the Golden Horde at last broke, and Tokhtamish once more fled away. This time there would be no way back for him. He would never again threaten to attain the heights he had once reached. His power broken for good, he would eventually die an ignominious death in faraway Siberia.

Despite this triumph, the most glorious pages in the history of Timür were yet to be written. However, the story of Timür is much more than just a tale of wars and battles. He had an architectural vision that was never matched in his era, and possibly in no other, certainly amongst any of the Mongols. Throughout his empire, great cities would be constructed. There were palaces with towers 200 feet high. There were mosques of a magnificence unrivalled anywhere else in the world, with blue tiles making their roofs appear like a shimmering reflection of the azure sky. One word above all other describes these achievements: monumental. This was what set Timür apart from other Mongols, even Kublai. They had never envisaged anything on this scale.

But it is not this for which Timür is remembered, though the people of Uzbekistan, who worship him as a hero, would beg to differ. One event more than any other seared the image of Tamerlane, as his enemies called him, into the consciousness of people both now and then. The chain of events that would end in one of the bloodiest pages in Timür's history was about to unfold. India had so far played an inglorious part in Mongol history. Several expeditions had been launched there, going right back to the time of Genghis Khan. They had all ended in failure. Even the Mongols had been unable to conquer the rivers that jealousy guarded India's frontiers, or the fetid jungles that protected her heart. Timür was about to take his men to heights that not even Genghis had scaled.

The attraction of India was simply understood: great wealth. The fact that few had conquered it, not even Genghis nor Alexander the Macedonian, possibly added to the attraction for Timür. The current state of the country did nothing to dissuade him. It was torn apart by internal dissent and there could not have been a better moment to unleash the dogs of war on it. Before it was reached, the soaring heights of the Hindu Kush must be crossed, snow-capped buttresses acting as a fortification more daunting than any castle could be. Unfortunately, here their timing went awry. The mighty peaks were beset by raging blizzards which turned the tracks into icy death-traps, sending off-balanced horses over the edge of precipices, falling thousands of feet to their deaths. Timür, now getting on in years and increasing immobile, at one stage had to be lowered 1,000 feet down a cliff on a litter.

He arrived in Kabul in August, where he was greeted with a display of all the treasure recently won on campaigns in Persia. It was a welcome fillip after the horrors of the mountains, and it put the men back in good heart. From here, they headed south. One wing of the army was led by Mahmud Khan, head of the Chagataids, installed by Timür some time before as a puppet ruler.

As this leviathan of an army lumbered on, a shimmering sheet of water was seen in the distance. The men moved towards it, a great river opening up before them as they got closer. It was the Indus, the guardian of India's frontiers. It was here that Genghis had watched Jalal ad-Din cross over to safety all those years before, but Timür would not be turning back. Instead he ordered bridges to be built across, and his men made their way over to the far side and India.

The city of Multan fell and Timür now moved on towards his ultimate objective, Delhi. The Punjab was ravaged as he advanced. By December, the outskirts of Delhi had been reached. Timür set up his camp close to its suburbs. There was an initial skirmish, from which a small group of Timür's men managed to escape relatively unscathed. There was however a horrific consequence of this small-scale fight. There were reputedly 100,000 Hindu prisoners with Timür. They had shouted their support for the attackers in the fight. Their enthusiasm was their death warrant. Worried that they might rebel in the bigger battle that loomed, Timür put them all to death. So great was the slaughter that even many of his own men did not want to perpetrate the crime. It was said that some had tears in their eyes as they carried out Timür's awful command. His men were afraid too, for the Indians had a secret weapon, which they had proudly boasted that they would unleash on them, mighty war elephants that would crush any who stood in their path.

On 17 December 1398, the armies of Delhi marched out of the gates to face up to the invader, a move of doubtful wisdom, given Timür's impressive track record in open battle. Timür arrayed his army in traditional format, with a left wing, a right wing, a centre and a vanguard. His left was the first to come under attack, and the fighting here was heavy. However, his vanguard was deployed to smash into the Indians here and they were triumphant. First blood to Timür. It was in the centre that the crunch would come, for here the Indians had assembled all their elephants. Timür had instructed his archers to fire at the *mahouts*, but despite this they continued to come on. Timür now called into action his secret weapons: camels. He had loaded some with bundles of flammable materials on their backs. He had set these alight, and then sent them careering towards the elephants. When they saw the panic-stricken camels charging towards them, the elephants ran wild. They charged blindly to the rear, trampling their own side underfoot as they did so.

The battle quickly turned into a rout. The gates of Delhi now lay open before Timür. He entered in triumph, through the streets of a city now quivering in fear. The elders of Delhi did homage to him and for a time it appeared that it would escape the worst ravages of his army. Small groups of soldiers made their way in, but all seemed calm, if fragilely so. Timür set his officials to the task of cataloguing the vast wealth he had won in what was a fabulously rich city.

That, it appeared, was that. No one seemed to notice that more troops were making their way into the streets of Delhi, not in any organised fashion but in small groups. Then there was an outrage, the details of which are lost. The strongest hint we have is that there was a case of rape, isolated perhaps, against which some of the citizens of Delhi reacted violently. The troops in the city struck back in kind. It was a spark that ignited a huge conflagration. Timür's troops launched into an orgy of rape and violence. The sack that then unfolded shocked the world in a way that was marked even in Timür's history. The streets flowed with blood. It took Delhi a century to recover from the shock, and the outrage seared itself into the imagination of India for far longer. The city was a wreck, which explained perhaps why Timür abandoned it soon after.

The conqueror made his way back to Samarkand, to his greatest ceremonial entry into the fabled city yet. Time, however, was catching up with him. Tumours on his arm caused great anxiety amongst his entourage. He was so ill that he had to be carried most of the way on a litter. Unlike Genghis, he does not appear to have thought himself immortal, or to have had any chance of becoming so. He was clearly slowing down. This makes the fact that his greatest triumph was still to come all the more remarkable.

Yet for all that, an analysis of the febrile last few years of Timür's life makes it hard to avoid the conclusion that, with the passing of the years, there came a bitterness, a resentment that death was coming. The cities conquered in that time paid heavily for their loss. There was a brutal anarchy about the slaughter that was about to descend on some of the great cities of the world. Delhi for one, had paid extravagantly for the mere fact that its wealth acted as a magnet to Asia's greatest warrior.

Other famous cities further west were about to follow suit.

The gaze of Timür was drawn inexorably towards the lands surrounding the Mediterranean. Here two renowned regimes in particular caught his eye: to the north the newly-founded and still evolving Ottoman Empire, and to the south, wealthy and famous but volatile Egypt and its Mameluke rulers. The fact that both were Islamic regimes would do neither any good, for both were Sunni states, inimical to a man who espoused the Shi'a cause like Timür.

The campaign that Timür was about to embark on was given the ironic title of 'The Pilgrimage of Destruction'. It is difficult now to be certain what motivated it. The name might suggest that it was religiously motivated, and there may have been an attempt to give it such a gloss. But by far the stronger emotion seems to have been a lust for plunder, for wealth, and (the risk of sensationalising the acts about to happen being duly acknowledged) an almost psychopathic thirst for blood.

Timür was about to set out on another extended campaign. In latter times these would become ever longer, often measured in years. The vast resources of manpower available to him meant that he could replenish his armies, though men of humble origin recruited to his armies would of course lack the skills of his elite and would be, in modern parlance, little more than cannon fodder. Another large force was assembled for the expedition that he now planned to lead west with Egypt the ultimate target. This would be a challenge, for in between him and Cairo was Syria, in many parts a land of deserts, where it would be hard to provision his forces adequately.

Timür bade farewell to Samarkand, to which he was an increasingly infrequent visitor, and set his course towards Damascus. However, he had another target to strike before he reached there, and this was one that would give him no pleasure. His son Miranshah had been given a large part of Persia to rule over, and their were disconcerting stories emanating from there about his actions. They came from an impeccable source, his wife Khan-Zada. She was held in high esteem: the blood of Genghis ran in her veins. She had appeared before Timür with a harrowing tale to tell. His behaviour had been reprehensible: he had turned to debauchery, and it appeared to some that he had even lost his faculties. All this might have been forgiven, but most worryingly of all he had reputedly set his eyes on his father's throne. Sensing the fact that Timür was ageing, it was claimed that Miranshah was plotting to have him deposed. 'Plotting' in fact, would seem to be the wrong word, for one chronicler, Arabshah, wrote to Timür in the following vein:

Certainly through your advanced age and weak constitution and infirmity
you are now unequal to raising the standards of empire and sustaining the
burdens of leadership and government and above all things it would befit
your condition to sit as a devotee in a corner of a mosque and worship
your lord, until death came to you.[6]

If Miranshah did indeed write in such a manner, then he surely must
have been out of his mind. It is fair to say that Timür was not used to
being addressed in such a manner. It was unequally unlikely that he
would laugh such insolence off with a shrug of the shoulders, even if
Miranshah was his own flesh and blood. And so, en route to Syria,
Timür stopped off in Persia with his vast army to pay his respects.

Miranshah was deposed but escaped with his life. His blood-ties with
Timür undoubtedly saved him, for if it were not for these then he would
almost certainly have been executed. In this instance, blood was indeed
thicker than water. His advisers were not so lucky. They were made the
scapegoats for his temerity. Some were executed, others imprisoned.
Miranshah would be forced to accompany Timür in the forthcoming
campaign so that he could be kept an eye on. Before reaching Syria,
Timür made a diversion to the north. Of all the countries unlucky
enough to be in the wrong place at the wrong time when the Mongols
were at their peak, Georgia was one of the most unfortunate. Time and
again it had been overrun, its cities burned, its people pillaged and killed
by the thousand. In early 1400, Timür moved on the country again. The
king, George VII, was giving sanctuary to Timür's enemies, something
of a dangerous thing to do given past history. Retribution was now at
hand.

The Georgians retreated to the mountains, realising through bitter
experience that to stand and fight would be catastrophic. Unusual
tactics were needed to deal with this move. Archers were lowered over
cliffs in baskets until they were level with the caves in which Georgian
troops were hiding. Flaming arrows were then shot into the caverns,
effectively smoking the Georgians out. Soon after, Tiflis – that tragic city
so frequently devastated – was a ruin once more. Captured Georgian
Christians were given a choice of converting to Islam or death – a very
un-Islamic thing to do, for the tenets of the religion frowned on forced
conversion. Most chose the former.

With Georgia subdued, the army moved west again. The stakes were
now rising. In Asia Minor, Timür's empire was cheek by jowl with that
of the Ottoman Sultan, Bayezid – 'The Lightning'. Timür sent envoys
to him, asking for peace, though in terms so patronising that he must

have known they would be rejected. Equally dismissive replies were received from the Sultan. A confrontation loomed between the two greatest powers in the world. The opening shots were fired soon after. The Ottomans pushed on to Armenia, into territory on the periphery of Timür's empire. He responded in the only way he knew how to: with overwhelming force. He laid siege to the city of Sivas, an Ottoman stronghold of some importance. The walls were strong, but miners were set to work to bring them down. After three weeks, the walls of the city began to crumble. The city elders sued for peace.

For the Muslims in the city, mercy was at hand, and Timür allowed them to live. Not so for the Armenian Christians, who had provided many of the soldiers defending the city. A huge pit was dug outside the city, into which 3,000 captives were thrown. They were then covered up and buried alive. It was a fitting if gruesome start to the campaign that was about to begin in Syria.

The first to feel the wrath of Timür's armies as they moved south was the city of Aleppo. Overlooked by a massive and impressive citadel, still today one of the most impressive military fortifications in the Islamic world, the city was at a wealthy crossroads on the road linking Asia Minor to Egypt. It would be a great prize to take. The governor of Aleppo, Damurdash, sent frantic pleas to the Mameluke Sultan in Egypt, urging him to send help, but none came. The tactics of the defenders were foolish in the extreme. Rather than stay behind their stout walls, their army came out into the open to fight. The result was an all-too-predictable rout. Damurdash made for the mighty walls of the citadel. Outside in the city, a massacre began. Damurdash, knowing that hope was gone, surrendered in the hope of saving some at least of the citizens. He was safe. Others were not half as lucky.

Timür's men helped themselves to all they wanted in the city. Women were bound and dragged off into a none-too-pleasant life of captivity. Children, considered useless, were slain without pity. It was said that women were violated in the great mosque. Gang rape was committed in the streets without shame. The Jews who had sought sanctuary in their synagogue were burned alive. The usual pile of heads was left behind. It was said that a number were left as evidence of the gruesome end of Aleppo, fifteen feet high and thirty wide. If Timür truly believed himself to be a champion of Islam, he had a strange way of showing it.

But this was only the beginning of the outrages. The reports of his barbarity may have been exaggerated; one chronicler said that the excesses were rather mild compared to others committed by Timür, a clue perhaps as to how awful the benchmark was that he had set. Now he moved south again, taking Hama with its water mills, next Homs and then diverting into the Lebanon to take Baalbek. It was blindingly obvious where the next stop would be: Damascus, one of the truly great cities of Islam. Its mighty walls had proved impervious to the attacks of Crusaders a century and a half before, but this was not so later on for the Mongols of Hülegü, who forced its people to cower. More pleas were sent to Egypt, but they were again ignored. The Sultan, Faraj, was new on the throne. He was very young and his position was precarious. Better by far, his advisers reasoned, for him to hang on to what he held.

So Damascus was left to the dubious mercy of Timür. The Damascenes were distraught as Timür's mighty host hove into view. They prepared for the inevitable. Cautious heads advised surrender in the hope of escaping with a crippling tribute. And then, a miracle. From nowhere, a relieving army appeared. The Egyptians had changed their minds, and had sent help after all. The Damascenes were euphoric, and prepared to fight. They set about Timür's rearguard, the great warrior having decided to retreat in order to regroup. There was ecstasy in Damascus that night, unconfined joy that Allah had been merciful. But when the citizens rubbed the dust of sleep from their eyes as they awoke to the next dawn, their hopes were shattered. The Egyptians, seeing the size of Timür's army, had fled. He would obviously be back. In fact, he was back already. His army stood ready once more to lay siege to the great city. Timür looked on, with a determined and angry stare.

Timür, though, preferred an easy victory to the heavy cost he would have to pay if he attacked. Negotiations were held. The Damascenes realised now that they were on their own, and therefore sought terms. These were agreed. They were heavy, a fine of one million dinars. It was raised and paid over. Not enough, said Timür – the price was now ten million. He was determined to squeeze the city dry of its wealth. Any of his soldiers caught plundering were crucified in the city square. This had nothing to do with protecting the Damascenes, and everything to do with him protecting all their wealth for himself.

An air of desperation descended on Damascus, a pall of hopelessness embracing its terrified citizens. Then a dreadful order was given by Timür. His army were to take Damascus, and do with it as they wished. Its fate would be awful. Drunken soldiers seized citizens in the streets and tortured them so that they would reveal where their treasures had been hidden. They competed with each other in a gruesome competition to see who could come up with the most ingenious forms of torment. The screams of the dying rent the sky. Even the dead were run through with swords, to make sure they were not faking. Flames soon took hold of Damascus. At its heart was one of the most sacred sites of Islam, the Umayyad Mosque, one of the oldest and most beautiful of all such holy places. In its shadow lay the earthly remains of Saladin, one of Islam's greatest warriors. Now it was put mercilessly to the torch.

One of Islam's greatest cultural landmarks was destroyed. It was a Sunni monument it is true, but within its walls, at one time, had been placed the head of Ali, the founder of the Shi'a movement. It was sacred to all of the Muslim world. This was no act of piety; it was abject sacrilege, which brought shame to all of Islam. And so the bitter fate of Damascus was sealed. It was the greatest blot on Timür's career, even worse than Delhi. But it was not the last. A few hundred miles to the east, across an arid desert, stood Baghdad. It had retained a precarious independence whilst the shadow of Timür had blotted out the sun across the Middle East. Now it too was to be pillaged. It was a pale imitation now of what it had once been, its walls still shattered in vast numbers of places following its destruction by Hülegü over a century before. No matter, it too must feel the wrath of Timür.

When its citizens knew that Timür was coming, they did their best to patch up the walls. It was like trying to bail out a sinking ship with a sieve, a hopeless task. Timür ordered his men to storm the city. Its citizens defended it gallantly, but the ferocity of their efforts only signed their death warrant. When Timür captured it, he was enraged at the numbers of men he had lost in the process. Each warrior was ordered to decapitate at least one citizen (some accounts say two) and return to Timür's camp with it, in return for which they would receive a bounty.

Then the city was set ablaze. Mosques, hospitals and colleges were to be spared, but all the houses were to be destroyed. At least that is what the chronicler Yazdi said. The claim is totally unconvincing after what had happened in Damascus. Timür's thirst for blood needed to be quenched, and scruples over colleges and hospitals in particular seemed unbelievable. His men were now tired, and wanted to go home. But Timür had one last challenge for them yet, the greatest they had ever faced. He had only three years to live, but his last glory would also be his crowning one.

It was obvious that the world was not a big enough place to house both Timür and Bayezid. As Timür's rise had been impressive in large parts of Asia, so too had that of Bayezid further west. Launching himself across the Bosporus and into Europe, he had won two stunning victories. The first of them in Kosovo in 1389 had opened up the Balkans to the Ottomans. Then, when a large Crusade had been sent to drive them back into Asia Minor in 1396, it had been crushed. The whole of Christendom trembled before the mighty armies of the Turk. This meant that Timür had some unlikely bedfellows, inspired by the concept that 'my enemies' enemy is my friend'. The emperor of Constantinople, Manuel II, had confirmed his submission to Timür. Friendly messages were received from King Charles VI of France. A couple of years later, the usurper King Henry IV of England would follow suit. Timür had an impact on Western consciousness which was different from any of his predecessors. Even Geoffrey Chaucer gave him a mention.

Bayezid had been further annoying Timür by giving succour to his enemies. As a result, messages had been sent to him, stating that Timür did not wish to attack him because the Sultan was busy attacking the Infidels and that was to be welcomed. However, if he were to continue offering sanctuary to his opponents then Timür would have no choice. With no other immediate enemies to fight, the battle against Bayezid could not be put off any longer. Another huge force was assembled. It was truly a global force, with men from all over Timür's mighty and still-expanding empire. It set its course for Asia Minor, the heart of Bayezid's lands.

A mighty battle was looming. In the build-up to it, Bayezid was cautious and conventional, leading his men slowly towards where he believed Timür to be. The contrast with his opponent could not be more stark. Timür was by now an old man, but he acted with a vigour and flair that no soldier of his day could emulate. He marched straight for the heart of Asia Minor. The crops were out and ripe for harvest; the local population did not benefit from this at all, for Timür's men helped themselves to them. This was just about the only time of the year that an army could live off the land, and Timür took full advantage of the fact.

Whilst he was dallying in the east of Asia Minor, Bayezid 'the Lightning' was struck by a thunderbolt from Timür. His enemy was even now approaching Ankara, the heart of his kingdom, and threatening to cut him off. Panic-stricken, Bayezid hurried back. Just outside of Ankara on 28 July 1402, the two armies faced each other at last. On the one side there was Timür's host, his men confident in their leader, well-fed and rested. Included in their ranks were the great war elephants captured in India, there were the greatest horse-archers in the world, and in totality a mighty force where every man believed in the legend of Timür's invincibility. Opposite them were the armies of Bayezid, tired, hungry, thirsty, demoralised. It is true that they had themselves seen years of uninterrupted triumph, but they knew full well of the reputation of the man before them. This battle was over before it had even started.

During the opening gambits of the battle, the Ottoman left was shattered and fled. The rest of the army began to crumble too. Bayezid's

Janissaries, his bodyguard, fought heroically to protect their master, but it was in vain, as the battle ended in a complete triumph for Timür. Bayezid was led into his presence, the only time in Ottoman history that a sultan fell into enemy hands. Bayezid lived on in captivity for just a few years. His treatment during that time is part of the Timür legend. Some accounts describe how he was kept in a cage, like a wild animal, how Timür used him as a footstool by climbing on his back to sit on his throne, of how his wives were made to become his cup-bearers. If these are true, then this was pre-planned humiliation. Not everyone concurs that these accounts have been based on fact, but they are consistent enough to make them plausible.

The world of Christendom now appeared to be ripe for the taking. Messages of congratulation came in from the courts of Western Europe, not based on any sincere affection, but more a panic-driven hope that sycophancy would protect them from conquest. News came in soon after that would have increased the sense of desperation. Smyrna, on the west coast of Asia Minor, was in the hands of Hospitaller Knights, on the front line of Christendom. Timür moved on the port, and demanded its surrender.

The Knights, confident in what they regarded as an impregnable defensive position, refused to submit. Timür instructed his engineers to build platforms across the sea, cutting the castle (which was offshore) off from the city itself. Volleys of Greek fire rained down on the city, which was soon overrun. The captured Knights shared the fate of so many others across Asia, being beheaded without mercy. When shortly afterwards a relieving force from the west hove into view, they were bombarded with the heads of their comrades fired from Timür's catapults. They turned around and fled back west.

Europe lay ahead of Timür, but there were other more lucrative conquests that he had in mind. The heartland of the Mongol empire had been China, and he determined to return it to what he saw as its rightful owners. This would be the biggest challenge he had faced. The emperor of China had huge resources at his disposal, both in terms of materiel and manpower. He was three thousand miles away from Timür too, protected by mountain and desert. Nothing that Timür had attempted so far would come close in terms of the size of the challenge that was presented by the campaign he now planned.

His past relationship with the Chinese emperor had been ambiguous. As the owner of some territories that had been in the Chinese sphere of influence in the past, he had been required to pay tribute. This he had scrupulously done for a number of years. But in recent times he had stopped doing so. This was a significant move. It was not the size of the tribute that most attracted the emperor's interest, it was the fact that it was paid at all. By paying it, Timür was acknowledging him as his overlord. By stopping the payment, he was sending a crystal-clear message.

But another army had to be made ready. Timür had been away from his beloved Samarkand for five years, and wished to return to it. He was increasingly infirm; as well as his semi-crippled status, he was also losing his sight. Age was catching up with him. It would be good to go back to Samarkand and relax, at least for a short time. On his way home, Timür stopped off on a diversion. It seemed impossible for him to bypass Georgia without visiting yet more death and destruction on it. So he launched another raid on that tragic kingdom, the sixth of his reign. The result was a formality: more deaths, more robbery and rapine, more forced conversions to Islam – all in a day's work for the mighty Timür.

At last, the minarets of Samarkand came into view, the beloved city was close at hand once more. There was a great outpouring of joy from his people as he returned in triumph. Timür sent out his commands to raise a new army and provision it, whilst he returned to the business of government for a short time. There was much to be done. Grandiose building schemes had been in train when he had left the place. A great new mosque had been built, planned to be the most impressive in Islam. Now he found, horror of horrors, that it was not as big as some of the mosques elsewhere in the Muslim world. Such a situation would not do. The officials responsible for the building were summoned into his presence and asked to explain. When they did not do so to his satisfaction, they were summarily executed. Then he ordered that the façade of the mosque should be demolished and rebuilt on an altogether grander scale. Other officials were accused of corruption. They too were sent to the gallows, including the man who had been designated governor of Samarkand in Timür's absence, an old acquaintance. Even if he was frail, there was no doubting that Timür was still the boss.

During his sojourn here, an ambassadorial delegation arrived from Spain. Led by a man called Roy Gonzalez de Clavijo, it did not make much of an impression on Timür, who was much more interested in the altogether grander party that arrived from Egypt at about the same time, accompanied by, amongst other things, a giraffe. However, Clavijo's mission is invaluable in noting everyday aspects of court life, which gives a glimpse of how things were changing. For example, he witnesses first-hand marriage ceremonies, clearly using Islamic rites, which have unmistakable evidence of Mongol culture underlying them.

This period of peace and partying (for such it was – there were some huge feasts with copious amounts of alcohol consumed) was a heaven-sent respite for Timür, but now it was time to move on China. He was unwell, and perhaps hoped that a burst of energy would revitalise him. And so his great army marched out into the middle of one of the harshest winters any of his men could remember. It was January 1405. The snow was so deep that man, horse and camel all struggled hopelessly to make progress. It was an unforgiving task, and China might as well have been on the far side of the moon for all the progress that they were making towards it. Already unwell before he left Samarkand, Timür worsened. His physician advocated a strange treatment for his ailments: covering Timür's body with chunks of ice. Instead of getting better, he gradually got worse. And then, irony of ironies, in the midst of this most bitter of winters, a delegation arrived. It was from Timür's old adversary Tokhtamish, who was fulsome in his grovelling. He had done great wrong, he admitted, and would do anything to reingratiate himself with his old mentor. Timür sent back a message that, once he had dealt with China, he would restore the fortunes of Tokhtamish. At heart it seems Timür was unable to bring himself to dislike the duplicitous former *khan*. Perhaps he sensed a kindred spirit.

By now, though, it was clear to nearly everyone that this was optimism beyond reason. There would be no future restoration of relations with Tokhtamish because, for Timür, there would be no future. He was clearly dying. In his tent his followers and family came in to pay their last respects. Timür's breathing became laboured, his sight dimmed. His last words were those required by the Koran: 'there is no God but God'. The great man, slayer of millions both Christian and Muslim, died a model death. Like most of the Mongol *khans*, Timür died in bed, so to speak. It is ironic that Timür and Genghis, two of history's mightiest warriors, died not with a sword in their hands, but surrounded by grieving relatives and courtiers in the relative comfort of a tent. The ironies did not end there either. Genghis had announced himself to Western Asia nearly two hundred years before, by responding to an atrocity committed against his people at Otrar. Now Timür, in so many ways his successor, died in virtually the same spot, close to the city whose governor had called down the wrath of the Mongols on his people with such terrible results.

CHAPTER 13
The Mongol Legacy

With the death of Timür, the great age of Mongol expansion came to a halt. Although he has often been compared to Genghis, the differences between the two men were profound. In contrast to the first Great Khan of the Mongols, Timür was a city-dweller, a Muslim and a man who spoke in Turkish. He was very aware of the great heritage that Genghis had left behind, but the two men lived in different worlds.

The Mongol clans in Central Asia became increasingly incidental in international affairs thereafter, in what was essentially a backwater, though it should be noted that their kinsmen founded the great Moghul Empire in India. But these later generations were unrecognisable from their forefathers, sharing little in common with them. Further north in Russia, the Golden Horde was parcelled up into ever smaller sub-clans. From time to time there would be a flare-up, as when for example the Tartars (men of Mongol descent) sacked Moscow in 1571. These were isolated incidents, no longer representative of the great might of the Mongols which had gone forever.

The Tartars set up their home in the Crimea. In 1783, the region was incorporated into Russia. In the twentieth century, they suffered hugely from the purges of Stalin and they were at last broken up, one of the last residues of the great Mongol era. The last reigning descendant of Genghis Khan, Ayid Alim Khan, the emir of Bokhara was deposed in the 1920s, dying in exile in Afghanistan in 1944. But his state was the barest shadow of that governed by his illustrious ancestor.

The impact of the Mongols is often measured by their destructiveness. Extraordinary figures are quoted for the numbers of deaths that they were supposedly responsible for. Medieval chroniclers are notoriously unreliable, and when they quote figures of say one million dead in a Mongol massacre, we should assume that this is not literal, but shorthand for rather a lot of people. This makes the numbers meaningless, but although there may be damned lies and statistics, human beings nevertheless like numbers, for they enable them to gauge the true scale of things. Allowing for exaggeration though, it is likely that the Mongols were directly responsible for the deaths of millions of people across Asia from China, through the Central Asian states, into Persia, Syria and Asia Minor, and of course north into Russia and the eastern borderlands of Europe. However, it is possible that they were indirectly responsible for the deaths of many millions more. In Persia for example, the concentration is inevitably drawn towards the horrific and graphic fate of great cities. However, the effect on agriculture may have been even more devastating. Persia relied on irrigation canals for the water supplies required to grow the crops and, in a land denuded of peasants, these would quickly have fallen into disrepair.

It is an oft-repeated cliché that the Middle Ages were a violent era, but it is important to note that the Mongols were not the only destructive culture to mark the era. The Crusaders, for example, committed terrible massacres in Jerusalem when they captured the city in 1099. Sultan Baibars was renowned for his savagery. The Turks too could be savage. This was a horrific age to live in if, as many peoples were, populations were a target for conquest.

All this is true but what is remarkable is how terrifying an impression the Mongols made on all those they came into contact with. The fact that they stand apart from others in what was a violent age says something. In part, this was an inevitable consequence of using terror as a tactic of conquest; again, not a unique stance, one employed frequently in the era when a town or castle taken after siege could expect slaughter and rapine to follow when it fell, in the West as much as anywhere else. But the scale of the devastation was unique.

The last word on the subject of the destructive impact of the Mongols should perhaps go to one of the leading experts on the subject, who said that 'the shock induced by the scale of the catastrophe [referring specifically to Genghis' campaigns in Persia] had no precedent. This must imply that the death and destruction which produced that shock had no precedent either'.[1] It is an apposite conclusion, and incidentally one that Genghis or Timür would have been pleased with, for the main purpose of their tactics was to terrify their opponents into submission. The fact that those who resisted them lived in a state of abject terror would have caused neither of them to lose a wink of sleep. Other indirect effects of the Mongols might have been no less catastrophic either. By uniting the trade routes of Asia under one master, the Mongols facilitated trade and the movement of goods, but also the transportation of something far more sinister – disease.

It has been suggested that the origins of the Black Death, the greatest killer in medieval history, can be traced back to Central Asia, to the heart of the Mongol empire, in around 1338. By Lake Issyk-Koul, part of modern Kyrgyzstan, the death rate in that year and the following shot up alarmingly. Nestorian graves discovered in the area refer to death by plague at the time. bubonic plague emanated from some quite remote areas, including the Gobi Desert. There is a body of expert opinion that reckons that the prime carrier of the plague in Asia was not the rat but the marmot, a strange animal that still lives in large numbers on the steppes today. It lives in burrows in the ground, popping its head up frequently to see what is happening. It looks decidedly cute, but even now local Mongolian folklore insists that they are the carriers of bubonic plague.

At any rate, experts believe that from its beginnings in Central Asia, the Black Death spread east to China and west to the Crimea, both prime Mongol trade routes. Apocryphally the Mongols were laying siege to a Genovese trading-post in the Crimea. During the battle, they fired the corpses of those dead from the disease over the walls. From here, an escaping Genovese ship carried the plague with it back to Italy and from there the Grim Reaper made his way across Europe, bringing devastation in its wake. It is too sensationalist to blame the Mongols for the Black Death, but they may have played an important part in its spread, given their control and the fact that they opened up the channels of trade that criss-crossed Central Asia.

In more recent times, the reputation of the Mongols has suffered much at the hands of various other races. Europeans took a dim view of their ravages and increasingly looked down their noses at what were termed 'Asiatics' of all types. Asian peoples were regarded as naturally servile, and of an all together lower stock than so-called Caucasians. Not everyone thought this way; the great eighteenth century historian of Rome, Edward Gibbon, had a high regard for the Mongols. However, in the next century not much respect was shown for them, and they were often regarded as mere barbarians. In case this statement might be thought to be the ramblings of a guilt-ridden Westerner, one might consider the fact that handicapped children with Down's syndrome were often called 'Mongol'. Going back to 1844, we find Robert Chambers writing of 'offspring of the Mongolian type',[2] positing that such handicaps arise as a result of incest where couples who have been too closely related have parented a child. Later theories included the bizarre claim that children with such handicaps born to apparently 'normal' Western couples were in fact a throwback to a time many generations previously, when a distant ancestor had been raped by a Mongol warrior.

This was not always so, as at one time the Europeans had been in awe of the Mongols. It was not just the military triumphs that caught the eye, but the mighty trading network that they created too, a merchant's web that stretched across from the mystical lands of distant and largely unknown China, right to the shores of the Mediterranean. Columbus was looking for China when he found America, that is the China of Kublai and his successors, lost from view since the Mongol empire had disintegrated a hundred years and more before. In his luggage was a well-marked and well-thumbed copy of Marco Polo's travelogue. In my view, their accomplishments, though characterised by violence and destruction, represent an amazing military achievement. Just how the Mongols came to conquer so much of the known world is a matter of debate. That it was down in the first instance to Genghis Khan is, in my view, not. He was not a complete innovator. The manpower he had available to him fought in broadly the same way that steppe warriors had for hundreds of years. Consider the following quotes for example: 'scarce had the infant learnt to stand without his mother's aid, when a horse takes him on his back'. Not, in this instance, a comment on the Mongols, but on the Huns nearly a thousand years before.[3]

Other quotations about the Huns hammer home the point. The fourth century observer Ammianus Marcellus tells how they 'are almost glued to their horses' and that they have 'extraordinary rapidity of movement'.[4] The Huns were exclusively cavalry, relying in the main on horse archers; very similar, in other words, to the Mongols. What Genghis added to this raw material was an iron discipline, and a breadth of strategic vision that few other military minds in history have been able to match. Military theorists have, in recent times, become very appreciative of the Mongols. The great military innovation of the twentieth century in terms of land warfare was the evolution of the tank. After the Mongols declined, so too did the cavalry arm of military forces all over the world. The infantryman became all powerful: long, static lines of riflemen standing ramrod-straight in a line, not moving, regimented, shuffling slowly around the battlefield. The ultimate evolution of this line of thinking was the trenches of World War One, and the rat-a-tat-tat of the machine gun.

The tank changed all that. It was the modern successor to the Mongol cavalryman, fast, quick, able to come crashing through the lines of stationery, scared infantry who did not know where the next blow was coming from. The weaponry was different of course. Where once a hail of arrows would come raining down, now it would be an artillery shell. But many of the tactics were similar enough for some of the leading military thinkers of the twentieth century to look back at how the Mongols fought and seek to copy them. German strategists in particular showed great interest in the way that Genghis fought. *The Secret History* was painstakingly translated into German so that the generals of the era could learn from a master of war.

Russian generals too were interested in learning from the Mongols. As mentioned earlier, Soviet strategists lured the Germans into traps in ways that the Mongols at the Kalka River would have recognised. Stalin was interested enough in Genghis to send several expeditions into Mongolia seeking in vain for his grave. Timür was not so lucky: everyone knew exactly where he was buried. So in 1941 his body was exhumed and leered at by Russian archaeologists, as if he was little more than a freak show at a circus. Inevitably, legends accreted to Timür even centuries after his death. Rather like an Asian version of Tutankhamen, it was said that disturbing his tomb would lead to terrible consequences. It was perhaps inevitable that just days after he was exhumed, the Germans stormed into Russia without warning. Shortly after he was buried again, the Germans were defeated at Stalingrad.

This toying with the bones of the great reflected something of the Russian attitude to the Mongols. They were seen as the great demons who had held back Russian development for centuries (though in fact, internal divisions within Russia itself played a much greater part in doing that). The skull of Timür became a toy, and Genghis, that other great conqueror, was most definitely *persona non grata*. Even today, there are frequent racist incidents perpetrated by 'white' Russians against those of Central Asian extraction. For a while the Russians were the unofficial masters of Mongolia itself, through a puppet Mongolian Communist government. During the 1930s, largely out of sight and out of mind of a Western world, and much more interested in the excesses of the occupying Japanese forces in Manchuria, Russian stooges destroyed Buddhist monasteries, and imprisoned or murdered Buddhist monks.

Also in the 1930s, one of the great battles of the century took place in Mongolia. Little mention of it will be found in any Western history book, but it was crucial. Shortly before the outbreak of World War Two, a large Japanese army invaded Mongolia. The Mongol army was tiny and completely incapable of fighting off the invaders. A large Russian force came to its aid. On the distant borders of Mongolia the Japanese army was heavily defeated. As a direct result, it abandoned its plans to move further west. Instead they turned to the Pacific and the path that led directly to Pearl Harbour. It was a supreme irony: a Russian army coming to the aid of the Mongols.

The Mongols also had a considerable effect on the history of their enemy that day. For centuries, the Japanese had remained insular and resistant to outside influence. The Mongol invasions of their sacred homeland and their miraculous release by the *kamikaze* winds lived long in the memory, and fed the sense of insularity. But as the twentieth century progressed, the Japanese became increasingly interested in Genghis, an Asian warrior with a matchless military pedigree. They too tried without success to find his grave.

The Chinese in the meantime used the legacy of the Mongols to stake their claim to lands long lost to them. Tibet moved to the top of their shopping list, based in part on the claim that it had formed a branch of the empire when the Yuan ruled (that is, when Kublai the Chinese, as opposed to the Mongol, emperor was *khan*). The Mongol legacy to China was to re-unite it into a powerful and unified state. It is a bequest that many of China's neighbours must feel distinctly ambivalent about. There is no doubt that at the time the impact of the Mongol invasions on China was catastrophic in terms of the loss of life. A modern estimate of the Chinese population is suggestive. At the beginning of the thirteenth century, it has been calculated that there were 100 million people in the Song and Chin areas of China. By the end of the same century, it had fallen to 70 million. It fell again in the next century to 60 million, though the bubonic plague must have played a big part in this. The decrease in the previous century, though, is staggering. Even allowing for the effects of natural disaster, to which China has always been susceptible, this was a horrific decline.[5]

Nowadays there are more Mongols living in Inner Mongolia, a province of China, than there are in Outer Mongolia, an independent state. But it is in the latter that the legacy of Genghis lives on most vividly. Ulan Baatar is a sprawling, messy city, a rather grimy part of the modern world. Move a few miles outside of it, though, and you are back in the lands and the time of Genghis. Focus your eyes on the steppes and you may well see the horse herds, gainfully trying to eat grass from the dry and arid hillsides. Here and there a rider cracks his whip, bringing the semi-wild stallions and mares to order. In the valleys, the felt *gers* still hug the lower slopes of the hills, moved on from time to time when the grasslands have been exhausted. Genghis is there still; his voice echoes in the wind and his eyes look down on the world from the hilltops. He is there in the mighty eagles that soar high above in the endless, eternal sky. He is there in the rock shrines, the *ovoos,* that mark the summits of the hills. They say that Genghis and the Golden Kin are dead, consigned to history and lost from view. Tell that to a proud Mongolian, and he will look back at you with a smile in his eyes. He for one knows better.

The end of Timür marked the end of Mongol greatness. He had spread terror in his wake, as had his Mongol predecessors, but the full extent of the Mongol empire had not been restored. China and Persia were both lost to the Mongols forever. Increasingly, the Mongol powers that remained were constricted into smaller territories, and their influence on international and even regional affairs diminished. As time passed, they fragmented and became ever more parochial. But the legacy that Genghis and the Golden Kin left to the world survived, perhaps largely unrecognised, but there nonetheless. It lives on to this day.

Notes

Prologue

1. Saunders, p171
2. Boyle, p24

Chapter i

1. Boyle, p39
2. Though not everyone agrees. Professor Urgunge Onon, the translator of *The Secret History*, dates it to 1162 as does Hildinger in his translation of Carpini. Some publications quote 1167 as the most likely – see for example RL Storey, *Chronology of World History*. However, opinion is bitterly divided with many historians also opting for 1162. The Mongol calendar used a twelve-year calendar based on animals, in a similar fashion to those used by the Chinese into modern times.
3. Boyle, p23
4. *The Secret History*, p31
5. The *Secret History*, p34
6. Carpini, p65
7. Carpini, p37
8. Boyle, p21
9. Carpini, p52
10. Boyle, p21
11. Carpini, p37. The present author can vouch that summer lightning remains an issue, having been nearly struck on the top of a mountain by a bolt of it. The windstorms too, which whip up clouds of dust, are as real as ever.
12. Runciman vol. 3, p248
13. Boyle p27
14. Boyle p30
15. Morgan, *The Mongols*, p107
16. Gareth Jenkins, *A Note on Climactic Cycles and the Rise of Chinggis Khan,* Central Asiatic Journal 18 (1974)

CHAPTER 2

1. Baabar, p1
2. Gabriel, p48
3. Gabriel, p49
4. Morgan, *The Mongols*, p65
5. Chambers, *Genghis Khan*, p72
6. Gabriel, p54
7. Lovell, p175

CHAPTER 3

1. Chambers, *The Devil's Horsemen*, p4
2. Chambers *Genghis Khan*, p91
3. Boyle, p107
4. Boyle, p116
5. Boyle, p131. Men from further west applied the word 'Tartars' or 'Tartars' to any eastern nomad warriors. They were also, as we have seen elsewhere, a specific tribe in the far reaches of Mongolia and the borders of China. Generally, references made by western writers refer to the more generic use of the term. The word derives from the Latin *Tartarus*, which translates as 'hell'.
6. *Marco Polo*, p74
7. Now in Afghanistan and famous for the vast rock-cut statues of Buddha that the Taliban recently destroyed.
8. One of the more conservative estimates. Juvaini estimated that 1.3 million died there.
9. Boyle, p134
10. Morgan, *The Mongols*, p17
11. Maalouf, p235

CHAPTER 4

1. Gabriel, p94
2. Nicolle and Shpakovsky p46
3. Nicolle and Shpakovsky, p60
4. Chambers, *The Devil's Horsemen*, p34
5. Chambers, *The Devil's Horsemen*, p37
6. BBC website dated 3 July 2004 – *Genghis Khan DNA test is offered*
7. The cause of Genghis' last illness is disputed. It is *The Secret History* that speaks of the fall from the horse, but Juvaini and others talk of a disease brought on by the 'insalubrious climate'

8. Chambers, *The Devil's Horsemen,* p49
9. Juvaini, p182
10. *The Secret History,* p136
11. Carpini, p47
12. Carpini, p64
13. Report on BBC website, dated 7 October 2004 in article entitled *Palace of Genghis Khan unearthed.*

CHAPTER 5

1. Boyle, p271
2. Turnbull *Genghis Khan etc,* p33
3. Turnbull, p47
4. From the *Vokresensk Chronicle*
5. Suggested by Pentti Aalto, quoted Jackson, p40
6. Turnbull *Genghis Khan etc.,* p49

CHAPTER 6

1. Morgan, *The Mongols,* p1
2. Morgan, *The Mongols,* p179
3. Jackson, p60
4. In Chambers, *The Devil's Horsemen,* p123
5. Discussed for example by Jackson, p72
6. Carpini, p101
7. Carpini, p64
8. Carpini, p51
9. Carpini, p66

CHAPTER 7

1. See p26
2. Carpini, p43
3. An interesting anthropological resemblance can be found in another warrior race, the Zulus, who would not by choice fight when the moon was dying.
4. Joinville, p283
5. See for example Saunders, p176
6. De Joinville, p283
7. De Joinville, p287
8. De Joinville, p288

9. Rubruck, p10
10. Rubruck, p12
11 Rubruck, p16
12. Rubruck, p45
13. Rubruck, p68
14. Rubruck, p106
15. Man *Kublai Khan*, p246
16. See Morgan *The Mongols*, p176
17. Boyle, p627
18. Boyle, p723
19. Boyle, p725
20. Waterson, p67
21. Runciman vol. 3, p304
22. *Marco Polo*, p11
23. Figures in Waterson
24. This is the romantic version of his end given by some chroniclers. Some historians opt for a more prosaic end, believing him to be killed in the battle itself.

CHAPTER 8

1. See Halperin, p18
2. The first line of which is '*In Xanadu did Kubla Khan a stately pleasure-dome decree*'. Coleridge never went within thousands of miles of the place and is popularly supposed to have composed the work whilst under the influence of drugs.
3. Rossabi, p31
4. Chambers *The Devil's Horsemen*, p189
5. *Marco Polo*, p81

CHAPTER 9

1. See Bradbury *The Routledge Companion to Medieval Warfare*, p305 and Keen *Medieval Warfare*, p116
2. From the *Yuan History* in Mann *Kublai Khan*, p217
3. Rossabi, p87
4. Man, p226
5. Man, p 246
6. From the *Hachiman Gudokun* in Turnbull *Genghis Khan etc.*, p66
7. This is an average of sixty-nine per annum. Amnesty International estimates for 2005 gave a figure of 1,770 executions in that one year alone. Even allowing for a population that is now ten times as large in

China as it was in the Mongol era, this gives an execution rate per head of a population which is three times greater in modern times than it was when Kublai was *khan*.

CHAPTER 10

1. *Marco Polo*, p39
2. *Marco Polo*, p 117
3. *Marco Polo*, p122
4. Axell and Kase *Kamikaze*, 141
5. *Marco Polo*, p97

CHAPTER 11

1. *Marco Polo*, p101
2. Morgan *The Devil's Horsemen*, p173
3. Gascoigne, p147
4. Gascoigne, p150
5. Halperin, p50
6. See *Russia and the Golden Horde*
7. Davies, p389

CHAPTER 12

1. In Marozzi, p70
2. Marozzi, p99
3. In Marozzi, p103
4. In Marozzi, p147
5. In Marozzi, p189
6. Marozzi, p279

CHAPTER 13

1. Morgan in Bosworth, vol. 7, 231
2. Weatherford, p257
3. Sidonius in Maenchen-Helfer, p392
4. Ibid
5. Langlois, p20

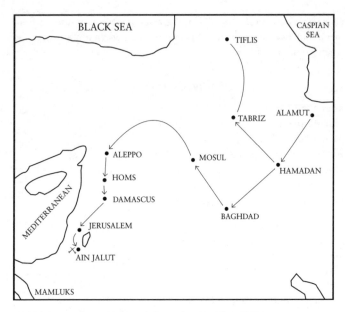

39. Hülegü's invasion of Syria and the road to Ain Jalut (1250s)

40. The dividing Mongol Empire (end of thirteenth century)

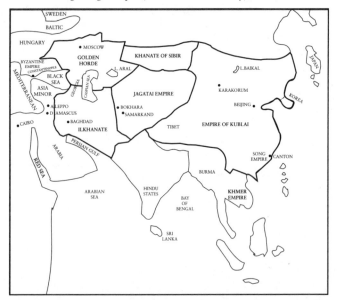

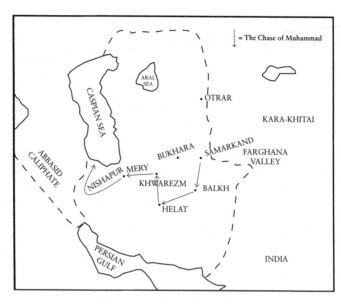

42. Genghis' invasion of Khwarezm: early 1220s

42. The Mongol invasion of Europe: early 1240s

Acknowledgements

I would like to acknowledge the assistance I have received in writing this book. Firstly, to all those who have helped in my research and for forwarding photographs. I am truly grateful. To family and friends also, for putting up with my frequent absences (maybe they enjoy them!) when I am writing, I thank you for your tolerance and understanding. You are entitled to complain much more than you do.

Also, for all those at Amberley who have helped finish the book. Thanks for your comments and hard work in this. Especial thanks to Jonathan Reeve for his unstinting support and encouragements.

Lastly, I would like to say perhaps the biggest thank you to all those in Mongolia who have made my several trips there so special. I went to Mongolia by accident and fell in love with it the first time I walked in the hills. Yours is a beautiful country. Your friendship too was appreciated, and will always be a part of me. I would like to think our paths may cross again but even if they do not I would like to say a sincere "bayarlalaa".

List of Illustrations

role in developing the toughness of the Mongol warriors (W.B.).

23. The statue of Genghis Khan erected in Ulanbataar in 2006 to mark the 800th anniversary of the founding of the Mongol state (W.B.).

24. Tourists stroll along the Great Wall of China where once Chinese soldiers looked out for another Mongol raid (W.B.).

25. The splendour of the Forbidden City in Beijing. It was erected by the Ming dynasty that conquered the Mongol Yuan dynasty and destroyed most of the city that they had constructed (W.B.).

26. Louis IX, King of France, sets out on Crusade: the saintly Crusader 'enjoyed' a problematic relationship with the Mongols (W.B.).

27. Western knights attack a Muslim city, exemplifying the state of Western arms at the time in a medieval manuscript (W.B.).

28. A romanticised view of a Mongol shaman from an old French manuscript (Wayne Bartlett).

29. A Persian manuscript illustrating lamellar armour as used by the Mongols (W.B.).

30. A hunting scene from Khwarezm illustrating the tactics of the 'Great Hunt' employed by the Mongols so effectively, both in peacetime training and in the heat of battle (W.B.).

31. This Chinese manuscript, showing the court in China, shows some rather fanciful illustrations of the Mongol *yurts* transported on the backs of wagons: the wagons tended to be much bigger and the *yurts* less Oriental in appearance (W.B.).

32. Genghis Khan, the founder of the greatest Empire the world has ever seen (W.B.).

33. An early twentieth century photograph of Mongols wrestling: the Mongols loved their wrestling (and still do): breaking a troublemaker's back in a wrestling match was one of the more bizarre and painful ways of execution employed by the Great Khans (W.B.).

34. A Mongolian horseman with a lasso to capture a horse from the herds that roamed the steppes (W.B.).

35. An early twentieth century Mongolian princess: a picture that captures both the beauty and elegance for which some medieval Mongol princesses were renowned (W.B.).

36. An early twentieth century Mongol prince, a successor to the great Khans such as Genghis, though by the time that this picture was taken, Mongolia was a pale reflection of the great empire it had once been (W.B.).

37. An old photograph of the great mausoleum of Tamerlane in Samarkand, his opulent capital (W.B.).

38. The coronation of Henry IV of England – he was nervous enough to correspond enthusiastically with Tamerlane (W.B.).

39. Hülegü's invasion of Syria and the road to Ain Jalut (1250s). Amberley Archive.

40. The dividing Mongol Empire (end of thirteenth century). Amberley Archive.

42. Genghis' invasion of Khwarezm: early 1220s. Amberley Archive.

42. The Mongol invasion of Europe: early 1240s. Amberley Archive.

Select Bibliography

Axell, Albert and Kase, Hideaki: *Kamikaze – Japan's Suicide Gods,* Pearson Education
Limited (Harlow, 2002)

Baabar: *History of Mongolia,* University of Cambridge (Cambridge, 1999)

Baabar: *History of Mongolia,* New Era Magazine (Ulaanbaatar, 2005)

Barber, Malcolm: *The New Knighthood; A History of the Order of the Temple,*
Cambridge University Press (Cambridge, 1998)

Bartlett, W. B: *The Last Crusade,* Tempus (Stroud, 2007)

Bartlett, W.B: *The Crusades: An Illustrated History,* Sutton (Stroud, 1999)

Bartlett, W.B: *The Assassins – The Story of Medieval Islam's Secret Sect,* Sutton (Stroud,
2001)

Bosworth, C.E et al: *Encyclopaedia of Islam,* E. J. Brill, Leiden (New York, 1993)

Bradbury, Jim: *The Medieval Siege,* Boydell (Woodbridge, 1998)

Bradbury, Jim: *The Routledge Companion to Medieval Warfare,* Routledge (London and
New York, 2004)

Bronstein, Judith: *The Hospitallers and the Holy Land,* Boydell (Woodbridge, 2005)

Boyle, J. A (translated): *Genghis Khan: The History of the World Conqueror by Ata-Malik
Juvaini,* Manchester University Press (Manchester, 1997)

Chambers, James: *Genghis Khan,* Sutton (Stroud, 1999)

Chambers, James: *The Devil's Horsemen: The Mongol Invasion of Europe,* Cassell (London,
1988)

Curtin, Jeremiah: *The Mongols – A History,* Combined Books (Pennsylvania, 1996) (reprint
of 1908 edition)

Daftary, Farhad: *The Isma'ilis – Their History and Doctrines,* Cambridge University Press
(Cambridge, 1995)

Daftary, Farhad: *A Short History of the Ismailis,* Edinburgh University Press (Edinburgh,
1998)

Davies, Norman: *Europe – A History,* Oxford University Press, (Oxford, 1996)

Fossier, Robert: *The Cambridge Illustrated History of the Middle Ages 1250 – 1520,*
Cambridge University Press (Cambridge, 1997)

Gabriel, Richard A: *Genghis Khan's Greatest General: Subotai the Valiant,* University of
Oklahoma Press (Westport, 2004)

Gascoigne, Bamber: *A Brief History of the Dynasties of China,* Constable and Robinson
(London, 2005)

Halperin, Charles: *Russia and the Golden Horde,* L. B. Tauris (London, 1987)

Hildinger, Erik: *The Story of the Mongols Whom We Call the Tartars by Friar Giovanni
DiPlano Carpini,* Brandon (Boston, 1996)

Holmes, George: *The Oxford Illustrated History of Medieval Europe,* Oxford University
Press (Oxford, 1991)

Hooper, Nicholas and Bennett, Matthew: *Cambridge Illustrated Atlas: Warfare – The Middle
Ages 768 – 1487,* Cambridge University Press (Cambridge, 1996)

Jackson, Peter: *The Mongols and the West,* Pearson Education Limited (Harlow, 2005)

Jotischky, Andrew: *Crusading and the Crusader States,* Persian Education Limited (Harlow,
2004)

Keen, Maurice: *Medieval Warfare – A History,* Oxford University Press (Oxford, 1999)

Lamb, Harold: *Genghis Khan – The Emperor of All Men,* Doubleday (New York, 1927)

Langlois, J. D: *China Under Mongol Rule* (Princeton, 1981)

Latham, Ronald: *Marco Polo: The Travels,* Penguin, (London, 1958)

Lewis, Bernard: *The Assassins,* Saqi (London, 1999)

Lovell, Julia: *The Great Wall: China Against The World,* Atlantic Books (London, 2006)

Maalouf, Amin: *The Crusades Through Arab Eyes,* Saqi (London, 2006)

Maenchen-Helfen (ed. Knight): *The World of the Huns,* University of California (Berkeley/ Los Angeles/ London, 1973)

Man, John: *Genghis Khan: Life, Death and Resurrection,* Bantam Press (London, 2004)

Man, John: *Kublai Khan: The Mongol King Who Remade China,* Bantam Press (London, 2006)

Marozzi, Justin: *Tamerlane: Sword of Islam, Conqueror of the World,* Harper Perennial (London, 2005)

Morgan, David O: *Medieval Persia: 1040 – 1797,* Longman (London, 1992)

Morgan, David O: *The Mongols,* Blackwell (Oxford, 1986)

Nicolle, David: *Medieval Warfare Source Book,* Arms and Armour (London, 1996)

Nicolle, D and Shpakovsky, V: *Kalka River 1223,* Osprey (Oxford, 2001)

Oman, Sir Charles: *A History of the Art of War in the Middle Ages,* Greenhill Books (London, 1991) (reprint of 1924 edition)

Phillips, E.D: *The Mongols,* Thames and Hudson (London, 1969)

Rockhill, William Woodville: *William of Rubruck's Account of the Mongols,* Rana Saad (Maryland, 2005) (reprint of 1900 edition)

Rossabi, Morris: *Khubilai Khan: His Life and Times,* University of California Press (Berkeley and Los Angeles, 1988)

Runciman, Steven: *A History of the Crusades,* Penguin (London, 1952)

Saunders, J.J: *A History of Medieval Islam,* Routledge (London and New York, 1996)

Shaw, M. R. B (translated): *Joinville and Villehardouin: Chronicles of the Crusades,* Penguin (London, 1963)

Turnbull, S.R: *The Mongols,* Osprey (London, 1987)

Turnbull, Stephen: *Genghis Khan and the Mongol Conquests 1190 – 1400,* Osprey (Oxford, 2003)

Turnbull, Stephen: *Mongol Warrior 1200 – 1350,* Osprey (Oxford, 2003)

Vaughan, Richard (translated and edited): *The Illustrated Chronicles of Matthew Paris,* Alan Sutton (Stroud, 1993)

Waterson, James: *The Knights of Islam – The Wars of the Mamluks,* Greenhill Books (London, 2007)

Weatherford, Jack: *Genghis Khan and the Making of the Modern World,* Three Rivers Press (New York, 2004)

Index